MARRIED TO THE BLACK WIDOW

MARRIED TO THE BLACK WIDOW

A chilling true story of lies and deception

Rob Parkes

SEVEN DIALS

First published in Great Britain in hardback in 2023,
this paperback edition published in 2024 by Seven Dials,
an imprint of The Orion Publishing Group Ltd
Carmelite House, 50 Victoria Embankment
London EC4Y 0DZ

An Hachette UK Company

3 5 7 9 10 8 6 4 2

ISBN (Mass Market Paperback) 9781399603836
ISBN (eBook) 9781399603843
ISBN (Audio) 9781399603850

Typeset by Born Group
Printed and bound in Great Britain by Clays Ltd, Elcograf S.p.A.

www.orionbooks.co.uk

For Grace

Contents

Part One:

Can We Be Civil?

Prologue

'Hello? Can you hear me? Is this working? Hello? Can we get someone in there to check the connection, please?'

I looked up and saw the clerk leaning over the desk. She repeated herself, speaking slowly and loudly into the microphone and checked the large video screen on the wall above the press desk. It had been over ten minutes since that screen had initially flickered into life, but the image had remained stubbornly frozen ever since.

With an imminent start to this, the final hearing and sentencing of the figure on the screen, appearing unlikely, I took a moment to survey the room. The courtroom felt empty without the jury, despite the rows of police officers, lawyers and reporters packed onto the long wooden rows between my chair and the judge's bench at the far end.

'Hello? This is ridicul . . . I don't know why it's not working. Hello? We need to get started, we can't wait any longer. Can you hear me?'

The picture showed a woman with long brown hair that hung past her shoulders, dressed in a grey-blue tracksuit top. Her eyes were blank and dull. Her face was slack, expressionless, as if she had been unplugged. Totally still and unmoving, Victoria stared straight into the camera as if looking through a window into the courtroom itself. As if looking directly into *me*. She was sitting in HMP Peterborough in a blank room with white walls, a chair and a desk. I had known the woman on the screen for twenty years, ten of which we had been together and six we had been married. But, despite the trial itself having gone on for an interminable ten days, this was the first time I had actually seen her face in over seven years and I had to stop to take a moment to consider how I felt about that.

The longer I looked, the more she resembled the woman I used to know: her features, her expressions and mannerisms all swam into focus. I remembered the way she would touch her hair and her cute, sideways smile; her laugh and the scent of her favourite perfume. Then I started to remember some of the other things: the constant expressions of disappointment, the looks of patronising contempt, the crack and roar of fire, the smell of smoke and the stabbing, electric shock of fear.

I shuffled the papers in front of me, unable to decide what I was feeling or even how I was supposed to feel. Angry? Should I be trembling with fury when confronted with the face of the woman who had put me and my family through so much?

But I wasn't angry, I was confused. I studied her more intently: Victoria was older but still familiar. How could I ever have thought that I would forget that face? She had aged better than me, I thought, as I tried to mentally reach out to get through the flat picture on the screen. But her lack of emotion made her somehow even flatter than the two-dimensional image in front of me.

'We've got it, someone's coming in now.' Suddenly, Victoria blinked and looked over to her right as the clerk hung up the phone. 'Can you hear me?' the clerk asked her again, puzzled.

4

'Yes, loud and clear,' replied a female prison guard as she stepped into the room from the left of the screen, her uniform making the blank walls behind Victoria seem even more austere. 'Everything's fine this end, she heard everything you said.'

I blinked as that sunk in. Victoria had sat frozen in her chair for over ten minutes, watching and waiting. I shuddered and remembered just who we were dealing with. Even now, from almost a hundred miles away, she had found a way to dictate the pace and tempo of her own sentencing.

'All rise.'

No sooner had the connection with the prison been verified than Mr Justice Chamberlain strode into court, barely waiting for the clerk's hurried instruction, which sent the assembled professionals scrambling into their positions.

'This is the sentencing hearing for Victoria Breeden,' began Judge Chamberlain in a hard, factual tone belying the emotion of this life-changing moment. 'Victoria, over a period of five years between 2014 and 2019, you actively sought out a series of men whom you felt could help you kill Robin Parkes. Of the four counts put to the jury, three of those men have testified in this trial.'

I swallowed hard, trying to decide where to look. Should I watch the judge or Victoria? I swung feverishly between the two trying not to miss a reaction from either.

'During the trial, the jury were played a recording of you and one of the men discussing your intentions, options and your preference for how Mr Parkes was to be murdered. The men who testified in this court gave evidence that you actively targeted them and emotionally and psychologically manipulated them into serving your intended purpose: that of ending Mr Parkes's life.'

An entire room of heads turned to the screen on the wall, where Victoria sat, quiet and still. There was silence as we waited. The pause stretched out uncomfortably. 'Ms Breeden, do you understand?' The judge turned to his clerks as they checked their computer screens: 'Can we please check that she can hear us?'

The prison officer came into view once more and Victoria glanced to her right, shook her head and whispered in an anguished, gasping breath: 'No.'

'No, you don't understand or no, you can't hear me?' enquired Judge Chamberlain, suppressing obvious frustration.

'She can hear you, Judge,' confirmed the prison officer.

Victoria remained mute, her face now starting to contort in anguish.

Judge Chamberlain referred to the notes in front of him. 'Victoria, the psychiatric evidence from your recent assessment shows that you are not suffering from any condition or impairment that might diminish your awareness or judgement. I have no reason to believe that you are anything other than fully aware of your actions at this time, just as you were when you approached and asked those men to kill Mr Parkes.'

Light, space and time contracted and narrowed into a tractor beam between Judge Chamberlain and myself. The room around me seemed to grow dark as he looked up from his notes to address Victoria directly. 'Ultimately, you have been found guilty of three counts of solicitation to murder and I hereby sentence you to nine years and six months' imprisonment.'

The whole room rushed back in an almost overwhelming flood of sensation, I experienced a sharp choking feeling and suddenly realised I had been holding my breath. My chest shuddered as I drew in a shaky gulp of air.

6

On hearing the judge's words, Victoria sagged. She slumped in her seat and then looked back up at the screen. She knew I was there: she had seen me through the video link give my victim statement detailing what she had done to our daughter Grace, to my second wife and to me. Through my confusion rose relief after all the years of trying to compromise, trying to do the right thing for Grace, battling moral condemnation from a society that sees only an absent father who abandoned his family. And now, after all of the threats, fear, manipulation and sorrow, I finally allowed myself to believe that we might at last be safe.

The courtroom buzzed with the quiet rumble of half-whispers and shuffling papers as the barristers started to prepare the paperwork that I hoped would allow me to find some closure after twenty years.

In the years that followed the verdict, I have come to recognise that I have struggled to cope with what happened to me and my family, and that gaining closure has been unexpectedly difficult. What it has helped me to understand is that in order to deal with our experiences, our daughter deserves to know her story. What she read in the newspaper or saw on TV in the days after the verdict only created more questions for both of us and so to provide those answers, uncomfortable as it may be, I knew I would have to go back to where everything truly began.

Chapter 1

The sequence of events that led up to Victoria's sentencing in court began twenty years earlier and two hundred miles away in a dingy, drab theatre hall at Teesside University. One of the original buildings added to the growing faculty through the 1960s and '70s, it had been used for events and presentations before new buildings and halls were constructed to cater for the increasing numbers of students on campus. When I was there in my late teens, the theatre hall was mainly used for exams and was the regular base of the university's various clubs and societies. I loved that space: it smelt of polish and dust just like my old school hall and for a boy who had recently moved out of home for the first time, I was torn between craving and rejecting anything that reminded me of my school days.

My first year at university was fantastic and there were so many positive things about that time that I carry with me even now. It gave me lifelong friendships, the sort that, thankfully, I could come back to after many years and still rely on. I also developed a BMI of 37, became 'morbidly obese' and very nearly found myself thrown off my course for doing . . . well, essentially nothing except having a good time. I learned life lessons the hard way (although in the case of my BMI, it was all too easy considering the 2-for-1 pizza deals in Middlesbrough in the late 1990s). I was living the student lifestyle and a part of that was attempting to hook up with any woman who showed an interest. But as strange as it may seem, it turns out not many young women were looking for a relationship with an insecure, overweight, underachieving late-bloomer, whose questionably eclectic music taste existed at the centre of a Venn diagram between bubblegum pop, operatic rock and nineties electro dance. Who knew?

But, as with most students, I found my place: a clique of people who, like me, enjoyed the thrill of playing spin the bottle at three in the morning after an evening of shot promotions and too many pints of Carling at the Student Union karaoke night. That first year was great, I had an absolute blast. I started to grow up and get an education of sorts, even if I didn't get laid.

My point is, in that first year I made the most of every second: drinking, partying and eating without any appreciation of what the future would bring. I made a conscious decision to leave my childhood behind and seize as much new life as I could possibly get. When I arrived, I joined the amateur dramatic society so a year of socialising and showing off on stage inevitably ensued. I was exploring who I was and loved every minute of it. By the time we came back from the summer break ready to start again, I found myself leading the entire society. I still don't really know why I volunteered to take charge but I'm certain a combination of blind enthusiasm, misplaced tenacity and alcohol probably helped.

The club always promoted itself hard at the Freshers' Week and there were a few ways that people usually found us. There was a steady stream of members who signed up during the week itself, those who stumbled into our first few meetings afterwards and those brought along by their friends for moral support.

At the start of the 1999–2000 academic year I was sitting on the side of the stage in the main hall. The vinyl floor was squeaky underfoot and smelt of the fresh coating they had applied over the holiday. I was running through some ideas about what we might want to do over the year, when Victoria walked into the room with her roommate.

That first day we met, Victoria held herself with a shy confidence that captivated me. We noticed each other immediately and I went over to introduce myself and invite the two of them to join us. That night and for several nights afterwards, as we continued to meet in the bar with mutual friends, she flirted with an infectious laugh that I was drawn to. She had long, dark brown hair, which she was rightly proud of and would tuck away, push back, twitch and pull on to accentuate her face and impish smile.

We hit it off straight away and undeniably a big part of the attraction was how she actively pushed for my attention. Our relationship evolved quickly and easily from acquaintance to friendship, close friendship and then to physical attraction without me really noticing. I was unbelievably nervous as I contemplated the prospect of only my second real relationship ever (the first being confined to terrible kissing and embarrassing fumbles – both on my part – with an incredibly patient but ultimately disappointed girl at school two years previously).

Those early days were filled with promise, excitement and sex. In retrospect, there was probably more of the first. However, for a naïve teenager whose previous liaisons had been limited to the thrill of holding hands and trying not to break a tooth while kissing, this was closer than I had ever come before. The thrill of a new experience, while incredibly flattering, exciting and sexy, would become something of a double-edged sword.

So, clearly my second year at university had started out very nicely. Things were going to plan and my love life at least existed!

Victoria and I began spending more and more time together, a *lot* of time. We would see each other most days or evenings and in my enthusiasm, nineteen-year-old me didn't want to waste time actually studying when there was someone who wanted to be naked in the same bed as him. In all honesty, there was nothing else that I, as a horny-yet-sexually-gullible teenager, was ever going to do.

After I moved out of student halls, I lived in a shared house with three other friends and it wasn't long before Victoria was spending more time in our house than her own, and the year flew by. It was so fast in fact that when the summer came around, I was starting to get a little overwhelmed, a bit claustrophobic. My housemates were telling me, 'She's just around too much', 'slow down a bit', 'give yourself some time'. Everything had gone from zero to one hundred miles per hour and I thought that sounded like good advice. When the summer holiday arrived, we could go our separate ways and take a breath. That was the plan. Breaking it to Victoria went as well as could be expected: she was disappointed but agreed that we needed some space so we both went off in our different directions.

But while we were apart, Victoria started to call and leave messages on my voicemail, not creepy per se – just insistent. We ended up seeing each other a couple of times over the break and by the time we came back to university, we were together again. It felt like she had attached some kind of physical connection to me and dragged me until eventually I was manoeuvred back onto her life path. Trying to haul in the opposite direction was more emotionally, even physically difficult, than anything I had ever experienced before and I didn't have the words to say what I wanted and needed. It became easier to simply agree with the suggestion that we should meet up alone because Victoria had a headache or didn't fancy seeing friends; often she had something important to tell me but could never quite remember what it was after I'd changed my plans to hear it. Sometimes, we would arrange to meet others but then she would delay and push back the time, then cancel at the last minute and ask me to bring something of previously unknown but suddenly vital importance to her because somehow, she knew I would.

None of these things are indictable offences. They are all reasonable and understandable when taken in isolation, indeed I suspect there are parts of this description that are represented in many, if not most early relationships. But if I had only stopped to consider just how many evenings were lost or how demanding she had been, would I have made a different choice? With the benefit of hindsight, I realise now that I just wasn't comfortable being alone and, because of that, I would run the errands, jump to the requests and answer the calls . . . all of which connected me to Victoria and validated her (and therefore my) view of what a boyfriend should be and do.

I had been brought up to be polite, fair and honourable and while I still believe in these values today, my application of them is very different. When we first met, Victoria saw something in me that I hadn't: I knew that I was an enthusiastic and sociable networker who liked to be part of the bigger picture and get involved, but, crucially, she saw that through all of this ran a strong protective streak.

Over the course of October 2000 to May 2001 (my final year at university), back with my friends around me, I started to see that the relationship wasn't mutual or healthy. I tried to call things off at least a dozen times, but no matter what I said or how I said it, sooner or later we were always back together.

My relationship with Victoria consisted of a steady layering of issues that built over time. Each inconsequential or even acceptable in isolation, it wasn't until I brought them all together that I really started to see what a mess I was in – and that only came a long time later. Gradually, our relationship shifted from one of mutual respect and equity to me becoming a source of support, someone she came to rely on and finally to total dependence. But if there's one instance I can point to which gives an understanding of where all this definitively tipped, it was a night in February 2001.

Student life in my house share was chaotic at best and there were always people asleep in most of the rooms – on sofas, chairs or sometimes even the stairs. It wasn't unusual for them to turn up at the door and ask to crash. Not long before the night in question, I had managed to successfully negotiate a breakup with Victoria and earlier in the evening, I had met up with a friend, Alice, who I'd always got along well with. One thing led to another and we'd ended the night back in my room, which had been a pretty big ego boost. I was riding high on life, my uni work was coming along, I had time to see my friends again and I was finding out how this whole dating thing was supposed to work.

But later that night as the temperature dropped and the town started to wind down, Victoria turned up at the house, claiming to have lost the keys for her place; she couldn't get in and was insisting that she had nowhere else to go. She wasn't expected and none of my housemates were keen on indulging her so they explained that I wasn't available as I was hosting a visitor upstairs.

Unfortunately, this did not get the response they were hoping for as she started to break down on the doorstep. Seemingly unable to get her to leave, they called me to come and deal with the situation. I came downstairs to find her curled up in the doorway, blubbing with rasping, stuttering breaths. She looked like a rag doll that had been thrown away. With broken, choking sentences, she cried that no one believed her, that she couldn't get in at home and that she didn't feel safe. Why would no one help her? Why did no one care?

After twenty minutes of listening to her wailing on the street, begging and pleading, I broke. I couldn't send her back out into the cold, so instead I brought her inside and found her a spare bedroom to stay in until morning. Closing the door behind her, I went back to my room. I was furious with myself: she was back in the house and *I* had brought her in. Why couldn't I just say no? But, I reasoned, what else could I do? I never actually found out why she couldn't get in at home but I wasn't about to kick anyone – especially a woman – out into the street in the middle of the night, alone, when they were so upset. What if something happened? What would that make me? My protective instincts simply wouldn't allow me to abandon a woman in distress and for whatever reason, she was clearly distressed.

The house started to quieten down. The people downstairs either slipped away or drifted off to sleep and with the romantic mood well and truly broken, Alice and I started to relax, talk and joke about what we would do the following day.

Sometime later, when the muffled talking and the clinking of beer bottles had finally stopped, there came a faint knock at my door followed by a shivering whisper of my name. Victoria was trying to see me. I ignored her, pretending that we were already asleep. It seemed to work as after another, more assertive hiss of my name (which remained unanswered), the quiet creak of footsteps marked her passage back across the landing to the room that I had left her in. I relaxed and drifted off to sleep.

'What the FUCK?!'

I woke the next morning to a very loud and very unexpected exclamation. 'What the hell are you doing?'

At first, I thought Alice was talking to me. 'Wha . . .? What's the matter?'

'I *said*, what the fuck are you doing? Get the fuck out!'

Alice was looking past me and down. I turned and my heart stopped: Victoria was lying on the floor beside my bed. She looked up at me, I stared back, utterly confused.

'What?' I managed to stutter.

Slowly, calmly, deliberately, Victoria got up and left the room. Alice dressed in ferocious silence. At the door, she turned back to me, still sitting up in bed with what must have been an absurdly comic look of dazed confusion on my face and shook her head: 'You have *got* to deal with that.'

Alice walked out of that room and out of my life. I never saw her again and as the door closed behind her something clicked deep within me. Victoria had found my kryptonite: the inability to refuse a cry for help. My weakness was *her* weakness. Later, when I asked why she had crept into my room to lie on the floor where her ex-boyfriend was sleeping with another woman, she would tell me that she had felt afraid and threatened in the room by herself, that someone had tried to get into bed with her. I asked my housemates but everyone denied it. At best, there had been a misunderstanding about the fact that the bed had been, up until the point that Victoria had arrived, empty. At worst, this was an attempted assault: a genuinely horrific experience for anyone to go through.

But just the accusation itself opened up a world of suspicion and started to drive a wedge between my friends and I. After all, I told myself, *something* must have happened to make Victoria act in such an extreme way and was I going to be the one to say that it wasn't true? Surely, she wouldn't lie about something as serious as that, would she?

This was the technique she would come back to so many times in the ensuing years: she found a way to create an impression of vulnerability, ensured she had a captive audience and then turned the heat up to eleven. Each time, her explanation was always plausible and her reaction always understandable. I had no idea what had hit me.

Chapter 2

After I graduated in 2001, and with my relationship with Victoria seemingly only strengthened through adversities such as the one described in the previous chapter, I moved out of the shared house. By this point, my friends weren't subtle in making it clear that Victoria was unwelcome. And because she wasn't welcome, Victoria convinced me that neither was I. We moved in together while she finished her degree. The bedsit we lived in was an attic room with nothing in it except the bed itself, a hob and two windows.

I remember the tiny dual-aspect windows looking out over the main street at the front and the side street on the right. It was from there that I spent hours watching people walking in and out of the hairdresser's just down the road. I remember the flock wallpaper, the brown lino floor that was peeling at the edges of (what was generously referred to as) 'the kitchen' and the old TV sat on a chair with its wire aerial precariously balanced with millimetre precision to achieve a grainy broadcast.

After the hectic nature of the house share, this bedsit was far more mundane and that suited Victoria down to the ground. She loved the evenings when it was just us: no friends, no family, just the two of us talking. We would talk about the future and about each other. The longer we talked, the clearer it became that in order to stay in Middlesbrough until Victoria finished her degree, I needed to make some money. It was time that I stepped up and provided for us. This would be our start to success and happiness.

I got a job at a local council improving road safety with schools. I've always been comfortable talking to groups of people, so getting a school full of primary-aged kids excited about being safe while walking to school seemed like a 'good thing' even if it wasn't exactly long-term career material. As time went on, Victoria seemed to prefer those evenings alone more and more often and as a result we became isolated even further. We practically stopped going out at all and the closest thing we had to friends was an emotionally interdependent goth couple living in the flat below. My life was divided between the bedsit, work and Victoria's family home in Ely.

I first met Victoria's family in the summer after we had got together and as the three-hour trips from Middlesbrough to her parents' house in the East of England became more regular, I got to know the family well. The building in which Michael and Marie lived was a semi-detached house that sat on the side of the road in the middle of farmland. The building itself was a solitary citadel of red brick standing in the middle of the Cambridgeshire Fens and Victoria's parents once told me that they had fallen in love with the place on the basis of its south-facing garden with undoubtedly beautiful uninterrupted views across the Fens all the way to the distant canal and railway line.

Michael and Marie, and Victoria's two younger brothers, were friendly and enthusiastic in welcoming me. It was always tricky to find common ground with Victoria's father (he is football mad, I am emphatically not), but we usually made it work as we would sit and chat through the evening. Although his sporadically explosive and intimidating temper might some-times bleed into the evening, with such huge skies and incred-ible rainbow sunsets to escape to, I usually managed to avoid all but the most acute arguments.

Back in Middlesbrough, my uni friends invited me to lots of parties and nights out. They wanted to see me and I was eager to share the hot nights and lazy mornings of my early twenties with them. But Victoria didn't get asked to come along very often and when she did, she usually had to work or was too tired and wanted to leave early. It started to become a running joke. They would ask me to join them, I would say yes but not actually make it. Then after a while it wasn't funny anymore, it was something they saw as a problem. And they were clear about what they thought I should do: detach myself from Victoria.

Easier said than done. Every time I tried to create some space of my own, to claw back the slightest measure of inde-pendence, Victoria knew exactly how to keep me reined in. I received constant messages asking me where I was and what I was doing. She needed me to help her with her studies or collect the shopping because she hadn't eaten. If I went home to see my family, Victoria would often refuse any invitation to come with me and simply didn't leave her bed until I returned. I was also expected to phone and check in on her throughout the day. These 'checks' would sometimes last for hours as she kept me on the line and away from anyone else. This moral obligation grew ever more oppressive: I was always the one who had to disconnect and then felt guilty about leaving her to suffer and struggle on her own yet again.

Mentally and emotionally, I was outgunned at every turn. Who could I talk to? I knew that something wasn't right, but I couldn't articulate it to myself, let alone anyone else.

Victoria's expectations were like a blanket smothering me, but with every demand, there came a comforting reassurance that she loved me and we were right for each other.

I was starting to believe, really *truly* believe, that the ominous feelings of danger were *my* problem, but no matter how hard I tried, I couldn't get a grip on it. Sometimes I tested the boundaries of our relationship and started going out anyway. Maybe I thought that if I brought the issues to the fore then it would force confrontation and the problem would resolve itself. I had a few late nights. I tried to change my attitude, found some new bolshiness, but then Victoria also started to change. She developed puzzling illnesses. First, it was sickness, then overwhelming tiredness and headaches. She had always complained about period pain for as long as I had known her but then it became worse – a lot worse.

Endometriosis[1] can be a terrible and debilitating condition. Sufferers go through horrific experiences every month and while I can sympathise, I acknowledge that, as a man, I can never truly understand exactly how it feels. And so I facilitated and enabled our lives to continue, adapted in whichever way was needed to ensure that Victoria could take part in whatever she chose to do in whichever way she chose to do it. Episodes of pain seemed to come and go, usually over the course of a weekend, but holidays also became times of great difficulty. Away from work and having already moved away from family, separated from friends and with absolutely no reason for us to be apart, it was just me and her, twenty-four hours a day.

I was never *stopped* from going out. I was never *asked* not to see my friends. However, the consequences of doing so

1 A condition where tissue similar to the lining of the uterus grows in other places, such as the ovaries and fallopian tubes.

became ever more severe: before, during and afterwards. For every drink at the pub or snatched hour out of the house, there were five conversations about how Victoria couldn't get to the toilet by herself or how she cried herself to sleep because she couldn't reach the paracetamol. I had left her; I wasn't there and she had needed me.

It's only with the benefit of a lot of time (and even more space) that I can see the pressure that Victoria put on me in those early days. I understand that young relationships are often intense and vibrant – they have energy, excitement and immediacy – but ours didn't seem to be like that. With all the hours of conversation alone in our flat, she created and reinforced the cast-iron belief that I was the only person who could support and protect her. We lost whole weekends in talking about how I was the only one who truly had faith in her, who really understood her, right down to her very core. To refuse that responsibility was to condemn her to a life of perpetual suffering, physically, emotionally and mentally. Without me, she would never be able to live a normal life; I was the person who was enabling her to live.

I wasn't prepared for that level of intensity or responsibility. I'd been brought up with the sure and certain knowledge that when people ask for help, you should help if you can. I'm not a saint by any means, but I do believe that the world is a nicer place if you put nice things into it. In the face of constant yet unpredictable spells of total and utter dependence, I felt I couldn't (and certainly didn't) say no.

Back then, I didn't know what a 'trigger' was. All I could see was that while we made plenty of plans, they pretty much all fell through just at the last minute: the night before, the morning of, or even during the car ride to the party, day out, or afternoon at the pub. But what was the pattern? One day we were having a great time but the next she was doubled over and begging me not to leave her alone. Did I choose not to see it, was I too lazy to do anything about it or was I already just too beaten down by her demands to consider myself to have any other option but to stay? Ultimately, the likelihood of being able to remove myself from the relationship in a positive way was becoming increasingly remote.

I'm not saying that Victoria didn't (or doesn't) have a medical condition that might require support and which left/leaves her with limited mobility. I also acknowledge that, at their extremes, sufferers of chronic endometriosis or adenomyosis[2] (both of which were queried in Victoria's case) might well need full-time care. However, as difficult as it may be to consider, imagine how advertising that you *could* be suffering from any such condition might, for some people, bring a certain amount of value and advantage from the attention and concern that it would understandably create. What I can say with complete certainty is that, despite the decade of medical intervention that I personally was involved in, I was never presented with a single piece of medical evidence to explain why such issues would strike with such perfectly coincidental timing to facilitate the outcome that Victoria wanted. Every. Single. Time.

We did, however, receive plenty of opinions. Victoria and I started to travel to hospitals and care centres to see a variety of specialist consultants, but the problem was that they told us that they could find nothing wrong. Middlesbrough, Cambridge, Newcastle, Oxford, London . . . We would move from one to the other as soon as the discharge letter came through with the same result: sorry, all the tests and investigations are negative or inconclusive.

---

2   A condition where tissue from the lining of the uterus grows into the muscular uterine wall.

Even back then there were signs, of course there were. I would be a fool to pretend otherwise. A consultant once took me to one side and asked what I considered Victoria's pain threshold to be. It seemed, as he very tactfully intimated, to be surprisingly low and to curiously fluctuate with the number of people in the room. In hindsight, I can see that he only wanted to help and was looking to get a grip on the mysterious condition that his patient presented with, but at the time I couldn't, or wouldn't, hear him.

There were other questions that he had about the nature of the problem: if a physical cause couldn't be found, could the issue be psychological? These types of discussions were dismissed very quickly. Victoria was very clear that the pain was real, exasperated at any suggestion to the contrary and absolutely not interested in any form of psychological assessment. Even with all this information available to me at the time, I didn't listen. I didn't listen to my friends, my family or my work colleagues, so why on earth should I listen to a know-it-all consultant who couldn't see the bloody obvious? Victoria said she was in pain and no one was helping. No one *could* help, except me.

Victoria graduated and we moved to Cornwall. I had a brave vision of my future as an advertising copywriter – I wanted to be one of the guys who created clever adverts that made people chuckle while admiring the nimble wordplay and astounding wit of a poster on the London Underground. I had managed to secure a place on one of only two postgraduate courses on the subject in the UK at that time (the other was in London but I had missed the application deadline so it was Cornwall or bust) and considered myself on the launchpad of a rocket-powered creative mission to the stars. Victoria wasn't keen from the off; in order to afford to live in Cornwall for a year, she would have to work and jobs that aren't connected to farming or fishing in that area are tough to get at the best of times.

Those first few months in Cornwall were rough. We rented a tiny fisherman's cottage for the winter, which was so cold that the milk froze *inside* the house but we were young enough for it to be an adventure. The cottage had thick stone walls covered in shingle and more vegetation inside (and attached to) the place than in the stone-walled boundary that the estate agent had very generously suggested was a 'garden'. The stairs, such as they were, only seemed to be held together by the carpet that lay (very loosely) on top of them. Every third board seemed to shift, threatening to give in to the forces of gravity at each step and after one particularly adrenaline-spiked near-miss, we learned not to put any weight on the handrail.

Double glazing was a luxury that had never been afforded to the property and the only source of heating we had was a single oil radiator on wheels that we moved from room to room with us. Well, I say moved from room to room . . . Pragmatism led us to quickly conclude that if we confined our life to the living room then that minimised the likelihood of losing a finger or toe to frostbite. Keeping the radiator in the one room also meant that all personal toilet habits were either performed at college or else very quickly.

Realising that we were ill-equipped to really make the most of this type of 'country living', we swiftly moved into a flat in town and for a time we were doing well. No hospital visits had been needed since the previous summer and it was just the two of us, far from any other family, friends or competing demands on my attention. Things had never been better, both between us and in terms of Victoria's health. She landed a job at the local health trust with a salary of £21,000 a year, which felt like an absolute fortune. Back in Middlesbrough, my job was barely more than half that and so it felt like we had won the lottery. I was so proud of her. Victoria's success in achieving her dream job supporting vulnerable families and adults had taken us both by surprise. For a moment, my unwelcome masculine pride struggled with the idea of her being the breadwinner as I had spent the last three years becoming 'the man' within the relationship. However, these issues soon became inconsequential as Victoria became more excited and my head filled with dreams of *both* of us contributing to an exciting life together, busy and full of purpose.

Flush with newfound cash, we bought my first mobile phone and a car. The pleasure of slipping into our new (second-hand) cherry red Rover 200 with optional sunroof and electric windows is an experience never to be forgotten and made me feel like a king: the gravy train had come to town and it felt great.

But the excitement that held me on that crest of a wave was not to last. Within three months, Victoria started taking sick days. Within four months, she was asking me to help her dodge phone calls from the office and within five, she had stopped pretending that she was even trying to go to work. I had almost managed to convince myself that this was to be the start of our future, success and riches were only a step away, but one day in bed became two, turned into three and so old routines returned: the doctors, the hospitals, the inexplicable symptoms and the expectation that I step up to the plate and be the 'man' that she needed me to be.

Clearly, Victoria building a career in Cornwall wasn't to be the start of our new life and I graduated in the same week that she received a curt message on our answering machine informing her that her P45 was in the post. I loved Cornwall but our time there had come to an end. I've been back to the area many times since (even eating fish and chips on Falmouth dock, just like I used to) but I've never tried to go back to that cottage or find that bedsit again.

Perhaps I feel ashamed of the associated failure that I carry for facilitating Victoria's ability to control me and our lives; the way she simply took what she wanted and the way I let her. It all seemed too easy, with every decision simply connecting to the next. She had explained it so well: I had had *my* year and even though I had found something I really enjoyed, that was hard but exciting and stimulating and which filled me with energy, it had failed to provide the career I had promised.

Considering 'our' circumstances, 'we' concluded that – with limited finance, opportunity and options – moving back home to the village where I grew up was the only option. Victoria confined herself to our room in my parents' house and provided nightly commentary on how I should be working harder to create a home for ourselves. This was never done in front of my parents, who loved me with the 'everything-is-fine-if-we-don't-talk-about-it' type of well-intentioned support that is so deeply rooted in the British psyche.

After Cornwall, Victoria continued to seek out consistent medical interventions in between looking for, getting appointed to and then losing various unskilled care jobs which were well below her skill and qualification levels. Being intermittently bedbound for six months at a time is difficult to explain and so I became well versed in defending, justifying and advocating her many medical conditions to anyone who dared question 'our' motives for not being more independent.

But being independent was part of the confusing and contradictory spiral that was my life. Victoria felt that moving back home with my parents was a wholly unnecessary and unpleasant consequence of my desire to move to Cornwall. It had been my choice to go and as a result of my failure to make an immediate career following the advertising course, we were now forced to live with my parents.

Living in my old room with a girlfriend who hardly got out of bed meant that I was faced with an array of dissonant messages: the disapproving words that were *not* spoken by my parents, the increasingly infrequent messages from old friends and colleagues (which I ignored) were all set against the constant need for me to cater to Victoria's every whim. Objectively, I could see the farcical nature of my position, but with every conversation she and I had, and with every hour that passed, I knew she was right: I *had* failed. I had failed to provide Victoria with the life she wanted. Failed to build a career. Failed to show the world that being with her was what I wanted.

I also failed to understand at the time that it didn't matter how good I was at doing something I loved, how many different futures I could think of or how much time I was committing to achieving them, it would never satisfy her. Instead of using that situation as an opportunity to re-evaluate my life and consider if that was truly the future I wanted, I decided that the only thing left for me was to double down . . . and I fell deeper into the rabbit hole.

Victoria was always looking for *more* and many years later, I realised that I had failed to make that break because while I was busy trying to understand the rules, she was busy changing them. My failure to comprehend what was happening to me was only matched by her success in making sure I never did.

Unbelievable as it might seem to anyone who hasn't been in that situation, I genuinely felt like I was unable to change my life. It came from a lack of control: control of my own life and control of the future. At the time, I *thought* that I had both but as I was about to find out, I wasn't even close to either.

I tried to consider my situation dispassionately: I was an educated and enthusiastic young man with a world of potential and an amazing future ahead of me. However, I was also living at my parents' house with a girlfriend who apparently wasn't able or prepared to take responsibility for her own life and who suffered seemingly unpredictable/inexplicable bouts of debilitating pain, requiring intense near-constant emotional support. But sitting at my old desk and staring up at the Blu-Tac stains and brown, peeling Sellotape marks on the walls which once held posters of my childhood heroes – Meat Loaf and the Chemical Brothers – the contradiction of life felt utterly overwhelming.

As couples should, Victoria and I talked a lot about our situation. Not to anyone else, though; it was only ever between the two of us and usually just before or just after she was struck down by moments of seemingly crippling, but indeterminate, pain. After one particular twelve-hour discussion, punctuated with long periods of Victoria weeping and repeating that I didn't, *couldn't* understand, the solution became so clear and so obvious that it was incredible that I hadn't seen it before. It's true that I had started out that weekend resolute in the decision that she needed to move out because our relationship had reached a point where it was no longer working, I had become the person she expected to solely rely on for the rest of her life and I was no longer prepared to support that. But as we talked and Victoria wept then coaxed her way through that day, she opened my eyes. She showed me that rather than her moving out, what we *actually* needed to do was rent a new house and move back in just the two of us together so that there were less distractions between us. That way we could concentrate 100 per cent on being together. After all, even if it hadn't ultimately delivered the future we'd planned for, hadn't our time in Cornwall been the best our relationship had ever been?

Don't get me wrong, when I write it down like that, I can see how it looks. I'm not delusional or shirking responsibility, but being there in that room, at that time and after being led to believe what I believed, 23-year-old me was as trapped as if there were bars on the windows and locks on the door. Control and choices: when you lose one, you lose the other, and back in 2003, it wasn't looking good for me.

Chapter 3

I remember the first time Victoria told me that we should get married. She was visiting her parents for a few days and we were talking on the phone. I was trying to calm her down after a particularly fraught conversation about going to my cousin's birthday party.

We discussed it a few times, it started easily enough: 'You can go,' she told me, 'just go. I'll be fine at home in bed here until you can come back and get me.' When I wasn't taking the hint, she offered a back-handed solution: 'If the pain gets too bad and I can't get hold of you, with nobody to help or hear me, then I can take more painkillers and sleeping tablets, then maybe just cry myself to sleep.'

Her intentions had become pretty clear, but I was still fairly confident that I should be able to leave for the afternoon. I would be back quickly, I reassured her.

'Sure, I understand but I might need the toilet too,' she went on. 'It will be fine, though – I'll just crawl across the landing and try not to fall down the stairs. Don't worry, go and have a good time. Don't think about me.'

I paused; the line crackled with an awkward silence that lasted just long enough for her to deploy the killer blow: 'Seriously, go and enjoy yourself. Also, I think we should get married. I know that we've not managed to talk about it yet but we both want to, don't we?'

It all sounds ridiculous now and, of course, it was. Why couldn't I just stop everything there? She was already in her parents' house for goodness' sake, why couldn't *they* take care of her? I was a hundred miles away yet somehow, I couldn't even conceive of anyone else being responsible for her. I've asked myself so many times, how did I accept that warped version of reality for so long? I can admit now that I just didn't know what a relationship should be. If you don't know how to recognise your own worth and a bad relationship is your only frame of reference, then how do you know when to say no?

So, I said . . . yes.

Getting married without any money while living with your parents is not a fun experience and don't let anyone tell you otherwise. We were married at Rockingham Castle in April 2004, with the ceremony taking place in the rose garden and the reception in one of the small halls. We wrote our own vows and my older brother Tim used the occasion as an excuse to buy us a large amount of fireworks. Victoria hadn't been exactly enthusiastic about the pyrotechnics and didn't lose any sleep over the fact that we were told at the last minute that we couldn't set them off anyway because it would frighten the local cow population. When I did finally manage to try to light them years later, on my twenty-seventh birthday, in the dying days of our relationship, the badly-ageing fireworks (those that fired at all) only just about managed a couple of mediocre pops before they exhausted what little life they had left in them. I couldn't help but reflect that Tim's generous present whose original intention was to create what should have been a beautiful, spectacular moment was instead, much like our relationship, disappointing and tinged with regret.

At the wedding itself, any thoughts of separating were dismissed as pre-wedding jitters and inevitable nervousness about making such a long-term commitment. I hadn't been involved in the preparations and hadn't been asked to make any decisions. Victoria had revelled in the opportunity to organise, co-ordinate and direct all the requirements of the big day. I was able to make only one stipulation: I refused to get married in a church. Victoria tried to push me towards agreeing but I was not to be moved. It felt like a small but meaningful act of rebellion.

Victoria didn't like me challenging her like that – she was never particularly religious during our time together, but it was one of the few occasions when I got her to compromise.

As parties go, this one was fairly sedate and didn't last long either. As night fell, the barely-touched buffet stretched across the length of the wall, piles of sandwiches going uneaten next to the mini Scotch eggs and cold sausage rolls. There was a DJ downstairs in the flag-stoned cellar and a few select guests; I extended a few invitations to a couple of old friends from my life before Victoria, but it was just too difficult to speak to anyone who knew her and justify over and over again why I was marrying someone who so obviously made me unhappy.

More than the speeches, the food or even the vows, what I remember most vividly is thinking, *it's legal now*. Another invisible layer of control that fixed me into place and tied the two of us together. It should have been a wonderful day and in many ways it was. Victoria looked stunning, her hair curled into ringlets, and she looked absolutely amazing in her dress. We exchanged vows in the castle rose garden and for those minutes we were connected as perfectly as we ever possibly could be.

But even back then I knew that something was pulling at me. It was like a gigantic tug of war with the world on one side, Victoria on the other and she was winning. Even as early as the reception that evening, my memories are filled not with happiness and joy, but instead with groups of expressionless men in grey and blue suits nursing their free champagne flutes, while similarly blank-faced women adjusted their wedding hats and pulled at their scarves and cardigans against the chill of the stone castle walls. I appreciate that may give a measure of disservice to our extended family who were the guests of the day but with hindsight, perhaps more people could see what was coming than I thought.

With the (admittedly already dim) 'post-wedding glow' persisting during the following months, the next stage in the slow dissolution of my identity was underway. I had been locked down, secured, bought and paid for, and I wasn't listening to anyone or anything because nobody knew what I knew, and nobody could look after Victoria like I could.

We moved out of my parents' house when I got a job in marketing for a small theatre company in London; while Victoria got a bit of work here or there as a house-visiting care worker for elderly clients and became involved in local volunteering, which meant that she could work intermittently. My life felt so heavy and distant but I can't deny that I made the move willingly and put any disquiet down to nerves; the truth is that by now I was very good at keeping any emotional turbulence locked down tighter than an Olympic swimmer's trunks. If anyone asked, I reassured them in a calm, measured and pointed fashion.

'I'm fine. Thank you for asking.'

We moved to Flitwick, a small town in Bedfordshire where we didn't know anyone. My family were two hours away and my friends had long since stopped calling; no social life, no family life, nothing except work and Victoria. But it was fine. Relationships are supposed to be tough, aren't they? I was separating, detaching from everything and everyone. I didn't feel anything about my life – it just 'was'. Things happened around me and I went through every day in a haze of apathy. I became almost robotic, blocking out any emotional connection to the night after night of Victoria's desperate sobbing brought on by me cooking the wrong thing, asking permission to go out for a couple of hours or not loving her the 'right' way.

The more she took from me, the more I emotionally pulled away from everyone else. I cooked, cleaned, worked and slept. I would give her medication and drive her wherever she needed or wanted to go, which was usually to the hospital or to see her parents. It was a mechanical existence as my understanding of what it meant to be a man was shaped and moulded. A man was a tool, an object or machine of necessity, my function and purpose to care for Victoria. But that's not to say she didn't give anything back: night after night she delivered whispered whimpers, desperate requests for attention masquerading as affection, which she chased with sleeping pills.

But it was fine. She loved me. I . . . loved her, I could do this, I was meant to do this, everything was fine. I was *fine*.

Flitwick is on the London commuter line just south of Bedford and I started travelling three hours a day into and out of Croydon. The house was small, but it had a garden, was bigger than the Cornish cottage and the weighting of London pay meant that I could afford the commute. My office was full of young staff and I felt guilty for enjoying my time away from the house. The office was so far away from home, it felt like another world filled with noise, laughter, music and fun and completely different to the hours I spent back at home.

From time to time, I had to stay at work in the evenings to manage various events and on one occasion, after we had shut everything up, we went out for drinks. I glanced at the time and said, 'I'd best get going now, I'll see you tomorrow.'

'What's the issue? You always run off so quickly after work,' my colleague Tracey challenged.

'Victoria just prefers me to be home, that's all,' I muttered apologetically, collecting my bag. I had found it best to move fast and leave the building before anyone could realise I had gone.

But this time Tracey caught up with me. 'She could come out too, we should all meet up,' she suggested.

'Yeah, that would be great. We should do that.'

A master of these platitudes, I had loads of them: 'Great! I'll see if I can organise that', or, 'We should definitely try to get something in the diary.' The point was to acknowledge the question but also leave as quickly as possible without committing to anything that I would have to row back on later. However, Tracey wasn't letting me off the hook this time.

'You always say that. What's going on? What's her problem?' she pressed.

'She doesn't like me to be late. She . . . she likes me to be home in case she needs me.'

With a confused shake of her head, Tracey left it at that.

Soon enough, I was being offered all sorts of new challenges and how many did I take? None. Zero. I would come home full of beans, a great new opportunity or idea alive in my head, but by the next morning, I was back on the train catching up on the sleep I had missed after spending six hours rocking Victoria backwards and forwards in bed until she woke at two in the morning and told me I needed to go and sleep downstairs because I was disturbing her.

Making the most of an opportunity means taking a risk, and risk was something that had been entirely removed from my life. But not content with wearing down my soul, there was one other thing that Victoria wanted from me: money. Looking back, it's clear that she didn't want the money *for* anything. Her dreams and aspirations were all incredibly pedestrian; she never pushed for a big house, never believed we needed a sports car (although she loved the idea of driving them). Even dream holidays were limited to the thought of following her parents to Tunisia once a year (which we never actually did).

I liked working in London even with all of its gritty-eyed, concreted glory. For me, it held promise and excitement – it still does. Even though I didn't particularly like my job, I loved kicking my way through the grey concrete streets during my lunch break – I felt as if I was part of the city. The town hall and high street were more utilitarian than aesthetic, but the chicken and kebab shops spilled warmth and light out onto the street as I walked past them in the gloom of a winter's afternoon. I had made a conscious decision at university to, if not enjoy, then tolerate the taste of coffee and here in East Croydon, I developed a love of the coffee shop.

Working in London was supposed to be a step forward for me in my career, my relationship and my life. It was new and exciting. I'm not a city boy, far from it, and I wanted to know what it was like to be one but even after dropping my dream of working in the industry I wanted, I once again found myself having to choose between Victoria and working in London. There was no room, no time for anyone or anything else: I had to choose between prioritising Victoria or myself.

Chapter 4

So, what happened? Fresh from a wedding I didn't want and feeling totally lost, I ran away from who I could have been and chose Victoria. I changed jobs (and my commute) from running the marketing department of a provincial theatre in London to selling cardboard packaging in Welwyn Garden City. I'm not really sure how I managed to achieve this position, considering my obvious lack of experience within the cardboard industry, but my desperation and the company's absence of other options seemed to match perfectly. The pay was good and at least the undertone of vicious ambition started as a shared goal within my team.

There on the third floor of an office block in Welwyn, I got another education. Whereas at university, my social circle all had my best interests at heart, this time the way my new work colleagues ensured that their own careers progressed was an altogether different approach. With the pressure to reach the unachievable heights that Victoria expected from me at home, and juggling to keep domestic life as separate from work as possible, I was somewhat distracted and inevitably ill-equipped for the cut and thrust of the competitive workplace.

By now I had pushed away all my old school friends. My family were spoken to with reluctance and suspicion, and I didn't give anyone in the office any reason to be nice to me. I didn't socialise, mingle or spend enough time at work to make any new friends. Victoria made me constantly concerned that I was doing the wrong thing if I wasn't with her, while simultaneously expecting me to squeeze more and more from my career although at the same time seeming to manage holding down only the most cursory of casual roles herself.

I started to see imagined scrutiny in the faces of everyone around me. How dare they make judgements about our life. They didn't have to stay awake through the early hours comforting their partner as they cried themselves to sleep, night after night. They didn't understand, they couldn't see how Victoria explained it. It was so obvious when she gave me that clear, totally focused understanding that I was the only thing holding her back from a life of agony, despair and utter hopelessness. I was the *man*; she was *my* responsibility; she depended on me and needed total commitment at all times. Of course, I was tired, and it *was* hard, but that's what being married means. Coming straight back home to cook dinner, clean up and put her to bed just demonstrates how much I love her. Because I *do* love her, don't I?

But despite all my best efforts, some people battled heroically past my defensive emotional barriers and constant excuses. One in particular who, to this day, I have yet to repay for her patience and tolerance. We worked in different departments and opposite ends of the country but started to speak after work several times a week. At first it was a way of blowing off steam, decompressing during the journey home. We would swap advice about how best to deal with whatever or whoever was causing us frustration in the office. Then, as we started to understand each other, our conversations became more open; in a funny way, it was the distance between us that let me talk about things that I never had before. Hers were the words that first allowed me to contemplate that I might not have to feel this way forever: 'I know that you feel like you don't have a choice. I know that you think there's nothing you can do and I know that you think you can't change any of this, but what if . . .?'

Now, that might sound like the beginnings of a new intimate relationship – after all, it's straight out of a secret affair storyline from a TV soap. But this was a purely platonic friendship, akin to a big sister attempting to protect and educate her little brother. Her emotionally smothered, horribly repressed, mentally restrained and physically burned-out little brother. It was a lifeline from one of the wisest, kindest people I have ever met and the beginnings of a friendship that has stood the test of time.

However, even as I secretly entertained the notion of not being with Victoria, I knew that it was, of course, ridiculous. Who else would take care of her? I was married now, which meant that I had even more responsibilities. She couldn't look after herself and what else could I do? I kept those conversations for myself. They were secret pockets of escape, moments in time when I could imagine the possibility of a completely different life. Totally absurd and crazy, but still, something that I could hold in my imagination, like winning the lottery.

Perhaps Victoria sensed a change in me – a subtle shift in my mood which indicated that I was again maybe a little bit too comfortable in spending time out of the house. Suddenly there was a need to move on and change jobs. More money, more responsibility and more flexibility were needed. The pressure mounted and we started talking about it a lot. I was wasting my time in that job – they didn't appreciate me or my abilities.

The Welwyn office was a satellite office away from the main manufacturing site and two of my work colleagues had made it very clear that they didn't like me. A clash of personalities, certainly, but it became more and more of a toxic problem the longer the situation continued. One day I cracked.

It was a Tuesday and intermittently I had to give presentations to customers in a dummy supermarket, showcasing new designs and the features of our cardboard products. This one was a biggie: a seasonal launch demonstrating the possibilities in front of the big knobs – buyers with significant cash to spend. It was a huge opportunity. I had created the presentation, working until the early hours for weeks, usually after getting Victoria settled, trying to be the best prepared person in the room, the guy in control. Desperate to prove to myself that I could handle it.

The day before everything was due to kick off, things started to unravel. My notes and my colleague had disappeared along with the sample products. Victoria kept calling, leaving desperate voicemails crying and begging me to come home, and my managing director told me that this was our 'big chance'. It was a pressure like I had never experienced. I was doing my best to hold things together but it seemed like the whole world was trying to tear me apart.

I left the office that day stressed and hurried. I had recovered the notes, found the samples and left a message for my colleague asking that they be moved to the presentation area first thing in the morning, while I would go straight to the store to make sure everything else was in place. On my way home, I got a text message to say that there would be no assistance coming. I couldn't expect other people to do my work for me and it was selfish of me to expect someone else to support me in a job that I obviously couldn't handle. If I wasn't appropriately prepared for the presentation then that was my problem.

I sat outside the house in the car staring at the message. For a while I couldn't read it and had to go over it a few times, I just couldn't understand why life was this hard. A light came on in the kitchen ahead of me and I looked up. There was Victoria looking at me out of the window straight in front. Her eyes were red, her face was pale and haggard. But her face was set hard with an icy stare and with a sharp jerk of the head, she ordered me inside. I took a deep breath and opened the car door.

I told Victoria what had happened and said that I had to leave extra early in the morning to make sure I could get everything ready. I showed her the message and she paused, considering it, before telling me to get on and make dinner. What did I expect? I must be horrible to work with. I didn't care about anyone. She had been calling me all day and I just ignored how much pain she was in. No wonder my colleagues wouldn't help. I probably forgot where I had put all the notes and now I was expecting someone else to solve all my problems. A real man could do it. A real man could fix it. A real man wouldn't complain.

I made dinner and held her in bed until she fell asleep, letting all the expectations in my life fill the darkness in the room with a rising storm of tension. The judgement of my colleagues, my customers, Victoria, my parents and her parents. This is just life, right? I should just shut up and get on with it. This was something that I should be able to cope with without making it such a big deal. I was being a baby and being selfish. Victoria was right. No wonder my colleagues didn't like me. I needed to sort this out, solve the problem. I needed to fix it.

My head felt full of cotton wool – tight, heavy and thick. Pressure built up and my thoughts were slow, travelling across my brain like sparks through glue. I don't remember falling asleep but I do remember the morning alarm buzzing after what seemed like only seconds after I closed my eyes. Fuzzy and disorientated, I sat up on the edge of the bed. I glanced across the room at the wardrobe and drawers.

'Socks, I need socks,' I muttered to myself but my legs wouldn't move. I tried to shake my head to clear it. 'I need to get up and put on some socks.' Nothing. Slowly, my brain started to clear but as the fog dissipated, I was left with a growing abyss inside my chest – a deep darkness that pulled on my hands and legs like an inescapable gravitational force. I didn't understand, I couldn't move. But, I told myself, I had to go to work: people were relying on me and I had so much to do.

I stayed there, sitting on the edge of the bed with Victoria asleep beside me for about ten minutes, arguing silently with myself. It felt like hours as I kept trying to move but couldn't. Inside my head I was shouting, screaming, but nothing was responding. My thoughts were hot, my mind viscous and jellified. I could feel prickles all over my arms, my face, my hair. They spread down my back and into my legs. My thighs and toes were tingling as the hairs stood on end. Shivering? No, I could feel the heat of the flush on my arms, face and neck.

Then suddenly, like an out-of-body experience, I felt my arms shifting. I saw the world start to move but I wasn't in control. I couldn't speak and I couldn't stop myself from sitting back and slowly, deliberately, lying back down in bed.

I knew I had to get up, I knew I had to go to work, but I couldn't – I couldn't control my own body. I lay there and my eyes closed. I didn't want them to, I tried to stop them but nothing would do what I told it to do. I could feel my body calming and shutting back down to sleep and I couldn't stop it. I wasn't afraid or worried, my thoughts weren't fast enough to carry that type of urgent message. It was, and remains, the strangest thing I've ever experienced. Something, somewhere right down deep inside was protecting me, *from* me. I woke up later that afternoon, called in sick and never went back. Within two weeks I had quit and found another job.

I recognise now that the experience was some form of mental breakdown. A psychological defence mechanism that had kicked in and stopped the entire day from happening for me. I thought that the problem was work and that by not going back, everything would be fine – but I was very, very wrong.

Chapter 5

Most of us have spent some time in hospitals or consultants' waiting rooms and will recognise that heavy, characteristic smell of mass catering and scented industrial disinfectant that seems to soak into the wipe-clean furniture. The shiny chrome and grey PVC coating of the trolleys and wheelchairs, the squeaky linoleum flooring and scuffed wall protectors lining the corridors. It's a source of comfort for some and pain for others. For me, it represents neither of those things. I have come to realise that the staff who work there are all just human beings, like the rest of us. They have chosen to spend incalculable hours, months and sometimes years of their lives dedicating themselves to the pursuit of helping others. Doctors, nurses, surgeons, consultants all have (to a greater or lesser degree) the same laudable goal. But they are not gods. Through the years of sitting beside Victoria and seeing the way she (or should that be 'we'?) framed and manoeuvred through the system, it's all too clear that they don't always have all the answers and they are not exempt from the frailties of human nature or the subtle twist of deliberate manipulation.

Victoria and I saw many new faces and heard thousands of kind words as we worked our way from doctor to doctor. Some advised further investigations, others prescribed drugs, but none of them saw two people in their office, none of them saw *me*.

I've already spoken about (what should have been) my first red flag: the consultant who questioned Victoria's pain threshold. He remains the only professional who took me aside and questioned me about the nature of Victoria's symptoms. But he didn't ever actually ask me what *I* knew. A lot of relationships are like that: there is so much information hidden just beneath the surface, but no one is asking the right questions to draw them into the open.

But if you do start to ask questions then you have to be prepared to see the problems: those multifaceted elements that may be the only thing holding a destructive or abusive relationship together. When your partner says she's in pain, you try to help them – anyone would do the same, wouldn't they? If the first doctor doesn't help, you'd find another. The second or third can't provide answers, so you crank up the effort.

We pushed to get into hospital; one consultant and then another specialist. One investigation. Two. Three. They can't find anything and nothing seems to help – she's still in pain. Painkillers: paracetamol is laughable, codeine doesn't touch it and co-codamol wears off too quickly. She can only take one sleeping tablet a day, so what's left? Come on, Doc, you have to help. Morphine? Surely that's a step too far, but she says it's the only thing that deals with it . . .

Having gone through practically all of the medical trusts within a two-hour radius, we were running out of doctors and drugs to try. There had been several exploratory operations too; investigations by keen, enthusiastic consultants trying to find out what was behind her symptoms. Victoria went through multiple laparoscopies but was given a clean bill of health each time and so we moved on to the next. Oxford,

Bedford, Cambridge and Milton Keynes . . . we became regular visitors at them all.

By 2004, I was getting tired of the constant drive to move from area to area, medical team to medical team. Around the end of January, I sensed that Victoria was about to push to try something different. Something new.

'You're married, correct?' I don't remember this consultant's name. I don't even remember which hospital it was. Oxford, Cambridge, Peterborough or Luton – it could have been any of them. Victoria confirmed that we were. 'We really can't see any reason why you have experienced such acute pain for such a long time.' It was the latest discharge following a string of appointments that had pushed us through yet another set of consultant registrars and specialists. 'All the surgery, all the medication and all the help you've had doesn't show anything wrong. Have you thought about having a baby? Some women say that it can help with undiagnosable abdominal pain.'

So that was a bit left-field. I'll admit, I wasn't convinced, but by now, you have probably realised that I had taken more than a few steps along the path of least resistance. To be honest, I was practically skipping along, carrying a bag of snacks for the journey, so it didn't take Victoria long to convince me that I was convinced. Couples who are in love get married, buy a house and have a baby. It's perfectly natural and reasonable. We were in love and married, weren't we? That's two of the four already, no more questions then. Be a man. Make it happen.

As a result of my last career change, I had managed to trade up a couple of notches and as there was much more finan-cial security back then, I found I could leverage enough of a deposit to buy an 80 per cent share of a housing association two-up, two-down semi in Milton Keynes. I've been back a couple of times since then and sat in the car looking at the door (not in a stalker/police stakeout kind of way, though admittedly I can see how that must seem), remembering that house and the life we had in it.

The house was a perfect first family home with the exception of the death-trap open spiral staircase. Installed, I'm sure, to save space but it was so steep, tight and slippery that it used to scare the bejesus out of me once our daughter, Grace, arrived. The front door opened directly into the living room with the stairs in front of you over in the right-hand corner. Straight ahead were a set of double doors leading into a kitchen, which dog-legged around before leading into the garden at the back.

I removed the double doors and we re-tiled the kitchen. DIY wasn't for me and remains one of my weaknesses, both in terms of intention and ability. The end result of the new-look kitchen was one that was passable so long as you didn't actually look at it too closely. Upstairs, there were two double bedrooms at either end of the house, separated by a bathroom and airing cupboard. If you are lucky enough to have a garden in Milton Keynes then you will probably have one of two types: tiny and overlooked by all your neighbours, or butted up against a tree-lined bank separating you from the nearest major road (of which there are hundreds – this is Milton Keynes, remember, home to a thousand roundabouts and an unfathomable grid system).

Our garden was an 'edger', which is to say it sat up against the edge of the estate and was therefore mere yards away from Vertical Road Number 5 (V5 for short). I think we can all agree that those civil planners who dreamed of a revolution in British urban infrastructure design really earned their bonus that year.

For all its faults (such as the lawsuit-waiting-to-happen stairs and modelling-clay-with-grass-on-top masquerading as a garden), I liked that house. I liked the size, I liked the area. I liked the neighbours, with whom I am still good friends now, and it was in that space, within those walls, that the last year of my old life and the start of the battle with Victoria really began.

People say that having a baby changes everything and that's true. They also say that you can't prepare for it and that certainly the first one will completely alter your perspective on life. I can testify that this is also true.

A baby is a wonderful thing, a new human being full of hope and promise. They have no expectations of you and bring no emotional baggage with them when they arrive. The parents, on the other hand, are a different matter. No parent is perfect. No one is able to say that their first child brings non-stop, constant and unmitigated joy into their life. New babies, in particular first babies, will drive any parent to their limits, specifically parents who have systematically removed themselves from all of their former support networks.

Let me be totally clear: I had absolutely no idea how to handle a baby. I was unprepared and frightened by the ante-natal classes, there in person but with a nodding, glassy smile that masked a denial to accept the impending reality. I didn't understand what it meant to have a baby or be a father. My frame of reference had been unfortunately limited to my own father, who taught me how to shave, drive and avoid any type of emotional responsibility.

So, I knew what kind of father I *didn't* want to be, but what kind of father *was* I? The question started to loop back around again and again like the songs on the tired old eighties Christmas playlist that gets dusted off in the shops every

November. Someone once told me that a child only needs one good role model in their life to give them the chance to truly flourish. But, when Grace was born, I was not that person.

I mentioned that I believe that having a baby will bring out the base traits in a person's character and in my case, when you strip back all the layers of sugar-coated social expectations ('Oh yes, I've taken to it really well'; 'It's tough but it's *so* worth it'; 'It's such a pleasure, I've never *been* so happy'), I had Victoria on hand to tell me that, if I was honest with myself, then having a baby should have made me realise just how selfish I was.

She reflected on how I always ensured that we only did the things that *I* wanted to do; I always thought of myself first and then tried to fit the baby and her in around me. I just didn't consider how unimportant and unnecessary my place was in the family hierarchy. My purpose was to get out of the house for work and then come straight back home in case they needed anything. That's not difficult, is it? Why couldn't I just provide the unconditional love and care that a man is *supposed* to have for his wife and child? Where was the support? The journey home from work was forty minutes maximum, why did it take me fifty? My wife needed me, my daughter needed me. I didn't understand the pain – that's why she was so tired and needed the pills.

I wasn't a good role model, that's true, but was I really *that* bad? With every dissenting thought, every question and every personal opinion becoming evidence of more selfish, self-centred and narcissistic personality traits that would be logged and filed for use at a later date, how could I possibly think of myself as anything else?

Perhaps through some vestige of a deep bulletproof self-confidence, no matter how often I was told otherwise, I still thought of myself as a good dad. Not the best, that's for damn sure, but if there's a better source of perspective in your life than looking down at a sleeping baby in your arms at three o'clock in the morning then I would love to know what it is. I was starting to see what being responsible *really* meant. This baby, this little person, is part of you. It doesn't ask, or demand or expect. It just needs you to do the best you can and loves you for that. The kind of love that both freezes and burns everything at the same time. Nothing else matters – not me, not you, not *anything*. Just this perfect little girl who looks up at you in the flickering darkness and yawns before slowly closing her eyes and drifting off to sleep again against your chest.

I worked during the day and then came home and played with Grace, bathed her, told her stories and put her to bed. When she cried, I got up, brought her to Victoria for a feed, then held her until she fell back to sleep. Holding her in my arms, I started to question how perhaps things in my life weren't going the way they were supposed to. How could I be doing so much wrong when there just wasn't enough time to do anything else?

One day, only a few months after Grace was born, I was sitting at my desk at work and I got a call. Victoria had been doing some ad-hoc freelance hours working for a company by writing 'example' essays for students. Well, I *say* she had been writing them. If I was being generous, then I would say that there was, at best, a significant amount of collaboration: she would edit the text that I had written (as and when she was able/willing/awake to do so). The very grey nature of this type of business tends to mean that companies appear and disappear quickly as they are identified and banned by schools and universities. At anywhere between £50 and £200 a time, though, it's a fairly profitable sideline if you can manage to write half-decent essays on topics that you only have a very limited understanding of.

The name flashed up on my phone screen: *Victoria*. My heart sank a little as it usually did, but I wasn't in a position to be able to accept personal calls outside of break times. My office phone then rang with a client and I was distracted by emails, calls and conversation. Then Victoria called again, a third, fourth, fifth and sixth time followed in very quick succession when I didn't pick up. I remembered what had happened the last time that I couldn't call her back and so I got up, pretending that I needed to go to the loo.

'Hi, what's up?'

'I've been calling you. Why haven't you answered?' Victoria seemed anxious and brusque.

I tried to calm her down and explain the situation: 'You know I can't take calls in the office. What's wrong?'

'I need you to come home now. Grace is screaming and I need to go to Bristol.'

The latest essay writing company that Victoria had been working for was based in Bristol and had been avoiding us for a few weeks. Evidently, Steve – the guy running the show – had cleared out and done a runner, owing people, including us, payment for work done. We were expecting about £150, which was a lot of money for us with a newborn baby and only one wage-earner in the house.

'What?! I can't, I'm at work. Wait, Bristol? What's wrong with Grace? Is she OK? I can't hear her crying?' The two disparate pieces of information knocked me off-balance, I couldn't think which to tackle first.

'I told you, I need to go to Bristol, right now. Are you coming home?'

At this point I should say two things: first, I couldn't hear Grace crying at all and second, I absolutely believed (and still do) that Victoria's genuine intention was to persuade me to drive her to Bristol. She had threatened some crazy things before but dropping everything in the late afternoon to drive to a city she didn't know, to find someone that she had never previously met, at an address that she didn't have and demand payment for a service that was barely even legal seemed to be a bit off the wall even for her.

There was a pause and then I heard Grace start to scream. 'There, see? She's crying. I told you. Are you happy now?'

'What's wrong? What happened?'

'Nothing. I don't know, I've got to go.'

The line went dead and I looked at the blank phone in disbelief. Did that just happen? Did she just . . .? Could she really have . . .? I'm sure that Grace hadn't been crying when she first called. Maybe she was in a different room? But then it was a very small house.

I immediately called back, but it just went to voicemail. I started calling round people who might be available to help while I thought about what I was going to say to my manager. Luckily, our neighbour was home and answered the phone to hear me breathless and practically incoherent, babbling about the need to check on Grace and Victoria, who was very obviously (to me, anyway) unable to take care of a baby by herself.

I drove home like a madman, but when I arrived, I found Victoria asleep on the sofa and Grace playing happily at the neighbour's. The events of that day secured another friendship that I'm thankful to say is still as strong as ever. It was an experience centred on the children and it was through them that I was starting to see things a little differently.

I spent some time giving Grace a bath and checking in case I could see what had hurt her earlier that day, but there was nothing obvious. Did I truly think Victoria would hurt her? All kids had scrapes and bumps. They cry because their teeth hurt. They cry because they are hungry. Sometimes they just cry. So, if I'm being honest with myself, did I really know what I was looking for anyway?

I got Grace into bed just as Victoria woke up. When she came through to the kitchen, there was no trace of the afternoon's profound emotional crisis and no discussion of what had happened. We ate dinner, made small talk and watched television. I was confused but ultimately, I accepted it. Bitter experience had taught me that it was so much easier to simply roll with the inconsistencies, ignore the conflicts and explain or excuse away the problems that they caused. We went to bed as if nothing had happened.

Of course, the people whom I had called to check in on her that day were not so happy to let the matter drop. They understood that I had been in a state of panic and that I had believed something very worrying was going to happen. One of those people was Jane, a friend that we had met in Flitwick before moving to Milton Keynes. She was also one of the few people who would continue to socialise with us, despite Victoria's disproportionate and active social friction.

Jane wasn't like anyone I had ever met before. She didn't seek conflict but she wasn't afraid of it either. She chose not only to challenge requests she disagreed with, but would actively confront inequality and inconsistencies, as and when she saw them. I was intrigued: here was someone not just 'talking the talk' but demonstrating just why it's important to understand yourself and then have the confidence to hold (and most importantly, act on) their morals every day. Furthermore, she was someone who still wanted to spend time with us even though disappointment and irritation were almost exclusively the only things we had to offer in return. After all, that's all we had given anyone else who came into our lives. We'd found someone who could see the consistent inconsistencies in our marriage and both Victoria and I were being called out on them. It certainly made for some uncomfortable times and the aftermath of 'The Bristol Incident' (as it became known) was one of those.

Chapter 6

I knew that Victoria could also feel things change. We started to see more of her parents and the hospital visits came back with a vengeance as the episodes of pain increased in regularity and intensity. They were no longer confined to any semblance of a monthly cycle; they stretched two or even three weeks of the month and were brought on by smaller and smaller events. To seemingly test just how far I would be willing to go to appease her, I would be asked to take unnecessary and extended detours while driving to avoid speed bumps or potholes that Victoria 'knew' were along the way or, where they were unavoidable, it was demanded that I traverse them at speeds normally reserved for pensioners on mobility scooters.

All the while, my perspective and function in life were changing before my eyes. Grace was bringing things that I had been unhappy about but willing to live with into stark, unrelenting focus. If my family had been a game of Top Trumps then Victoria had been beaten into second place – and she didn't like it.

As circumstances go, Jane split up from her long-term partner a few months later and moved temporarily into our house, sleeping on the sofa while she found somewhere to rent. Victoria thought that the short-term opportunity of a live-in babysitter might go some way towards helping the growing tension between us, but it didn't quite work out that way.

Jane's readiness to confront inequality and unfairness meant she and Victoria regularly clashed. She may have been a visitor in our house, but their strong and opposing personalities quickly created friction.

For my part, having someone to talk to of an evening was a change that I appreciated. To the outside world, my relationship with Victoria may have been considered difficult or perhaps strained but ultimately resolute. But when Jane saw it up close and personal, she recognised just how toxic it was and indicated as much to the both of us. She and I talked long into the evenings about what makes strong relationships: the principle of mutual support, the importance of balance, equity and equality. It was so different to the life I knew. Jane met me as an equal, asking my opinion and at times, particularly where my own self-belief had been beaten down, defended my perspective.

Jane never suggested I leave Victoria – her moral compass was and remains much too strong for that – but before too long, she had moved into her new house, leaving behind for me some unanswered questions and a newly opened door. I was able to question myself more strongly: what if? Could I leave? Would Victoria let me? Was I strong enough and crucially, what would happen to Grace if I did?

Those questions scared me. Scared me because after seven years, this was what I understood relationships to be. Scared me because it was who I believed I was and scared me because, quite frankly, I couldn't see how I could protect Grace and myself from Victoria's manipulations at the same time. So, I pushed all of those questions to one side. Shut them away, dismissed any notion that I was anything other than fine. But the more I refused to acknowledge my own emotions, the stronger they became. They would ambush me unchecked at two in the morning or driving home from work. They would cause me to physically catch my breath while in the shower, as if I had just sprinted a hundred metres. As my chest constricted and the water poured over my head as hot as I could bear, or while I fought the sudden urge to throw up during lunchtime summer walks around the park next to the office, one thought kept replaying in my head: *What will I tell Grace?*

What will I tell her when she's old enough to recognise all the times that I could have made a change but didn't? What will I tell her when she can see that my life is just filled with apologies and making allowances for somebody else? How can I be an example to her when I can't look at myself in the mirror?

Of course, talking to yourself is one thing, but putting anything into practice is very different. From the dawn of time, relationship breakups have been postponed, put off and shied away from because it's the 'wrong time'. But what was the right path to take? Should I be insensitive and to hell with it, or was there a 'right time' to do something so incredibly difficult? It all felt like a false choice: did I really have to choose between putting the divorce application in with a birthday card or forcing myself to wait eighteen years while slowly sinking into a blackhole of depression and misery? Either outcome seemed so fundamentally wrong.

But then, something crystallised in my mind – Victoria *owned* me and the certainty of what I had to do about that came so clearly that I knew it had to be right. Was it going to be right for all three of us? That would be debatable as I strongly suspected that Victoria wouldn't agree with the choice I was going to make, but right for me and Grace? Absolutely and without question.

Victoria told me where to go, what to do, who to see and what to say. The little of my own voice that was left was being used to reinforce Victoria's sense of identity. I was becoming an echo of myself. Victoria had been hinting that she wanted another child, but if that happened then the cycle would start all over again. While I had to accept responsibility for bringing this life on myself and Grace, how could I justify inflicting that on another baby? Grace had come along before I realised that I *could* choose, before when I felt the risk of doing nothing outweighed the risk of leaving. But now that I faced that same crossroad again, I wasn't alone: Grace could give me the strength I hadn't been able to find before.

I was capable of being a better dad. I *wanted* to be a better dad, but I just didn't know how to get away from Victoria. Back then, I had no idea what a coercive relationship was, beyond the media stereotypes that I certainly didn't recognise as a reflection of my life. Grace deserved that I be the best dad that I could be, but it had become clear that I couldn't do that with Victoria: she was too controlling and I was slowly but inexorably suffocating. Sooner or later, I wouldn't be able to take it anymore.

I had to leave.

Chapter 7

'I can't do this anymore.'

Victoria glanced over to me but didn't say anything. I couldn't tell what her reaction was as I drove down the road with my hands clenched around the steering wheel, as if trying to force myself backwards into the seat. Had she heard me? She brushed a few strands of dark brown hair away from her face as she looked over at me. Her deep hazel-brown eyes blinked slowly before she looked away and drew in a slow deliberate breath before letting it out in a deep, disdainful sigh.

I didn't know I was going to say it, I really didn't. The pressure inside me was so immense, so absolute, that I had no idea what was going to give first, our relationship or my sanity. I felt that if I didn't say it then, I would never find the courage to be brave enough again. But the ice-cold fear that gripped my heart and froze my tongue was so painfully real. There had been so many times during our life together that I had wanted to speak. I had tried so hard but just couldn't find the words, my voice had been taken away. The incongruous nature of that fear over something as simple as a conversation, a conversation that Victoria could and would dismiss so casually as if it wasn't even worthy of acknowledgement, would come to perfectly sum up the first years of our relationship.

'I can't do this anymore' is so easily said. People say it all the time: after deciding to climb the stairs to the fourth floor instead of taking the lift, when they are halfway through eating a tub of ice cream and the brain freeze hits, or when they're late for a meeting while standing in a queue for a coffee.

When I finally managed to say those words, it wasn't easy. It wasn't easy because it meant that I was about to change the lives of what I thought were three people. But actually, that sentence impacted so much more than I ever imagined. My perception of 'giving up' is the equivalent of taking the easy way out. The negative connotations are so ingrained that we are desperate to teach our children not to do it. We want them to keep going and to finish what they start. Perseverance against adversity is something to be celebrated, even revered. But if we just continue forever then how can we tell when enough is enough? How do we give those same children the ability to distinguish a temporary bad patch in an otherwise healthy relationship (which is something that is not unusual nor, usually, insurmountable) from the final straw in a decidedly toxic one?

But if that was to be my only problem then it could have been an easier one to resolve (although admittedly my previous attempts at leaving our relationship hadn't exactly gone to plan), but it wasn't. Like Nostradamus, a vision of my future stretched out ahead of me; I saw a court system and society that rewarded contact of children to their parents principally on perfected ideals of gender-based suitability. I assumed (just as I suspect most people do) that a mother is inherently more equipped to care for a child and my position, as Grace's father, was viewed through that perspective. Even if I ever believed that I could have left with her, my own feelings of inadequacy stopped me.

Other things also weighed heavily on my mind. The Bristol Incident, in particular, could have been a shout for attention but what if it happened again? What if it was worse? What if it was already worse and I had been missing it? Thoughtful, considered internal debate turned to awful thoughts that chased me through the night like a crazed never-ending marathon while I wrestled with the question of what to do next. The greatest irony was the realisation that to be there for Grace and give her that voice, I had to say goodbye to her. Not because I wanted to, but because I couldn't see any other choice.

It was a Wednesday afternoon and I had left work early to collect Grace. I spent a few minutes with the childminder hearing all about my daughter's epic adventures with her friends that day, before she had fallen asleep in her car seat in the sun, shattered from the day's hard play time. I was driving along in the early summer warmth, trying to keep my eyes on the road instead of looking in the rear-view mirror at my gorgeous baby girl. She looked angelic as the afternoon sun made her blonde hair glow like gold. The window was down, the sky was blue and I had plenty of time to work on my trucker's tan as I traversed across Milton Keynes in my white Volvo saloon, but I felt uneasy. My thoughts wandered between what I was going to cook for tea that night (I would be expected to cook for us both most nights, as Victoria was often in too much pain to stand for long) through to just how uncomfortable the upcoming weekend with the in-laws was going to be. It was 2008 and Grace was one and a half. I loved those times where everything seemed to stop; those were the moments that reinforced that Grace would always be my baby, regardless of how much she grew.

From the childminder's, I had to go to pick up Victoria from work. As I drew up to the kerb, unlocked the door and let her in, that sickly, uneasy feeling intensified in my chest. Perhaps I was a bit ill? *I hope I'm not coming down with anything*, I thought. We drove in silence for a few minutes as we had tended to do recently, but then the quiet was broken a few moments later by Victoria asking if I had thought any more about our recent conversation as I had seemed 'a little reticent' about the topic of trying for another baby.

I paused as the nauseous sensation morphed into a mental gut punch but outwardly just shrugged noncommittally.

She continued, 'I think another baby would be the best thing for us as a family. We've always wanted a big family, haven't we? Plus, there really isn't a "best" time, isn't that what you said?'

I knew from experience that this was a one-sided conversation. I was not required to give an opinion as Victoria was effectively talking to herself, working through enough of the rationale for me to then agree to her plans. If I offered any dissenting view, the topic would be repeated later in the same way but still approached with the same predetermined conclusion. So, I sat and waited until she had expressed enough of her thoughts to justify her decision. It was a routine that had been perfected over the nine years of our relationship and I would like to say that it hadn't always been like that, but I can't. Perhaps it wasn't as polished as in our early days, and it would take longer to reach the same inescapable conclusions, but in retrospect it had always been there.

However, this time something wasn't right. The heavy feeling had solidified and was deepening in on itself like a collapsing neutron star. I could feel the beginnings of the black hole inside me start to physically pull at my fingers as they tingled and my heart worked twice as hard to force blood around my body. It wasn't the same feeling as before, I still felt in total control but just very heavy and my limbs seemed numb and it was hard to move. But I continued to drive in silence, listening.

'Besides, Grace is going to be two this year and she needs a brother or sister to play with.' Another statement that did not invite comment. 'And the last pregnancy wasn't too bad, right? Having another baby really would be the best thing for the family, wouldn't it?'

The void in my chest had eaten my stomach, lungs and heart. My arms were anaesthetised, my fingers had moved from a tingle to a sharp prickling. In contrast to everything else, my head was getting lighter, not quite dizzy but fuzzy and hot. Then I said it. I opened my mouth and it just blurted out, I couldn't stop it:

'I can't do this anymore. Any of it. I'm leaving.'

She fell silent, mouth open mid-sentence, looked at me with eyes that expressed her disdain more than words ever could. Then she turned away and we finished the drive home in silence. No drama, no fuss.

That night, I got Grace bathed and ready for bed before I came back downstairs. The house was a morgue in those intervening hours as Victoria moved from sofa to kitchen to bedroom while maintaining that deliberate silence. I knew that those silent hours were only the start of my punishment. Her refusal to even acknowledge my existence used to exasperate me. It would make me angry that she knew she could annul my opinion so easily by simply ignoring it. Over the years, my periods of frustration had lessened in duration and intensity until only acceptance remained. Silence was her most powerful weapon and the more the silence grew, the worse I knew the repercussions would be.

But this time felt different. I'm not sure why. I'd finally said the words and I couldn't take them back. We both knew that the rules of the game had changed and I felt more confident than I ever had before. Nervous and petrified but stronger too.

'What are you cooking for dinner?' she asked me. 'I'll just have some salmon and rice. I'm not really very hungry.'

'Don't you want to talk?' I asked.

'No, I'm really tired. I just want dinner and to go to bed.'

So, I made her dinner. Victoria liked plain flavours, nothing spicy, salty or even too sweet most of the time. I love to cook and would do it most days; steamed salmon with plain rice was one of her favourites.

We had one of those metal steamers that held the water at the bottom and had two removable layers like a colander. With the rice cooking in the bottom, I could steam the salmon in the first layer and a couple of pieces of broccoli or even a few green beans in the top when Victoria was feeling adventurous. A little sprinkle of salt, no pepper and serve. It was a one-pot, one-plate solution. She liked to keep things clear, easy and simple.

Every now and then I had tried to liven things up a bit, but nothing seemed to enthuse or inspire her and she certainly didn't try to pretend for my benefit. It wasn't as though I *couldn't* cook anything else and I was never explicitly told not to. Instead, when faced with a plate of something she didn't want, Victoria wouldn't eat at all and claimed that she 'wasn't hungry anyway' or 'was too tired to eat'. Inevitably I would offer to cook her the dinner she wanted and she would reluctantly agree to pick at it over the course of an hour before going to bed without talking to me.

That night, I didn't eat but avoided Victoria as she finished her dinner before going upstairs to bed. I cleaned the kitchen and sat down to think about what I had done. Was this the right decision? Did I really understand what it meant and was it going to be worth it? I sat almost on pause, grateful for the space and time to myself. I was waiting for a pained, demanding cry that could come from either the baby or my wife. Despite the events, and the emotional impact of my own ultimatum earlier that day, I still knew I would react to either without thinking.

I know how it all sounds. Marital breakdowns happen every day. It's a fact of life and on first impressions, I wasn't exactly helping myself. The most obvious criticism is that I could have left at any time if I had wanted to. But go where? My whole life was focused on Victoria. We did what *she* wanted to do, went where *she* wanted to go and only saw who *she* wanted to see. I believed that she wouldn't be able to cope without me and so what else could I do? I would be lost without her because that's what a marriage was. At least that's what *our* marriage was.

I was daring to acknowledge those deep, dark feelings that weren't supposed to be there. Loneliness. Anxiety. Unhappiness. I'd been pushing them down, stamping them out and boxing them up. Storing them away so deep inside that they couldn't get out. But now I could hear them getting louder, asking me: *is this it?* Did I really want to leave and risk everything to have the chance of being a father who wasn't completely beaten? Or should I stay with her? I knew that if I did, I would end up staying forever and so this was the time to decide. Right here and right now.

In the end, I sat staring at the TV for hours. Not really watching anything but rather letting the light hypnotically flicker across the room. My thoughts jumped and skittered around, slipping away from me before I could make sense of what was happening. Eventually, everything started to slow down and come into focus. Sitting by myself, watching the news cycle round before me in the early hours of the morning, I realised that my choice had already been made. I had an unexpected but rock-solid certainty that I couldn't and *wouldn't* bring another child into the world within this relationship. If I was unhappy now, and another baby was the one thing being demanded of me, then capitulating this last time would ensure that our problems would never be over.

If I went back now, Victoria would have completed her suppression of the person that I used to be, so I had to seize this moment if I wanted the chance to be a positive part of Grace's future, to give her the life she deserved rather than the one of subservience and robotic pandering to Victoria's erratic and contradictory whims, which would stretch out ahead of us if I stayed. I realised that the best way I could protect my daughter, in fact the *only* way I could do that, was to paradoxically leave her. I was desperate for Grace to have the opportunity to be happier than I was; it was now or never and if I didn't go, Victoria would possess me for the rest of my life and so in April 2008, I moved out.

Chapter 8

Because I didn't know I was going to leave, I didn't make any plans. I didn't know where I was going or what I was going to do. After spending the night on the sofa, I left the house as early as I could and drove to my work that morning and then . . . just . . . carried on. I drove straight past the office in a daze and ended up in a Starbucks, drinking the biggest cup of coffee I could afford while staring vacantly out of the window.

All the repressed fears, hopes and anxieties now bounced and ricocheted around the inside of my head, coming at me from all angles so fast, I couldn't make sense of them. But I had no second thoughts, no reservations. I felt liberated: I'd managed to rescue myself so that, somewhere down the line, I could then be the dad Grace needed.

So, what plan did I come up with? It may not be very dramatic but the truth is: absolutely nothing. I sat in that Starbucks for four hours and came out with nothing but a parking ticket. I just had no idea where I was, what I was doing or who to talk to. I was convinced the world would open up before me as the weight of my toxic relationship with Victoria lifted, but nothing could have been further from the truth. I was terrified, frightened to death about what Grace would think of me. Would Victoria even let me see her?

Where would I live? How could I afford to live? I had so many questions and not a single answer.

I thought about whether I should tell work or if I should even tell my family. The latter might seem like an odd question. For most people the answer is straightforward: *yes, of course you should.* But, for me, it wasn't that simple for a couple of reasons. First, I had spent years systematically distancing myself from my family. Second, as much as I wanted to tell them everything, the man I had become, the man that Victoria had made me into, just wouldn't let me speak out. I use that phrase literally – I physically couldn't speak about it.

When I tried, my tongue and jaw would freeze. What sounds I could make were guttural and stuttering. All thought processes would slow and even as I reached out for the right words, they would slip away from me and nothing would make sense. My mind would dump everything and leave me in suspended animation, paused like a buffering YouTube video. Even now, all these years later, it can be difficult to talk about.

I had never realised that shame was such a frightening and powerful emotion. It is what other people in terrible situations suffer through. It didn't touch my life; it didn't affect *me*. I acknowledge now that I had lost any sense of pride many years before in accepting the lengths I was prepared to go to in order to protect Victoria, but shame isn't just the opposite of pride, it holds its own power.

I believed, and I mean *truly* believed, that I simply didn't deserve to ask for help. In leaving my wife and child, I had failed to live up to my responsibilities as a husband and father. Worse of all, I had *chosen* to do all of it and so I had to live with the consequences. It was ironic that, even in the act of leaving, I felt shame at the same time as relief and even though I had just turned my whole life inside out, my frame of reference was still based on my life with Victoria: 'real men' didn't need to talk about their problems.

And who in my family was there to talk to anyway? They were struggling themselves: my parents were in the process of separating and my brothers were just about holding their own lives together as best they could. I am the youngest of four brothers and as a child, I had always been chasing after them, trying to catch up and show that I could be a grown-up too. But, of course, by the time that I realised being a grown-up isn't all it's cracked up to be, I *was* one and I couldn't go back.

Although we spanned almost a ten-year age gap between us all (which, when you are seven years old, is the same as fifty), growing up, my brothers had always been a constant, a 'safe' place to turn to. Tim (my next oldest brother) is always available for an 'adventure' in whatever form that might take. Matt is an artistic genius who could cook up a storm for any size party, from two to twenty; and when, in my mid-twenties, I crashed and nearly flipped my car over the central reservation of the M4 in the early hours of the morning, with Victoria asleep beside me and Grace in the back seat, I called Adam because, well, Adam was the person I called when I was in trouble.

Adam was the guy who held us all together – he was *sorted*. At sixteen, he had left school, went straight into a job at the local hospital and worked his way up from a porter to the management board. He was a man who knew how to play the long game and I envied that.

But I'd pushed them all away to the point where we barely spoke and when we did, it was painfully superficial. How could I tell them just how badly I'd messed everything up? That emotional lock was incredibly powerful and I still don't entirely understand it now. Partly my own embarrassment at failing in the eyes of the people that I loved and admired the most, partly fearing their judgement and (without wanting to pass too much blame onto my own parents), partly the way that I had been brought up.

Second, Mum, while embarking on her own post-retirement life-changing experience, had travelled to Eritrea in East Africa at the time, volunteering to help organise and implement rural education programmes with VSO International. Unfortunately, the available methods of communication into and out of Eritrea were then, as now, difficult at best. She had been gone for a year or so by then and had settled in comfortably, which put a physical layer of separation almost impossible to overcome between us.

Dad, on the other hand, *was* around and it was to him that I did turn in the end. He has never been a man who's easy to talk or show emotional vulnerability to. It's probably best to describe him as someone who knows what empathy is (he has certainly read about it in the newspaper now and then), but who has never really managed to get to grips with the detail of it. His philosophy has always been in moments of high pressure, it's best to take a moment to shake yourself off and pour another glass of whisky. He took the news with characteristically stoic demeanour and then extended a financial lifeline. He didn't ask me to cover any of the more nuanced aspects of the situation, nor did he express an opinion or judgement (positively or negatively) about my actions, but he did provide help to me when I needed it most in the only way that he knew how and that's something I will always thank and love him for.

After sofa-surfing for a week, which is how long it took me to exhaust my very short contact list of people willing to house me, I found a house that was available to rent and which I could just about afford. I moved straight in and having always been one to prepare for the worst, spent the following week scaring myself stupid. I started to research the potential problems that single dads have and how others had made successful breaks from relationships where children were involved. I wanted to try to make sure that I didn't fall into the bear traps that separated parents faced, and realised that I needed to identify a few basics to make sure Grace could have a home from home with me.

First, one of the biggest complications that separated families run into is the lack of suitable space. Forced by either necessity or circumstance, financial or otherwise, the separated parent (almost always the man) finds themselves with only a single bedroom. If the split is amicable and civil then the kids, when visiting, are either placed in the only bed, or on the sofa or a blow-up mattress. I feared that if Victoria wasn't always going to play nice then I needed to make sure that I had everything Grace needed. That meant that she needed her own bedroom and *that* meant two-bed accommodation.

Second, it needed to be close by. Luckily, thanks to that unintelligible grid system you can cross the entire city of Milton Keynes within thirty minutes. Although I couldn't afford anything within walking distance, I could still easily be just a few minutes away.

Third, the new place had to be ready immediately because I couldn't hang around – I needed to be good to go, because one of the biggest issues I had read about was *delay*. If separated fathers took too long to get themselves sorted, and as a result couldn't see the children, then they ran into problems later down the line and I wasn't going to let that happen. It would be better (I reasoned) to get a crap house immediately and make it nice than wait for a nice place to become available and risk accusations of abandonment.

But that first house was, to characterise it euphemistically, a real 'fixer-upper'. I made sure that the parts Grace had access to were as clean as I could make them, but looking back, the rest might have been charitably described as a little ropey. The dark and foreboding garden blocked out most of the light at the back of the house, while the flooring of the kitchen/diner/conservatory was sticky even after the fourth mopping. I made sure that I took the room with the suspicious black mould creeping along the ceiling and the edges of the outside wall, but at least Grace's bedroom had some lovely pink wallpaper.

I attacked that mould with every chemical available on the shelves of Tesco, but it nevertheless continued its inexorable march towards the door throughout my time there. As is so often the case with landlords who are more interested in the rent than their residents' well-being, mine told me that the mould was exclusively due to the fact that I never opened the window. I tried to point out that I didn't think it unreasonable to be able to close the window during the winter without inviting poisonous spores to infect my daughter's lungs, but my pleas fell on deaf ears and quite frankly, I had bigger issues to concentrate on so I closed the door on the problem, literally.

And that was going to be my life. I had swapped owning my own nice, affordable two-bed terrace property in a quiet, family-friendly part of town within walking distance of some great schools and my work, for renting an overpriced but immediately available two-up, two-down detached house on its last legs.

At the time, I thought that Victoria had taken our separation well. She didn't argue, threaten or actively try to change my mind and although our split could never be described as amicable, as the first few months passed, we developed uneasy but fairly equitable arrangements to take care of Grace. It wasn't formally defined in writing and mainly managed through (often) tense conversations and emails. I was trying to accommodate the situation as best I could and it certainly wasn't simple. I saw Grace three nights a week (initially at her house) as well as through the school holidays, and while the handovers couldn't be considered exactly pleasant for anybody, we took each day as it came. Or at least, that's what I tried to do.

Being the separated dad, I approached Victoria almost apologetically and a subservient role was one that I fell into easily. After all, it was one I was used to. Even though I had gathered the courage to leave the marriage, the weight of social expectation as the man who had left also drove me to offer total flexibility. I agreed to anything and everything that allowed me to see Grace, on the principle that any positive outcome is a step forward. Victoria appeared happy that I seemingly understood that, although I had ended our personal relationship, I was utterly at her beck and call and she was still able to direct my life through the one thing I clearly cared about: Grace. Each request was small, perfectly acceptable for a couple trying to work together – a pick-up from her childminder's here or collection from a playdate there. But it was the sheer volume of contradictory requests that soon hit fever pitch and before too long there were just more times than not that Victoria's plans would change at the last minute. She would ask if I could have Grace on an evening only to cancel at the very last minute or ask me to taxi our daughter from one side of the city to drop her at the other, only to be told when we had got there that all the plans had changed and Grace had to go back home. The more I agreed, the more changes there were.

Conversations between Victoria and I were frosty at best as we tried to navigate through how the separation would work. We found ways to agree when it came to Grace, but in doing so, I seemed to swap one set of ground rules for another. The cost of no longer being there for Victoria was to simply be expected to comply with her every decision or arrangement. She was Grace's mother and she had the final word, no ifs, no buts. I no longer had even the pretence of being allowed to question her decisions.

Those early weeks and months were as confusing for me as they were exhilarating. I appreciate how that might sound, but I would rather be honest than pretend that I was totally broken or, on the flip side, living my best life. The truth is that I didn't know what to feel. I had been emancipated from a partner who told me what to do and what to think. However, without that bedrock of emotional dependence I was also lost. I was starting again from scratch, rebuilding and relying on myself for the first time in years (maybe ever) and when it came to Grace, I got a lot of things wrong.

For example, that first year the two of us pretty much existed on yoghurt, olives and Pizza Express, often in any combination. I think most people would realise that this was not going to work long-term but in a doomed attempt to reassure myself that I wasn't going to do Grace any permanent harm, I turned to Google for help. This was a mistake. I would voyeuristically trawl the comments on Mumsnet and Reddit (I certainly wasn't going to publicly announce myself as a separated dad who didn't know how to get his daughter to eat properly) to try to gain some insight and instead found what felt like an overwhelming number of parents proudly announcing that their children were happily eating kale and quinoa or spinach with flaxseed. This made me feel like even more of an abject failure than I already did.

The truth is that I, a single dad with nothing other than the constant barrage of totally contradictory advice coming at me from all sides, was bewildered into a standstill. Principles are all well and good, but when my back was against the wall and I had no idea what else to do, I didn't pause for a second when choosing which yoghurt to crack open for tea. Will the raspberry or peach melba taste best when mixed into shepherd's pie? Spoiler alert: it's the raspberry.

For most of the separated guys that I've spoken to, this is their lot. This is what they can expect from a family relationship breakdown. Divorce is no longer a taboo subject; rather, it is a topic that many families are learning to cope with. But while more and more families are separating, I think that as long as the parents maintain a sense of focus on the children, they can usually navigate their way through the uncertainties and confusion with minimal complications. There will still be problems – sometimes huge, seemingly insurmountable problems – but if both parents can understand the need to compromise, then hopefully whatever frustrations and issues drove them apart won't significantly impact the kids. Because life does go on and even though I sometimes felt I had just swapped the frying pan into the other hand, I had to remind myself that at least I wasn't in the fire. Yes, I worried about Grace even more than I used to. Yes, I lost whole weekends running around the country at Victoria's whim and would drop everything as and when Victoria needed a babysitter while she sporadically decided she wanted to socialise. But that meant there were also times when I didn't have to worry at all. I had finally managed to stop, look around and see what I'd been missing. I'd lost almost ten years and when I wasn't looking after Grace, I had every intention of taking them back.

Live music was an exciting thing to do again and pubs were places to actually spend time and hang around in. I rediscovered that making new friends and having fun were side effects of having conversations – and conversations were easy when I wasn't always looking over my shoulder or at the clock. I drank too much, mucked about too much and generally behaved like the twenty-year-old I hadn't been allowed to be. I was letting loose and enjoying myself. Looking back, I wouldn't change any of those (sometimes instantly calamitous) decisions. Well, maybe just one . . .

I was invited to a friend's wedding, an old school friend who coincidentally went to the same university as Victoria and me. He had met his wife at university and we all knew each other but lost touch during the intervening wilderness years. He saw on Facebook that I had separated from Victoria, so got back in touch and extended the invitation.

It was a no-brainer and I spent the next few months feeling excited about reuniting with the old gang. It was a chance to see friends from university and school without having to apologise any more, without feeling anxious or embarrassed about the unnecessary lies and excuses that I used to have to make.

It was a great wedding. Such a lovely day, the sun was gorgeous, the bride was stunning and my old friends were as diplomatic as you might want anyone talking to a freshly separated man to be. Spurred on by my newfound freedom, but without any ability to withstand even the smallest quantity of alcohol, there are two things that I remember about that night and two things only. I felt like I was the *master* of the dance floor. First out of my seat, I was pulling moves out of the bag that I didn't even think possible. Parts of me bent and flexed like they were attached with elastic bands and I knew that I would never move that well again. I danced the carefree dance of a man who has remembered what it's like to feel the rhythm again after completely forgetting what music was. I was at one with the beat and as I one-man-conga'd across the boards grinning from ear to ear, it felt fantastic, but I must have looked like a madman.

After a while, I walked outside to regather my thoughts before another assault on the DJ booth. Moving from the heat of the hall to the garden, the cool air hit my face and travelled to my brain like a shockwave. I managed to stagger to a bench just as I heard someone calling my name.

'Rob! How are you doing? It's great to see you!' The speaker's face swam into my field of view, a warm smile beaming out of the haze. It was joined by three others, another man and two women. Everyone hugging and having a great time. I knew them, I knew that we had been at school together, but the names became a mystery of cosmic proportions. I paused and decided to play it cool.

'Hey! I know you but I can't remember your names! These are my friends, but I can't remember their names either and also, I'm not feeling very well.'

A more cultured and refined re-introduction to adult society, I couldn't have hoped to make. At this point, the unsophisticated depths of my character took more direct control and made my excuses for me in the nearby flowerbed.

The point of this story is to highlight the fact that parents are people and people have flaws and while I left any sense of dignity in the garden that night, I had started to remember that there was a world outside of Victoria. I just had to work harder with her to prevent our problems from bleeding into

Grace's life. Of course, it's easier said than done. Almost every separated couple I know will say that they want to remain friends, but it doesn't stop them arguing and throwing their toys out of the pram every once in a while. As long as both sides continue to remain flexible, to be open to compromise and to endure the frictions that being tied to someone that, in other circumstances, you wouldn't choose to speak to, look at or even think about, then life goes on.

But it's hard. I mean it's really, *really* hard, isn't it? The human need for punishment and retribution is strong, particularly if you feel that you've been left holding the wrong end of life's shitty stick through no fault of your own. My case, just like the majority of breakdowns in the UK, was the result of me, the man, deciding to end the relationship. I've talked about my reasons, but however justified I may consider them to be, Victoria certainly did not see things the same way. As such, I understood that in creating this situation she would want to dish out a certain amount of payback. Speaking to others who have made the same decision (albeit for so many vastly different reasons), there is a similar expectation.

I could only hope that given time, Victoria would understand and appreciate that I had been such an important part in Grace's life to date – and for a while that was exactly what happened. Our separation was calm and settled and for the most part we managed to maintain a level of mutual civility. While no bed of roses, I genuinely thought that this new life could be maintained in a precariously balanced, awkward, if not downright suspicious at times, alliance. Trying to figure out what our new dynamic was, and working out how to connect with each other to make this new life work, allowed me to imagine previously unimaginable futures. Perhaps if I wasn't constantly there to prop her up, then Victoria would find her feet again and remember how to cope with the realities of life?

Regardless of whether she was with or without me, Victoria made no secret of continuing to want another baby. A series of boyfriends came and went in quick succession; I often met them at the house during handovers or heard about them from our daughter. Grace regularly came to me excited because she had been told to expect a baby brother or sister, encouraged to refer to each new partner in these relationships as 'Dad' and got used to new individuals moving in and then back out. However, by the end of the summer of 2009 there was a new, more potentially permanent, candidate in the picture.

Russell was tall. Taller than me by a good couple of inches. Lanky and fit, he was sporty in the relaxed way that people who have naturally good genes usually are. He would open the door and glare at me without even trying to hide his distrust and hostility. It wasn't unexpected – I don't know many people who consider their connection with their partner's ex as anything other than 'strained' at best. But at least with his honest and softly spoken demeanour, I found that I could engage with him during the times when Victoria was unable or unwilling to speak to me.

And there were plenty of those occasions that year when I found myself on the outside, looking in on my old relationship with Victoria. Only now it was Russell explaining to me the same old reasons why Victoria wouldn't be doing what she had previously agreed to do. Why she would be too busy to show up at the place we'd agreed for the handover, or why she couldn't take Grace to the childminder, to the shops or even speak on the phone. Where once it was me struggling to justify and excuse Victoria's tendency to avoid situations that she didn't want to deal with, now it was Russell scrambling to find the words. More often than not, he and I didn't speak. We simply passed by each other with the look and barely perceptible tilt of the head that men the world over use to acknowledge each other's presence.

And so, ironically, it was Russell who unwittingly helped me understand just how far Victoria and I had diverged from each other, both in terms of our relationship and our approach as parents. While my focus was on trying to work out how to be an effective positive-but-separated dad, Victoria was busy exploring a whole new arsenal of options that were opening up in front of her. Russell presented an imposing, silent figure as I waited on doorsteps or at school gates; Victoria needed a means to remind me of my place in this relationship and he seemed to be the ideal man for the job. If I wasn't going to see sense and accept that I should be with her, then she was going to find another way to get what she wanted . . . and that started with Russell.

Chapter 9

By summer 2010, Grace was almost four years old and I was at Victoria's every beck and call, and she knew it. Never was that clearer than one evening in the middle of that summer. I was driving up the motorway with some colleagues that I had collected from the airport an hour or so earlier. It had been unusually hot that week and we had the air conditioning blowing, even though it was eight o'clock in the evening. I was briefing them on what to expect from the meeting the next day when my phone rang. Normally I wouldn't take personal calls while I had work colleagues in the car, but the caller ID showed me that it was from Victoria and it was rather late. Concerned, I picked up.

What followed was a perfunctory but very difficult conversation where Victoria told me that Grace was ill and was being taken to hospital. She was short on detail but described a sudden change in Grace's temperature, a lack of appetite and an out-of-character lethargic disposition, which as most parents know, in a young child is a clear and immediate call to action. Victoria thought that although I wasn't around, I should know that she was going to go to the hospital. Obviously, in that moment, I couldn't do anything other than simply worry. I worried for the three and a half hours that it took me to cancel my part of the meeting, drive the rest of the way to Leeds, drop off the three people who had flown in and get back down the M1. The journey time for a one-way trip from Leeds to Milton Keynes is usually about three hours, but that night I'll freely admit that I did not drive as responsibly as I should have: my baby girl was in trouble and I needed to be there to take care of her.

I got to Milton Keynes hospital and went straight to the children's ward. It was close to midnight by the time I arrived so the place was quiet, with parents circling in various states of concern. Grace was asleep in bed. She was pale, her eyes were red and she was hooked up to a drip. Victoria saw me come through the door and looked up, her face fatigued with dark sunken eyes but a thin trace of a smile briefly flickered across her lips. It was just a split second, but yes, I'm sure there was a fleeting, ghostly glimpse of victory.

'How is she?' I asked softly.

'She's better,' Victoria replied. 'Sleeping.'

I went over to Grace and reached out my hand to touch her. 'What happened?'

'She just came over all clammy, said she felt sick and started falling over – I don't know.' Victoria was matter of fact. Not exactly emotionless, just a little cold, unlike Grace who had a raging temperature.

'OK, I'm staying. Are you staying?' I wasn't going anywhere and I could even put up with spending the night with Victoria if I had to.

'No, I'm tired. I think I'll go home and get some sleep, it's been a long day.'

I paused, not expecting that answer. 'Umm, OK.' I struggled to know what else to say. 'Will I see you in the morning then? What time will you come back?'

'I'll let you know.'

And with that, Victoria just walked out of the hospital.

If you have ever spent an unexpected night with your child in hospital, you will know that it is one of the worst experiences a parent can have. The children's ward is rarely dark, can be very noisy and most usually filled with a palpable atmosphere of anxiety. There is often a parent 'break out' room with a battered old TV in the corner that, in my limited experience, no one ever watches. Some parents walk the corridors all night filled with nervous energy, others sit at their child's bedside as if they can impart strength through the proximity of their presence alone.

I never left Grace's side that night but spent it trying to get my head around what was happening. I had seen her earlier that week and nothing had seemed wrong. Victoria and I had talked about how I would be travelling for a few days and wouldn't be available to have Grace midweek as usual but would call her in the mornings. I had left Grace bright and bubbly, without a hint of an issue. I know that kids can be struck down quickly with health problems, but what did I miss? Then there was that little smile that had flashed briefly across Victoria's face when I arrived. I had been distracted at the time but when I stopped to think about it, it just didn't make sense. But no one thinks reasonably or rationally in the early hours of the morning, particularly when looking down at their only child in a hospital bed, so I put it all out of my mind to focus on the only thing that mattered right then: my daughter.

Dawn came and as the morning sun broke on the sleep-deprived faces of the adults on the ward, Grace woke up. She was groggy and confused with little understanding of what was happening, looking around for her mum. But Victoria didn't appear before or after breakfast, and not even when normal morning visiting hours started.

In the light of day Grace still looked pale and weary. During the night I had asked the nurses what medication she was on and they told me the drip contained nothing but saline solution. It had been a great relief as it meant that they didn't consider anything was immediately life-threatening; the doctor had said as much on her morning rounds. The standard blood tests they had taken showed nothing out of the ordinary but Grace had been put on the saline drip as a precaution while they kept her under observation.

Victoria reappeared in the hospital ward just before lunch and I shared the doctor's views with her. She seemed confused and concerned that the hospital couldn't find what was wrong. I said that I would go home to freshen up and get changed as I was still in my work clothes from the night before. I left for a quick turnaround: a few phone calls to let work know that I wasn't available, followed by a shower, shave and a change of clothes, meant that I could be back in the hospital almost within the hour.

But by the time I was back on the ward, everything had changed. Suddenly, there were a lot more worried people, a lot more questions about all sorts of concerns and worries that Victoria had shared with the staff that I was not party to. I walked back into a scenario where *I* was part of the problem. I had left a little girl who had been poorly but was on the mend and came back to suspicious looks and loaded questions about my approach to caring for my daughter. When I replied that I hadn't seen any problems with Grace over the last few days or even prior to that when I had seen her, Victoria started to list multiple issues that she had taken Grace to see the doctors about. Issues with constipation, allergies, antibiotics and steroid creams were ticked off like items on a takeaway menu. I knew that Victoria went to the GP more often than I was comfortable with, but this range of symptoms and medications was new. I asked for more details but she shared a look with the consultant that spoke volumes about my position as the separated father. I had been very firmly, but very deliberately, put back in my place.

And that was all right, I could live with that. My priority was making sure Grace was OK and if that couldn't happen at home then this was the best place for her. To my shame, I remained quiet and didn't challenge any detail that had been provided in my absence. I didn't realise then that I had the option to challenge medical staff or the hospital as an institution and I certainly didn't want to impede them from providing Grace with the care she needed. What did surprise me, though, was Victoria's next move. Once the consultant had gone and we were getting ready for Grace to settle down for the evening, she asked: 'Are you OK to stay with her again tonight? I've got something to do. She seems much better now and if you can stay here, I'll be back in the morning.'

Victoria was calm. *Very* calm.

'Umm, OK,' I replied, 'I can stay . . . Are you sure you don't want to be here?'

'No, you know I can never sleep in hospitals and if you're here then she'll be fine.'

And then, with a kiss on Grace's forehead, she left again. It didn't make sense. Why make it so perfectly clear that I had no understanding of, or ability to care for, Grace's medical situation but then disappear so that her care became my responsibility? The nurses all seemed to look at me with warm-hearted pity as they went through their shift: *Ah, look at him: the dad who couldn't tell that his daughter was ill, barely managing to hold things together while Mum is getting some much-needed rest.*

Grace was in hospital for the best part of a week. Victoria and I spent the days alternating during working hours but I would take the majority of the evenings and overnights while she went home to sleep. Over that time, something weird and confusing would happen. Each time I would leave Grace, everyone seemed full of positive expectations. Grace was feeling better and full of beans; every day we thought that she would soon be able to come back home. But when I returned, there was a new concern. Grace would be sleepy, passive and apathetic, clammy to the touch and complaining of a headache. What was happening? What was I missing? I opened the window, took off her jumper and tights and made sure she had enough water, but every time I left, I had to come back and do the same thing all over again.

Over those days, Grace and I chatted our way through the hottest week of the year, while she was stuck in bed. We talked about why she had been feeling so poorly. 'Mummy tells me to wrap myself up tight in the big duvet to make sure I'm extra-comfy,' she said. 'Mummy shut all the windows in my room because she says that the noise from the cars outside will stop me from sleeping,' she told me. And: 'Mummy puts a hot water bottle in my bed every night.'

'All at once?' I asked, surprised.

'Yes, I get very hot and I don't like it very much. Can we read a book now?' Grace replied as we moved on and concentrated on other, less concerning things.

As the tests continued to come back negative, Grace was eventually diagnosed with simple dehydration and recovered well. For weeks after she had been discharged, I tried to keep as close to her as possible to make sure she was OK. I was

disturbed by Victoria's, on the face of it, strange and potentially dangerous change in behaviour. She had looked almost
triumphant to see me that night in the hospital, pleased that
I had come. But as she left a few minutes later, she clearly
didn't want to talk to me – so what could she possibly want?

At the hospital, Victoria and I had tried to discuss the need
for better sharing of information. I had asked to be informed
when she was taking Grace for medical appointments so I
could also attend if possible. As the volume of concerns grew, I
thought I might be able to ask some questions and understand
any underlying problems that I should be looking out for.

The questions I felt needed to be asked made me feel uneasy.
What were Victoria's motivations? Any possible explanations
ranging from malevolent intention or perhaps simple incompe-
tence were as confusing as they were unbelievable. The depths
of the twisted power play, things that I had seen first-hand
and more that I feared had happened when I wasn't there,
gave rise to the issues that I was being forced to confront.

Chapter 10

Back at the house, Victoria's new partner Russell was now the only person I saw opening the door to me. I rarely saw Victoria except to slip something she wanted (usually expenses for school lunches, clothes or utility bills) into the following week's arrangements. She and Russell were expecting a baby, but I understood that their relationship was becoming more and more tense and Russell would later tell me that he was starting to resist her pressure for a longer-term commitment.

Russell tended to keep his distance when it came to medical issues. I asked him on the doorstep a few times about various medications that Grace would have with her when it was my turn for contact, but he took a literal as well as a metaphorical step back from the topic and tried to get Victoria to answer the question, at which point she would refuse to speak to either of us as punishment for Russell's seeming lack of moral support.

As the friction between Victoria and Russell grew, I started to hear more and more about Grace's growing list of illnesses. They seemed to multiply during periods when Russell wasn't around. There were reports of doctors' visits and prescriptions for antibiotics, nausea, allergies, paleness and sweats so serious that they had needed immediate medical attention – a growing litany of medical requirements.

In early November 2010 I received a text message from Victoria to say that Grace wouldn't be available for my weekend with her – they had again attended the hospital through our local walk-in centre. Grace had a cough so Victoria had spent the morning driving between different pharmacists, all of whom had refused to provide the antibiotics that she wanted. She assured me that Grace was 'fine', but she had decided to go to hospital to obtain a prescription anyway.

It was difficult to find a pattern to the increasingly frequent inconsistencies, but this one was jumping up and down, waving its hands and spot-lit with neon lights and sounding a klaxon. If Grace was 'fine', why was Victoria visiting multiple pharmacists and then the hospital to get medication? I immediately called her back but got no answer; I tried for a second time but again it rang to voicemail. A few minutes later, I gave it one more try but once more couldn't get through. Given the concerns that had bubbled to the surface when Grace had been taken to hospital a few months earlier, the one thing that happened when Victoria told me not to worry was an immediate and urgent sense of worry.

By this time, my friend Jane and I had started a relationship of our own and as it happened, we were in town together only a few minutes away. My connection and subsequent relationship with Jane was as unlikely as it was unplanned but being so close to the hospital, it was an easy decision for us both to jump in the car and dash over. Jane drove and parked my car for me so I could make a run for the reception as soon as we arrived. I hurried inside and the receptionist showed me into the consultation room, where the doctor had already started to examine Grace.

Victoria explained that Grace had a persistent cough that had been going on for the past two weeks and she had been complaining of pain in her chest. She had a temperature, she was being sick and she wasn't sleeping, eating or drinking. Grace had come over to me when I entered the room and I held her on my lap. She didn't feel too hot and she certainly hadn't had any issue a few days ago when I'd seen her. The doctor listened to her chest and asked us a few questions. After a few minutes' deliberation, he told us, 'There's really nothing to worry about. She'll be fine. It's probably just a nasty cold. If her sinuses are blocked up and she's struggling to breathe, use steam inhalation to clear the lungs because we really don't give children this young medication if we can help it.' With that, we were shown the door.

We returned to our cars. By chance, Jane had unintentionally parked my car right next to Victoria's but hadn't noticed. Victoria put Grace in the back seat of her vehicle before coming round the back to speak to me – she clearly wasn't happy and started to work herself up. It was my fault that Grace couldn't get the medication that she needed, she snarled, so there was no way that she would be well enough to see me the next week. She told me that Grace had been assessed by a nurse at the front desk who had confirmed that, yes, she had a chest infection and, yes, the doctor would need to prescribe the necessary medication. My arrival and supposed intervention had stopped that prescription and therefore put Grace's health at risk (although, of course, she had said none of this in the treatment room). Throughout, her volume was increasing and people were starting to stop and stare as I explained that I hadn't prevented anything; it was the doctor's decision not to prescribe because, as the pharmacist had already told her, giving strong medicine to children is always very carefully considered and Grace was hardly at death's door.

While Victoria and I were embroiled in an increasingly heated exchange, concerned bystanders had gone inside and reported the incident. A member of staff had come out to check that everything was all right. Victoria turned at this intervention and left her in no doubt as to what the issue was. At the same time, Jane waved goodbye to Grace. Victoria caught a glimpse out of the corner of her eye and went ballistic, screaming at her to stop and pushing past me to get to the driver's side of her car.

She shoved Jane out of her way to get past, then turned and pointed a shaking finger at me. 'He pushed me!' she yelled. 'He pushed me into the car! I'm pregnant and you've hurt my baby!'

'But I was right here. I saw everything,' said the staff member who had come out of the walk-in centre. 'Nobody pushed you.'

'HE DID! HE DID PUSH ME! IT HURTS. I can't stand up.' Victoria started to double over before whimpering in loud rasping breaths. 'It hurts so much, I've got to go.' With that, she wrenched open the car door, jumped in and sped off.

The three of us stood for a moment trying to process what had just happened and then I turned towards the member of staff. 'Sorry about that,' I said in what might have been the most repressed, most typically 'English' apology ever uttered.

'Don't worry,' she told me, 'I saw what happened and we have CCTV. She came in and I was the one who met her, I booked your daughter in. Is everything OK?'

'You gave the initial assessment?' I replied. 'Victoria said that you'd diagnosed a chest infection, that's why she was so angry because the doctor wouldn't prescribe any antibiotics.'

'What? No, I can't. I'm not qualified to do that. She told me that she had been to multiple pharmacists to try and get medication. She said your daughter had been unwell for weeks.'

I clearly looked a bit dazed and confused as I tried to make sense of all this. Grace hadn't been unwell for weeks, had she? Or at least she seemed fine when I saw her a few days earlier. Given what had happened in the hospital before, I was really having to question my ability to recognise if my daughter was ill. The stigma that I had experienced weighed heavily on me because if I misjudged the situation, I wouldn't be able to make a positive change either way until it was too late. I was left with an inescapable question: was I truly missing Grace's illnesses or was Victoria misrepresenting things on purpose?

My concerns were growing and I needed a clearer picture of what was going on. I contacted Grace's doctor to request her medical notes. The bizarre altercation outside the walk-in centre reminded me of the way that Victoria attempted to obscure the information between various agencies and institutions years before with her own medical issues. I had no idea if she was still doing it to or for herself, but here was an example that she was starting to do it to Grace.

The next week, despite Victoria's threat, Grace *did* come to me without any new medication or additional instruction for therapeutic care. Was this justification of my decision to challenge her or simply another power play? I was tired of second-guessing what might happen and just wanted to enjoy the time with Grace as best I could.

Unfortunately, Victoria was in no mood to slow down. Once I started to take a closer interest in Grace's records, I discovered that for two weeks before the 'chest infection', she had already been in several arguments with Grace's childminder about the administration of medication.

Victoria had demanded that Grace should take a range of antibiotics, constipation and cold and flu medication throughout the day. When the childminders started to question the need for such regular medical intervention for a seemingly healthy child, their relationship with Victoria had become frosty, but they felt unable to speak to me about it as Victoria had told them that I had lost parental responsibility.

To put that into perspective, when it comes to being an active non-resident parent, losing parental responsibility (PR) is nothing short of disaster. Without it, you have no legal right to any information nor the ability to make an input into significant decisions except by the good grace of the other parent or guardian. It was a complete lie, of course, and one that I disproved immediately, but as I resolved the situation with the childminders, I could only shake my head at the pettiness of it all. Victoria was so determined to cut me out at any opportunity that she would even try to stop me from finding out if Grace had enjoyed playing with her friends.

We had been sharing the logistics of mornings and evening collections through the week when suddenly Victoria demanded to be the only contact with the childminder and changed the way Grace was transported to and from childcare. Our routine was reconfigured yet again, so that I had to literally drive past the childminder's door and then drop Grace with Victoria simply in order for her to then drive our daughter back to the childminder. If the situation seems ludicrous, that's because that's exactly what it was. Not only was Victoria trying to persuade someone else to administer copious amounts of potentially unnecessary medication to our daughter, she was also manipulating a situation where both Grace and I were spending up to an hour travelling around the city for what should have been a ten-minute journey.

It was an exercise in pure manipulation and control. Control of me, control of Grace and control of the situation. But I had no way to argue. As much as I wanted to push back and find some pragmatic compromise, I couldn't say no to these requests and Victoria knew it. The alternative – simply not seeing Grace at all – wasn't something I could even consider.

It's these small things that I, and thousands of other separated parents like me, tolerate on a daily basis. We acquiesce because it's better to suffer through than start another fight. And I agree with that: it's our lot, our place as separated parents, to suck up the crap and keep on smiling. I'm not just talking about men here: *both* parents should be expected to try to make it work, even when it clearly isn't. Both mums and dads can feel rightly aggrieved because the other person is being a bit of a dick. I get it and I *agree* because frankly, it's bloody hard, even in the best-case scenarios, to jointly brave the trials and tribulations of parenthood. At the end of the day, you have to love your child more than you dislike your former partner.

In other circumstances, if we were different people, those arguments between Victoria, myself and the childminder would have continued for weeks, perhaps months, before things either settled down or moved on. But instead, Victoria took those frustrations and resentments and chose a different route.

It was in that context that the confrontation at the walk-in centre took on deeper significance. I started looking back at conversations and events that, at the time, didn't seem important but which I should have been paying a lot more attention to. When I received a copy of Grace's medical records from her doctor, I took possession of an inch-and-a-half-thick catalogue of medical intervention, 80 per cent of which I had had no prior knowledge of.

That triggered an avalanche of questions. When they realised that Victoria had lied to them about the information I was entitled to receive, Grace's childminder then gave me the multiple pages of notes that *they* had taken. The notes listed all the times they had been expected to administer medicine that Victoria had provided, detailed the different types of medication involved (most often antibiotics) and chronicled the alarming frequency of those requests, alongside a child who presented to them for most of the time as entirely healthy.

I hadn't seen them before, not because the childminder had anything to hide, but because they had been told I no longer had any right to see them and, in any case, they simply assumed that I already knew. The comments Victoria had made about my seeming unwillingness to give Grace medication started to make sense. If she had been actively looking to medicate Grace for illnesses and conditions that, at best, I didn't know about and, at worst, I knew she didn't have, then of course there would be conflict between us. I knew then that I would need some formal guidance as to where the limits and responsibilities lay for both of us, so I started the process to get a Contact Order from the court.

It was with reluctance, but I had no other option. No matter how flexible I tried to be, Victoria wanted more. More compliance, more money and more contrition, and it was all on her terms.

I learned through Grace's notes that Victoria's combative insistence on medical care (and specifically seeking antibiotics) for our daughter had already raised professional concerns even prior to the incident at the walk-in centre. Staff at her local GP surgery had made a social care referral, specifically noting concerns around 'fabricated induced illness syndrome' (FIIS). Colloquially known as 'Munchausen by proxy', FIIS involves a parent or carer faking or causing an illness in someone else, typically a child or vulnerable adult. That referral was marked as '*no further action*'.

Crucially, the report didn't state that she *hadn't* been unnecessarily obtaining medication, but the end result was that Victoria hadn't reached the critical threshold required for them to intervene. It was a theme that I would hear time and time again from doctors, social services, court officials and others: 'It's bad, but not quite bad enough.' Of course, had I been aware of all these professional concerns at the time perhaps things might have been different but to my eternal regret, I never knew.

Around this time, I visited a local meeting of the charity Families Need Fathers (FNF). FNF is a charity whose mission statement is to 'help children and families to retain positive relationships after separation or divorce'. The guys at the group often talked about resistance within the family court system and the difficulties that they were experiencing in working their way through it in the hope of finding a resolution between the two parents.

Looking back at my time there, I think that I just wasn't ready to listen. I considered the meetings were tending to focus on the negative aspects of being in such a position, but I was blind and deaf to the support that these guys were offering. I saw myself as out of place and not ready to talk about the problems that I was dealing with. I can see now that I rejected the opportunity to understand my thoughts and feelings in an attempt to find 'a solution' that simply didn't exist.

I attended a few meetings looking for practical ways to engage Victoria and enable a conversation about how shared parental responsibility would be in Grace's best interests. I wanted to find a blueprint, a tool to use, but soon concluded that I was in a very different place to the rest of the room. I sat there looking around and listening to all the stories that these guys were sharing, horrific, emotional and enraging in equal measure. But rather than recognise the power in sharing these incredibly difficult experiences, I looked at the room and saw forty men whose individual stories held separate echoes of my own. I felt like I was the unfortunate combination of all of them put together.

I tried to take stock of what these men were describing but all I could see was that they had fought and lost. When I looked around, I saw dejected, angry men. If there was one thing that united them, it was the fact that not a single one had managed to achieve (what I considered to be) a successful resolution. It pains me to write that, because it's taken me so many years (and the process of writing this book) to understand that what I was actually looking at when I saw the men in those rooms was my own reflection.

I can see now that I was so busy trying to find a fix for my own life that I focused on the negatives that I saw in those meetings. A lot of these guys seemed resigned to their position, some were suffering various degrees of depression, others confused about the best route for them and their kids, but I mainly saw anger. Anger at a judicial system that assumes a child's emotional need for a father is limited to two days and a night every other week. Anger at what appears to be the systemic bias against men as non-resident parents within the family court system. But more than anything, they were angry about how everyone else saw them.

Groups such as these serve an important purpose: the opportunity to find understanding from, and solidarity with, like-minded people facing the same types of problems. But I refused to identify that opportunity. Instead, I saw these men as beaten down by their inability to make positive changes for their children within a skewed system that supported women over men, but that was me and *my* experiences that I was looking at: I looked at them and I saw myself.

I was overwhelmed and petrified by the reality of the mountain I had to climb and saw justification for my fears everywhere: co-workers, friends, neighbours all have negative preconceptions of a man who pays child support. Because even if he gives everything he owns, pays every penny he can and works harder than he ever did, he is still reliant on someone else to validate how good a father he is. And sometimes all it takes is one event, one argument, one word to bring everything crashing down.

For me, that catastrophic event happened a few weeks after Grace's half-sister was born in May 2010.

Chapter 11

Victoria and I had been awkwardly shuffling our way through the previous few months after the confrontation at the hospital. She had complained directly to the hospital trust about the staff member at the walk-in centre who had witnessed the incident, but her unfounded accusations didn't provide the leverage that she wanted.

We had, once again, managed to settle into a regular routine: Grace would come to me every other weekend; I would change her out of the clothes she arrived in and wash and dry them, ready for her to wear them when she next returned home. But then Victoria began asking me for particular items of clothing. Tops, shoes, socks or skirts – it didn't matter what it was. Sometimes Grace had been wearing them the weekend before so I was washing them ready for her return, but most often I simply didn't have (and had never had) what she was looking for. These requests continued and the tone of the emails or texts grew more and more aggressive as the list of 'missing' clothes became longer and longer. Sometimes to attempt to appease the situation I would, despite knowing that I had never seen or had the items, offer to replace them if she felt it was needed. Perhaps this increased or incentivised her behaviour, but I wasn't sure how else to keep the peace.

One afternoon, I dropped Grace off with Victoria, or more specifically with Russell, before returning home myself. An hour or so later, I received a gentle knock at my door. On the step was Russell requesting the return of Grace's clothes. Looking past him, I could see Victoria and the kids (Grace and her new baby sister) in the car and decided that, despite having not deviated from our long-standing arrangement, this was another reality of being 'the separated dad' that I simply had to accept. I retrieved the dirty clothes, passed them over, told him that clearly this previously agreed method wasn't working so we should rethink it and oh, there was a top of Grace's in the washing machine which I would send back with her next time. We said our goodbyes and he left.

A minute later there was another knock on the door and this one was significantly less polite. This time it was Victoria and she dispensed with the pleasantries.

'Give me Grace's clothes,' she demanded.

'I just gave what she was wearing to Russell,' I replied.

'Give me the rest. I want Grace's clothes!'

'I just did. She has a hoodie, but that's in the washing machine. I can't give it back to you now.'

'I want them back – you *will* give them back.' Victoria poked her finger at me, her face turning a blotchy red in fury.

'I haven't got any more – you know she wears back to you what she's come to me in the time before.' I didn't know what else to say, it was a swapping process that had worked up until now.

'GIVE THEM BACK!' she screamed in my face, spittle frothing through the air between us.

'OK, I can't be more clear: her top is in the washing machine. You've got to leave now.'

I tried to close the door but she stepped in to block it with her foot. One more step and she was in the house, bracing herself between the door and the frame.

'I'm not leaving.'

Well, that much was clear. The house had a small hallway, with a door between the front door and lounge. At this time, I still had hold of the front door but it was wide open and I was pushed back at an angle against the inner hallway door as Victoria forced her way in.

I looked up and could see Russell standing dead ahead, watching. Was he as confused as I was? He certainly wasn't rushing to stop her.

'Listen, whatever you think I have, I don't and this is not the way to try and resolve anything,' I told her. 'I'm going to count to three and then close the door.'

'I'm not leaving!' It was the statement of a petulant child, all that was missing was the stamp of her foot. 'You can't make me leave! I'm not leaving! GIVE ME HER CLOTHES! YOU HAVE TO GIVE ME WHAT I WANT!'

The intensity, energy and volume suddenly cranked up a notch and I leaned away. As I let go of the door, she sagged to one side as the force needed to keep me from closing it was suddenly removed. I stepped forward, put my hands under her armpits and lifted. We were locked together for the first time in years but as she kicked and thrashed for the second or two that it took for me to take her the three steps back outside, I knew this was clearly going to be a major change in the way things were between us.

As I put her down, she screamed and buckled at the knees, crumpling onto the ground. She reached out and gripped my jumper tightly, pulling me down with her, howling in pain. I extracted myself and stood up; Victoria remained on the paving slabs, trembling.

I looked up at Russell and he looked back at me, then down at Victoria. I stepped back and he came over from the car to help her up to her feet, as she moaned through bawling tears.

'I'm calling the police! Russell, call the police – he assaulted me! Did you see that? He assaulted me!'

I watched them both as she limped her way back to the car. Russell helped her down the path and opened the car door before lowering Victoria into the passenger side, just as I had done so many times before. As he crossed behind the car to the driver's side, she looked up at me. The tears hadn't yet reached her cheeks and for a fleeting second, her face was set as hard as stone. Then Russell got in the car and handed her a phone.

What Victoria had realised was that it wasn't enough to ask me to do what she wanted any more; I was starting to be able to refuse the more unreasonable requests as Grace got older. She needed another tool to be able to stamp her authority down, something that was unquestionable; a reason, something that would *compel* me to fall into line. It seemed that no matter how hard I tried to lift the weight of my relationship with Victoria, it just got heavier and heavier. I felt crushed, overpowered and totally overwhelmed by the sheer mental load of what my life had become, and for what? She had already taken everything she wanted, hadn't she?

That night, I had more uninvited visitors. Two uniformed police officers came to speak to me about what had happened and I confirmed that, yes, as per her statement, Victoria had come to the house asking for our daughter's clothes and yes, I had given over the clothes I was in possession of (with the exception of a pink hoodie, which had been in the washing machine). I agreed completely that I had asked her to leave multiple times and she had refused. Then, just as Victoria claimed, after she had refused to go, I had indeed lifted her out of my house exactly as described (I even re-enacted the scene for them). After which she had pulled me down on top of her as she fell and had writhed around on the floor, before getting up and being helped to walk to her car, where she was driven away.

From the start, a couple of things about this seemed a little strange. First, the speed at which Victoria appeared at the door: Russell had barely enough time to get to the car, let alone give her the clothes that I had passed over. Second, the way that Victoria had challenged me and stepped into the house. That wasn't like her at all – she usually avoided direct or physical conflict at all costs, preferring instead to defer or bypass arguments on medical grounds or by putting the impetus to find a resolution onto the other person. While I was surprised that Victoria had called the police claiming assault, I was reassured that at least her accusation did accurately detail all the multiple times that I had requested her to leave, as well as the clear warning that I was going to close the door, which she had ignored. The outcome of my conversation with the police and of her complaint was that I was deemed to have used reasonable, legal force and no further action was taken.

So, what was the point? I've spoken about patterns before, patterns that only become visible once you step back. Drawing connections between different events may seem easy with the benefit of hindsight, but at the time my biggest concern was how to stop this Hindenburg of a relationship from impacting Grace before any impending disaster. I'd applied for a Contact Order a few weeks before 'Hoodiegate' and the answer to any questions regarding Victoria's puzzling behaviour arrived through the letterbox within the week in the form of an appointment letter for the first mandated mediation session, which is a standard pre-requisite to the process of establishing contact of a child between two parents experiencing a non-amicable separation. She was ahead of me yet again and I'm sure you can guess what the first topic of conversation was.

It didn't matter that the police didn't take any action, just as it didn't matter that Victoria had no medical evidence for the catalogue of afflictions she said the event had caused her. All that mattered was that she now had an allegation of domestic violence against me on file. As effective as any 'dead cat' strategy, as soon as that kind of allegation is thrown on the table, the mood in the room changes palpably. Things suddenly became less about how to make the situation work for Grace and very much more about how to protect Victoria from the person she claimed to be afraid of. The outcome of the mediation was never in doubt: there was to be no agreement and the court date was set for three months' time.

Stepping through the doors of Milton Keynes Magistrates' Court for the first time on 24 August 2010 was a daunting experience. It's impossible not to feel a sense of formality from the building itself or to assume the ambient nervousness of those in attendance as futures are created or shattered several times a day.

Getting there hadn't been a comfortable ride either. Since the mediation, and since Victoria had successfully manipulated the police incident to legitimise her position, our contact with the police had escalated considerably. They were often now called in on a Sunday either to check that Grace was being returned, to retrieve some personal items which I didn't have, or to enquire about some other minor issue that Victoria had complained about.

I had also started to receive nuisance calls from an unknown number, usually in the middle of the night and often with heavy breathing. As anyone who has had that form of unpleasant intrusion can tell you, it's all about the not-knowing. Not knowing who was on the other end of the line. Not knowing why they had decided to visit this type of torment on you and ultimately, not knowing what they want to achieve from it. This time, it was me that called the police. Even though they traced the call, discovered who was on the other end of the line and spoke with them, they wouldn't tell me who it was. Of course, I had my suspicions, but I just couldn't pin it down past an older male with what sounded like a forty-cigarettes-a-day habit. Russell was obviously in the frame but try as I might, I couldn't see him with the kind of anger management issues needed to commit to such a sustained attempt at intimidation. However, I knew that any response in kind would have been to acknowledge that whatever they were doing was working: a bully doesn't stop being a bully just because they're hiding on the other end of a phone.

I couldn't afford to show weakness. I always attempt to measure myself to a moral standard that would make Grace proud of me, so I wasn't about to play any games. Retaliation would have also extinguished any hope of seeing my daughter on a regular basis as part of a formal agreement if the perpe-trators were who I suspected they might be. I knew what happened to guys who fought back like that: I had met them within the walls of the FNF meetings telling their stories, lamenting their frustrations. The man who can't show self-control, who snaps or threatens or scares his partner, *loses*. End of story.

Which is all absolutely, perfectly and completely right. As the sex who is generally deemed to be, at least within Western society, more physically dominant, men should rightfully be expected to be held to an acceptable standard of behaviour during disputes, although if that is simply to keep control of their temper, then that's a pretty low bar to set in my opinion.

I had used an acceptable level of force in a calm and measured way to remove Victoria from my home. However, it is self-evident that the family court is full of examples of the consequences of the inability to demonstrate self-control (on the part of both parents) and that the weight of expectation is focused on the man – and it was this expectation that Victoria was attempting to harness. Making it appear that I had already crossed that boundary put me in a losing position from the off.

Despite having spent years not rising to the bait, playing by the rules and dealing with the police so often that Grace, Jane and I were on first-name terms with the weekend shift, I was still incredibly nervous as I found myself standing outside a court, waiting for a judge to read the case before deciding what would be my daughter's future. It all seemed like such an anti-climax; years of difficulty and frustration, months of waiting, preparation and tension before a few short minutes were supposed to provide clarity and conclusion. I was ready to get on with my life, ready to hear something that I could rely on.

Chapter 12: The Lost Chapter

Due to the limitations and regulations in the British legal system, I am not allowed to tell you what happened in the family court. Family court proceedings are often protracted, acrimonious and damaging to everyone concerned, particularly any children caught up in the battles. I can understand that these constraints are in place for admirable and positive reasons. It would be counterproductive for everyone involved if I were to ignore those controls, as I could be fined or sent to prison myself.

Frustrating as it may be, I cannot give you the astonishing context and colour we experienced on this part of our journey. Our route through family court was a five-year, six-judgment, three-court case phenomenon, but I'm not allowed to talk about it. I'm not allowed to say who gave evidence or how that evidence was challenged. I can't tell you why there were so many delays or what detail we learned from inside the court during that time, and I can't demonstrate how Victoria was able to attack and needlessly protract the already incredibly difficult and damaging environment for our child.

Although it's true that I can't tell you what happened in the courtroom, what I *can* describe is what happened outside, both before and afterwards. I thought that the court system was so complicated and opaque that if I had to go to court then I needed a solicitor. The process of finding one had not been long or thorough. The firm that I'd used to buy my first house also provided family court services. They knew us both already as I had used them for our divorce and they were available immediately. It was a simple decision to make. The cost was a worry, but it was something that I would just have to deal with later; right now, my focus had to be on my testimony and gathering my own supporting evidence.

My rucksack was packed so full of files that it barely closed, the zip straining against the fabric as it stretched over multiple three-inch thick folders that I had stuffed inside. The weight of it was surprising and it was a relief when I had to take the bag off to walk past the security guard and enter the court building. Once over the threshold, I turned and tried to open my bag to show its contents but even as I pulled on the tag to let the guard see what was inside, the overly taut zip broke in my hand. The top of the rucksack peeled open, spilling papers out all over the desk. I stood with my arms full of all the hastily re-ordered paperwork and arguments and desperately tried to convince myself that I was a calm, patient and completely non-anxious person.

I was looking for a parenting arrangement which kept both Victoria and I involved, separately as necessary, but with equality at the heart of it. It was a simple position that I thought would represent the best option for Grace and I hoped exactly what the judge was looking for. While I had been forewarned that most decisions were made in favour of the mother, I was confident that, given my proximity (and the fact that Grace had spent more time in my care than her mother's during the preceding year), an agreement could be reached.

Victoria, by contrast, arrived alone and thirty minutes later, we filed back out of the courtroom with the judge having declared that it would be in Grace's best interests for her to live with her mum full-time. I would be able to see Grace from Saturday morning (9 a.m.) to Sunday evening (5 p.m.) every other weekend and we (Grace and I) were allowed to go on holiday together for seven days once a year (I should give a minimum of one month's notice with details of where Grace would be staying). Additionally, at Victoria's discretion, I could make a phone call to Grace each Wednesday and Sunday evening at 6 p.m. On the flip side, Victoria would be required to inform me of 'major events' in Grace's life, when and if they occurred.

I was gutted. Absolutely gutted.

It's very difficult to describe the type of disappointment that came from that judgment. Of course, looking back, I can see that this was the most I could have ever expected within our horribly flawed and unequal system. But like all those other guys that I had met, I had misguidedly hoped for, even *expected* more. I had expected the judge to see that my circumstances were different. *My* case was important and *my* daughter needed me. But I was wrong because as was so definitively demonstrated, my case wasn't any more important than that of any one of the thousands of others within the system and I certainly wasn't special. Despite having long-established and mutually agreed arrangements allowing Grace to be in my care for half the time and even with all the unsubstantiated accusations, needless police visits, silent calls, last-minute reversals, refusals to communicate and arguments about money, Victoria had been vindicated. She had all the justification she needed to dump me in with all those other men who had walked out on their wives and children for no reason other than because they were terrible excuses for human beings.

And this is the second point where so many more separating families' stories sadly end. This is the end of the road for all those guys who meet up at their local primary school hall on a Thursday evening to talk with other newly separated dads starting their journey towards, what will ultimately be, exactly the same outcome. Or those dads who do manage to hold everything together (without drowning in the bitterly cold waters of pious anger and self-pity) and who find new relationships and, hopefully, successfully navigate the complexities of blended families. I, like so many others, had held on to the hope that just getting to court would be the solution: it would provide fairness and clarity to a situation which had neither. But what I got was a catch-all proclamation that gave all the power and control in the relationship to one of us and then expected that we should share nicely.

It's a tricky road to walk, but there are so many men all locked into place by that exact same judgment. No wonder it was handed out to me. The odds were not in my favour with such huge regional and individual variances in the interpretation of legal guidance across the country. I don't blame the judge – how can I? There wasn't any other outcome I should have expected at that time.

What I saw right there in the courtroom was an environment built on assumption. An assumption founded on the belief that positive outcomes for a child can be better achieved by a woman than by a man. This is understandable, given the vast majority of caregivers in Britain are women and society regards this as the norm. However, equality in parenting simply cannot exist within this skewed view of family, where the role of a father is an un-required additional extra, and the way that the courts handle the care of children often reflects that. If both parents can't expect an equal footing when the futures of their children are decided for them (particularly in circumstances where they have already lost sight of the needs of their family), then surely it is that very inherent inequity that feeds the bitterness and resentment between separating couples, rather than calming it?

With those doubts and questions ringing in my ears, and the inability to do anything about them, I tried to put this part of my life aside and move on. That was what the court expected me to do, that was what everyone around me expected me to do. And you know what? I was looking forward to marking the end of a chapter that I would happily leave behind. Victoria and I had been left to work together: it may have been unbalanced, unequal and fundamentally unfair, but if that was the decision, so be it. I would have to find a way to live with it just like everyone else.

Chapter 13

We went out for dinner on the night of the court case. I didn't want to cook. My favourite Chinese restaurant in Milton Keynes is the Taipan and they did us proud. We didn't hold back and must have sunk the best part of a hundred quid into that meal. I was upset, dismayed and relieved in equal measure. At least I had closure and a plate of fried rice. Thoughts about what to do next, even though I knew the outcome wasn't best for Grace, would have to wait until the morning.

Jane and I would take Grace out for dinner to the Taipan on special occasions and it felt right to eat somewhere that was special for us all. We'd been working hard to move Grace out of her Petits Filous comfort zone and even though she wasn't with us that night, it felt strangely comforting to bring closure to this chapter by doing something we all enjoyed when we *were* together.

With a heavy heart, but a newfound determination not to let any opportunity pass me by, I set about making sure I could make the most of the time I had with Grace. Thirty-two hours every two weeks, 9 a.m. Saturday to 5 p.m. on a Sunday was what we had to build our relationship. However, I was *always* watching the clock, desperate to make sure that I stayed on time and never having enough time to really enjoy the moments that we had together. But the more reliable I tried to be, the more Victoria would test me. It started with changing the pick-up and drop-off locations, sometimes in and around the local area, maybe to her friend's house.

But as Victoria had previously relied on the fact I would move heaven and earth to be where she told me to be, now she felt even more secure in her position and that brought other benefits. With nothing holding her back and fully in control, she exerted that control to the maximum. She and Russell had separated and, newly single, she wanted to go out dating; with a reliable babysitter on hand at a whim, she started to let me see Grace a bit more. Sometimes, I could pick Grace up from school on a Friday again, or maybe take her for a Wednesday evening. Things were more complicated but I was managing to keep everything afloat. By complicated, I mean that while the heat of the conflict between Victoria and I seemed to have cooled (I refused to allow any request to prevent me from seeing my daughter, no matter how absurd), Victoria realised that she could dictate Grace's life with impunity as long as she didn't cross over into my weekend time too much.

I understood why, of course. Being given the keys to the kingdom must be an incredible feeling. Suddenly the powers that be have told you that you were right all along and there is nothing stopping you. You have the opportunity and the right to decide where, when and how things happen. It must be an amazing endorphin rush. And then, just like any rush, it dies away and you're left with only a memory of that feeling. Some of us take this as the responsibility that it is: the understanding that shaping a well-rounded adult is necessarily hard, but others carry on chasing that dragon, keep trying to find the depths of that power and wondering what's next. Perhaps she started to speculate: just what *is* the limit? How far *could* she go? Victoria had already secured the safety net; it's not as though she could go backwards. So, what did she do next?

Through all the calm(ish) handovers and smile-through-it-for-the-sake-of-the-kids conflicts, Victoria was trying to re-define who Grace was. Now that she had The Judgment, she wanted to make it clear that Grace was *her* (as opposed to *our*) daughter. I don't know when it happened, but at some point, she realised that a legal identity is really only a collection of documents with your name on. When you stop to think about it, it really isn't that hard to create the textual evidence of a new child: an application form here, a few sports clubs there. In the absence of any independently verifiable reality, the truth becomes simply a collection of what everyone believes to be true.

It must have been a few months after receiving The Judgment, and still riding high on the wings of authority, Victoria decided to push those boundaries. Despite repeatedly saying how afraid she now was of me, she insisted that I had to collect and drop Grace home and refused to consider letting anyone else support that process in order to reduce tensions. Grace had just turned four and was due to go to school the following year, so I was keen to be as active a parent as I could be, in the little part that I had to play. It was time to make her school application and we had to apply to one of two available local options. Following the dictates set out by the court, I was at least informed of the decision after the application form had been submitted, but when I asked for a copy, Victoria was less than keen to share it.

I pointed out that I didn't want to challenge or change the decision, I wasn't going to make a fuss or slow anything down. I just wanted to see what options had been offered to compare the standard of schools in the area. But Victoria wouldn't let me have the paperwork. She couldn't find it, then didn't have time to collect it all together or had just forgotten to pass it over. In the end, I had to wait until the confirmation came back from the council. It was at that point that I discovered that Grace's application had been processed in Victoria's maiden name.

A non-amicable separation gives rise to many potential problems but few are more contentious between a mother and father than a child's name. It is a topic that can be difficult, prickly or even weaponised. When I saw what Victoria had done, I thought I should start to make other enquiries and soon found many more examples. Grace's doctor's, her dance class and at the local swimming pool; Grace's friends, her nursery and even the local library had all been under the impression that her surname had been legally changed and was therefore now different to mine.

You might think that I'm going off-piste here and laying on the outrage a bit too thick. After all, the court judgment meant that I had lost the right to provide any significant input into that decision and, of course, Grace might decide to change her name when she was older or got married anyway. And if you think that wouldn't make me any less of a father to her, you would be completely right. But one parent unilaterally attempting to change the name of their child without the agreement of the other parent is a big problem for men in my position. First, from my own experience it reinforces the notion that all steps should be taken to exclude a separated dad from their child's life. The tried and tested 'no smoke without fire' reasoning: 'he *must* have done something bad if she's changed the kid's name. It's probably for the best. You just don't know what happened, do you?'

Second, with enough separation it would become easier for men to drift away. It distances separated partners and I think can exacerbate feelings of estrangement for both the child and parent. That distance might also lower the expectation of responsibility of the father and therefore make it easier for the parent and child to drift apart. I'd like to think most fathers wouldn't use a different surname as a reason to shirk responsibility, but we have to acknowledge that unfortunately there are examples of men who do exactly that. This hinders rather than helps, when surely we should be looking for and encouraging the exact opposite outcome?

Don't get me wrong here, there are plenty of situations where I understand that it is completely right to protect children by changing their names. But I, as a conscientious father, who wants to play as active a role in his child's life as possible, don't believe that this should be a universal, go-to tool, threat or strategy that one parent can hold over the other.

I pondered over what had prompted Victoria to change our daughter's name: was there a legitimate benefit to Grace? Maybe something in this that helped Grace, Victoria and the new baby be better connected as a unit? Or was this just another calculated move orchestrated to test my resolve? Paranoia was a very regular and unwelcome part of my situation. I tried very hard to stop myself thinking that Victoria was looking for ways to screw me over, or that she was going out of her way to create needless problems, just to see how I would react. But the issue was that there were so many examples. Every time I told myself that I was just being overly sensitive, something else happened that seemed designed to measure just how much of a reaction it would or wouldn't get.

For example, The Judgment limited my time to pick Grace up on a Saturday morning until after 9 a.m. I would drive across the city to collect her and we would spend the weekend together before I dropped her back home at 5 p.m. on Sunday. One particular week Victoria told me that she was intending to travel to her parents for the weekend and I would have to pick Grace up from their house in Ely, about an hour and a half's drive from me.

OK, let's do that, I told myself. It's not the easiest of situations (which would have been to just leave her with me before going), but I would have to roll with it. Such is life, right? I made the one-and-a-half-hour trip first thing in the morning to ensure that we made the most of the day. We managed to find a few fun things to do in the area before coming home that evening, no problem. I tried to make sure that Grace didn't perceive that this was anything out of the ordinary.

On my next weekend with Grace it happened again. This time Victoria left for Ely on the Friday evening before asking me to make the same trip some twelve hours later. She then returned home herself later that same day. Grace and I once more spent our time mooching about before coming back home, and I mentioned to Victoria that if this was something that was likely to be a regular occurrence then it might be more sensible to let me take Grace for the Friday night, rather than forcing her to make the return trip unnecessarily. Victoria was unambiguous in her response: the rules were clear. My time had been specifically defined, I shouldn't expect anything else.

The defining shot from Victoria in this exchange came through on the morning of our next contact. It detailed how she had already arrived at her parents' house so I could either pick Grace up directly from Ely (which even if I left immediately would make me late for our time together) or wait until she brought her home on the Saturday afternoon. An impossibly difficult choice for any dad in the process of being forcibly removed from their child's life and one which just keeps the rhetorical questions about Victoria's intention circulating.

Understanding at what point the reliance on flexibility between two parents becomes a problem is, at best, an annoyance for most separated parents. I don't know any who haven't ripped loose a few frustrated comments about their other half after a particularly badly timed or coincidental event has forced them to drop everything at the last minute yet again. But could this court order be being deliberately used to create rather than solve the existing problems between us? No, surely not. That was going too far, wasn't it? It just seemed so hard to make sense of. Who was Victoria fighting? She clearly didn't want to find a long-term working partnership or equal parenting plan, her constant and ongoing complaints made that very clear. But didn't she see that she had *already* won? Now that she had the court ordered responsibility, if she wanted to remove me from Grace's life she could just move away. But even when I was refusing to be provoked (or perhaps I might cynically suggest *because* of that fact), Victoria continued to up the ante.

It was a constant, infuriatingly difficult and completely unnecessary battle.

Chapter 14

Over the course of 2010 and 2011, the friction became a regular part of everyday life, but it was something that I and those closest to me simply had to accept. The pettiness over the contact arrangements continued and we became resigned to whatever nonsensical decision Victoria made next.

As Grace started school, Victoria, claiming to be a single parent, applied for free school meals. However, she then proceeded to cancel the application the following term and ask me for the cost of replacement packed lunches in cash. Why? Well, there seemed to be two potential reasons: maybe it was because Grace didn't like the school meals and didn't want to eat them at school, or perhaps it was another means of exploiting the stigma of absentee fatherhood – another way of making me look like a terrible dad if I disagreed with her. It could go either way, right? So, I spoke with the school and as far as they were concerned, Grace loved the school lunches.

These types of passive-aggressive run-ins peaked around Grace's fifth birthday. As everyone knows, birthday parties are a big deal when you are five years old and I wanted to make this one really special for Grace. I invited about twenty of her friends to celebrate at the Valhalla of Children's Parties: the soft-play centre (which for the uninitiated among you, is a warehouse filled with tunnels, swinging punch bags and several levels of foam-cladded scaffolding joined by padded steps and/or cargo nets). If you're lucky, you'll remember to pack enough food and water to avoid paying the eye-wateringly expensive prices and escape dropping twenty quid on a 'treat' size packet of popcorn and some chocolate buttons. However, the less fortunate parents among us might mistime their visit to the ball pool and discover an unattended toddler being sick in the corner. Every visit is a game of chance.

We discussed it and Victoria was clear that while she didn't want to get involved in the organisation of the birthday party, she was happy for me to take up the baton and so I arranged the food, cake and party bags along with the oversized dancing cartoon characters who seem to be a primary requisite for such events. Everything was going well and the kids were supercharged with enormous helpings of highly processed fats and sugars. The other mums (there were, tellingly, no dads present) were holding an audience between themselves and keeping their distance from me. All was proceeding as anticipated; the kids blasted around the place as I hoped they would and what little conversation I managed to engage the other adults in attendance with was as awkward as I had expected it would be.

Then, without warning, two newly acquired friends of Victoria arrived an hour early to collect Grace. I introduced myself and tried to make them welcome. However, they had been asked to collect Grace from the party immediately and return her home but, perhaps unsurprisingly, Victoria had omitted to mention this to me.

Trying to remain calm, I gave Victoria a call to establish the details but couldn't get through and so to avoid becoming the worst dad in the world by having an argument in front of all

Grace's friends (and more pointedly, their mums), I agreed to let her go. As I was getting her ready, I asked Victoria's friends what was so important that she had to leave her own birthday early, but was told that Victoria wasn't at home and wasn't intending to be home until later that night. I asked if they'd be happy for Grace to stay until the end of the party; they'd be more than welcome too and I could get them something to drink or a plate of food. Now conscious that I had not been aware of Victoria's expected plan, they were polite but reiterated their instructions that they had to take Grace straight away – apparently Victoria had been specific about that.

Victoria had asked her friends to come and take Grace away from her fifth birthday party and then babysit her at home for the next six hours while she was out for the evening. Surely, there must be some misunderstanding? No. I'll just let that one sink in . . .

I've come to believe that these examples of control and use of power, particularly in terms of such smaller micro-confrontations, were intended to serve two functions. First, to keep me off balance and remind me that the power in our relationship had not changed. Now that I had left our marriage, I was far more aware of what it had degenerated into in the time that we were together, but history ran deep. I still found myself facing an emotional firestorm that switched between anger and despair at a moment's notice and I simply didn't have the skills or ability to communicate with Victoria through it. For years, I would lock myself down and bottle it all up. Taking care of Grace and Victoria had been my sole purpose and it was incredibly difficult to turn that reaction off, even when we were separated.

Second, it was all about the show. Victoria's strategy was always to elicit sympathy in others, to somehow make them feel compelled to help or support her. Now she had someone to point at and to blame for everything that was going wrong in her life. She was being disciplined at work? That was my fault. She didn't have enough money? That was my fault. The children were playing up? My fault again.

But once more, like a snowball rolling down a hill, this one decision (born, I believe, out of the need to exert control over me and the time I spent with Grace) had ramifications which Victoria hadn't anticipated. All the other parents stood and watched as Grace was forcibly removed from her own birthday party. That decision was enough for them to start asking questions and to look at the situation with Grace very differently. No need for comment from me, the actions and intentions were enough. I made more than a few friends that day as the mums were all confused at how a mother could capsize their own child's birthday party in such a way.

But that was just a perfect example of how everything blew so hot and cold. It was all or nothing, or more often than not, it was all *and* nothing. Victoria hated me and made sure everyone knew it, but she also wanted to make sure I couldn't do anything except chase her.

In May 2011, Jane and I married at the Royal Garrison Church in Aldershot. It was a wonderful time and enabled us to temporarily escape the stresses in life that awaited us back at home. Victoria knew of our impending nuptials and had allowed us to have Grace in return for us providing her with Grace's bridesmaid dress, which Grace would re-wear for an upcoming wedding in Victoria's family. A wonderful thirty-two hours of love, fun and celebration with Grace maximised our time together.

Back home, 'normal' life seemed to be becoming a welcome reality as things thankfully slowed down. In February 2012,

Victoria appeared to be holding down a steady job working for the local authority to support their children centre delivery. As half term approached, Victoria asked if I could take Grace for the week because she had to work and it would save money on childcare. If ever there was a chance to have Grace for longer than usual, I seized the opportunity with both hands and didn't ask too many questions. I moved some holiday around to take the week off work and spend it at home with her.

It was an unremarkable holiday in many ways. We didn't go anywhere (I was desperately saving to get enough money together for the longer summer holiday) and just spent the week having fun at home. Going to the zoo, swimming and the cinema all seem pretty normal to most families, but the chance to do them *all* in a week was a real treat and we tried to make the most of it. We even started our daddy/daughter camp-out tradition, which I'm pleased to say is still going strong now all these years later, even if the most important thing in her life nowadays is her smartphone!

But just days after she returned to school, Victoria went to her school and informed them that following an allergy test, Grace had been shown to have a severe strawberry allergy and needed to be kept apart from the other children. As was their standard process for separated parents (and particularly separated families that were proving as difficult as ours was), the school ensured that both parents were aware of the measures they'd been asked to implement. But, no matter what I thought of the request, I couldn't change the situation.

The school were obliged to accommodate Victoria's demands and The Judgment allowed her the ability to make those changes unilaterally. Like so many children, strawberries were Grace's most favourite fruit and she'd certainly had her fill over the years, so it's fair to say I was highly sceptical of this request. Inventing something so random and easily disproved and then demanding that her own daughter be excluded from other social contact because of it seemed extreme even for Victoria.

It was the first I had heard or seen of anything connected to an allergy in Grace, so I needed to make sure my scepticism was justified and that I wasn't leaping to negative conclusions. Nothing would be worse than throwing my toys out of the pram only to discover that Grace had gone into anaphylactic shock after eating a jam sandwich. So, having attempted to explore this new development further with Victoria, but being stonewalled regarding any detail, I went to our doctor to ask about the allergy test Grace had received, but was informed that it was Victoria who had told *them* about the allergy. There had been no testing.

But the conversation didn't end there. As I was Grace's father, the practice also informed me that they had further concerns. Victoria had asked the doctor for more antibiotics for Grace, claiming that she had a urinary tract infection (UTI). However, she had declined for Grace to be examined because she worked in London and couldn't get back to the practice for an appointment. The staff were naturally concerned and asked me if I had any information about Grace's condition as no treatment had been supplied.

I struggled to pull together the strings that were multiplying in front of me: Victoria worked less than ten minutes away and it was the first I had heard of any infection, UTI or otherwise. These consistent inconsistencies were accumulating so many minor problems that on any given week I was seemingly navigating a minefield of paradoxes. I decided that if I wasn't able to prevent her from inflicting needless medical interventions on Grace, then I would need to step up my fight for equal access.

In April 2012, I applied to the court for a Shared Residence order. It was a tough decision because I knew I would be going back into the bear pit, but I couldn't think of another way to make a substantial (and sustained) difference to Grace's life and well-being. Forcing regular long-distance travel, isolating our daughter from her peers and continuing to demand medication to such an extent that the professionals had raised concerns, *again?* Victoria seemed hellbent on making life as difficult as she possibly could . . . and all of it at Grace's expense.

And then there was the holiday. The original court ruling allowed me to take Grace on holiday for just seven days each year, so I booked everything in January of that year and let Victoria know where, when and how I wanted to proceed. I had the idea to take the whole of our extended family away for a week in August to a farm in northeast Lincolnshire because if I had one shot with Grace for the whole year, then I wanted to make it special. Unfortunately, the first weekend was not my allocated time and so Grace would need permission to go at all and that meant negotiating with Victoria. As per the court direction, I had to give a month's notice minimum, but I actually let Victoria know before I made the booking, which was almost seven months in advance. She didn't acknowledge that I had requested the holiday and instead stopped communicating with me completely. Once more, handovers became silent affairs without the most cursory of acknowledgements.

The Shared Residence application kicked off a whole new range of Social Care reviews. CAFCASS (Children and Family Court Advisory and Support Service) is the department responsible for promoting the welfare of children and families in family courts. In essence, it assesses the suitability of any application to change the existing arrangements for children who are the subject of a court order. These applications are usually due to disagreement between the parents. In our case, the CAFCASS officer's role was to look at my application, weigh my circumstances against Victoria's, then make recommendations to the family court.

Although CAFCASS involvement is fairly routine in these cases, as you can imagine – based on the accusations that Victoria was continuing to make about me – an already difficult situation suddenly took on even higher stakes. She was still unwilling to engage and I continued to take Grace for the weekend where I could. The date of my requested holiday got closer but there was still no word from Victoria regarding if she would allow me to take Grace. Everything was dependent on how compliant I was.

I started asking about the holiday at each drop-off and pick-up. If I was lucky, I would receive a withering look, but more often than not, I got a slammed door in the face. Any written correspondence was similarly met with radio silence.

I considered my options:

1. Take Grace without permission (and no, this was not something I seriously considered, not even for a second).
2. Accept the situation, cancel the holiday, or go without Grace. Either way, this somehow felt like it would mark the beginning of a path that ended with me giving up completely and I wasn't prepared to take a single step down that path, not one. The holiday was, finally, my line in the sand.
3. Go back to court to apply for permission to take my daughter on holiday on top of an already tricky Shared Residence application.

★

Option 1 was clearly a non-starter: I could just imagine the kind of hellfire that would fall on me, should I try to take Grace away without prior agreement. That sort of thing puts people in prison. Option 2 was possible – upsetting, disheartening, frustrating and potentially clinically depressing, but possible. Ultimately, I considered that as soon as I put myself in that mental space to 'move on', I would probably never recover. I would have let Victoria control me all over again. She would have been able to change the way I felt about my daughter, because if all I was doing was wasting hours of my life complaining that I was trying my best for her, but not actually doing anything, what kind of a dad would that make me?

I was filled with a conflicted, frustrated energy and questions I couldn't answer. Very clearly, none of these options would provide an easy solution or positive outcome and to make sense of any of it, the only thing I could do was keep Grace firmly at the forefront of my mind.

Chapter 15

So, what kind of dad was I going to be? The kind that sat back and accepted being made to feel powerless when my daughter's welfare was on the line? It may not be a comfortable fact to admit to myself, but if she had stopped to talk to me, even then Victoria could still have dictated the situation. All she had to do was play the game and she didn't even have to play it very well. I was seeing ever more clearly the differences in 'acceptable' behaviour between parents with residence and those without. Every day non-resident parents, of which most (but not all) are fathers, are hamstrung by ex-partners who are prepared to put in just enough to avoid losing any inherent control as the resident parent.

In my case, just as in so many others, it was about control. I believe that Victoria was attempting to control me and when she felt she couldn't do that to punish, crush and humiliate me. And so, on 2 August 2012, we found ourselves back in court.

After the first two hearings my solicitor took me to one side and kindly suggested that as this was without doubt going to become a long-term situation, I should probably reconsider using her services. Unless I had recently come into a significant amount of (very) disposable capital that I had not previously mentioned, then I should probably start to think about representing myself.

It was a lesson in self-belief that I will always be grateful for. Here was a professional telling me that she considered me perfectly capable of advocating for my daughter's interests and more than that, that there probably wasn't anyone better to do it than me. Representing myself, dressed up in my best suit with a fresh shave and haircut for confidence, reading what amounted to a begging letter asking permission to take my own daughter on holiday taught me that I could control my nerves even with all the pomp and pageantry of the court. I could be proud of my accomplishments that day, regardless of the outcome.

The hearing came and the judge concluded that Victoria had not provided a justification to stop Grace from attending a court-ordered holiday with her dad. My very first success, it felt amazing. For years I had been on the back foot, following Victoria's directions, papering over the destruction that she left in her wake or at the very least trying to stop her from causing too much damage. But not this time. This time I was right. *I* had made a stand, said what I thought was correct and other people agreed with me. I had been restrained, accommodating and patient but also clear, tenacious and resilient. It might sound like an easy thing to do on paper, but I was proud that I had finally realised what it was to stand on my own two feet.

Of course, Victoria was never going to let things go so easily. Even after a last-minute affirmation of the holiday, there was a very tense moment where I genuinely wasn't sure if she was actually going to allow Grace to come. I certainly couldn't afford to relax until Grace was in the car and we were speeding our way north.

That holiday was, without doubt, one of the best I've ever had. The East Yorkshire coast is always pretty spectacular, no matter when you visit, but that year, at that time, and with those people, it was perfect.

It may have all happened late but everything had come together and I was on top of the world. And it proved that I did have a superpower: by being reasonable, consistent and reliable I could start to break free of Victoria's notion of what it meant to be a man and a father and start to achieve what was best for my daughter. It may have been slow-going but at least it meant that now I could look at Grace and tell her I did my best . . . And my God, that felt good.

But it didn't take long for Victoria to retaliate. The following week, the CAFCASS report was published in relation to the Shared Residence application. As I read the report, the incredible high of the week before crashed down around me. I felt the weight of the system against me: I was just fighting on too many fronts with what felt like both hands tied behind my back. Not only was I pushing back against ten years of control and psychological misdirection, I was also prevented from being a father by the very agencies that I had thought were there to encourage exactly that.

Victoria had once again trotted out all the old accusations but without being expected to provide any proof or evidence for these crimes. It seemed all I could do was submit a reply pointing out all the factual inaccuracies in the report and then wait. Was I hopeful? I think you can probably figure out the answer to that.

As I have explained, Victoria had begun moving Grace east across the country, requiring me to match her movements if I wanted any contact at all. She would ask me to meet her in Milton Keynes, St Neots, Cambridge and, increasingly, close to Ely, where her parents lived.

The last time I made that journey, I drove through the fields on my way to collect Grace and my mind darkened to match the clouds covering an otherwise bright and sunny sky. I had learned from years of previous visits not to pull into the driveway: it was short, steep and narrow, which made it almost impossible to pull away from quickly – and getting away from that house as fast as possible was one of my main priorities that day.

Instead, I stopped on the road and backed into a farm track that led to the entrance of the adjacent field and would take me across the front lawn to the house. I paused and gathered my thoughts before opening the car door. With nothing to hinder its progress across mile upon mile of flat farmland, the powerful wind sucked the heat out of the car and whipped at my jacket as I closed the door behind me. I crossed the twenty metres to the front door over the grass and driveway and stood on the porch, sheltering from the weather. I knocked at the door and stepped back. After a few moments, Michael – Victoria's dad – appeared.

'I want to have a word . . .' he started angrily. 'Never in my life could I have imagined you would do this to my daughter. To your own daughter. You are destroying your family. Do you understand that?' Michael was not one to shy away from a battle, and I had witnessed his temper on a few occasions.

'I thought you were a man,' he spat. 'I hope you're happy with the pain and suffering you're causing. You're doing that, you're choosing to put them through that.'

I stood, considering my options – this was not a time that I wanted to get into anything with him.

'Look, Michael . . .' I started to say, but he stepped in closer and hissed through gritted teeth.

'The way you have hurt your daughter, your own daughter.'

'Wait, hang on . . .' I tried to interject, but he wasn't finished yet.

'How can you stand here in front of me and look at me? How can you do that after what you've done? You are *evil*, Mr Parkes.'

I'll never know what Victoria told them about me. Maybe, unlike the subsequent friends or boyfriends who had no prior relationship with me, she didn't have to tell them anything at all and the simple fact that I had chosen to break the relationship was cause enough for him to react in this way. I saw in Michael's eyes the certainty that I was the cause of the pain that he truly believed had been dealt to his daughter, and the burning desire he had to hurt me for that. I can understand that, but if this reaction, which was co-incidentally also the last time I ever actually spoke to the man, gave me anything, it solidified my opinion that Victoria's heights of vitriol and hate weren't traits she had developed independently.

Grace had come to the front door now with Marie, Victoria's mother, and I stepped sideways to draw her over to me so we could go to the car. But Michael wasn't done with me quite yet: 'Did you hear me, Mr Parkes? You are evil. You are evil for what you are doing.'

'Michael, look, I'm not doing anything, I'm just here to collect Grace.' I managed to glance past him. Marie was holding on to Grace, who was looking at us both. Michael was jabbing at my chest, punctuating each word with a sharp stab of his finger, trying to push me back, to force me away from the house.

I planted my feet firmly and stood my ground. Michael came right up to my face and I could smell the sour stench of the roll-up cigarettes that he always smoked. I was a few inches taller than him but he raised his chin forcefully and

I looked down at him, trying to remain calm. I didn't raise my hands, I didn't push back and I didn't raise my voice. I realised right then that I didn't need to: all I had to do was not run – I would never run again.

Michael realised that I wasn't moving and as he stepped back, I wiped the venom and smoke-laced spittle from my face. Grace broke free of Marie's grasp and ran to me. As we turned to the car, Michael called out after us: 'The devil is coming for you, Mr Parkes. You had better watch out, the devil is coming.'

While he didn't know it at the time, this statement proved to be closer to the truth than he'll ever know.

Chapter 16

By 14 November 2010 I was back outside the magistrates' court in the same suit and this time I *was* feeling nervous. 'Eye contact,' I muttered to myself, 'confidence and clarity.' I had asked for pointers from family and friends and while these seemed like the simplest instructions, it was their actual execution that terrified me. I couldn't keep the growing demands of all the legal work quiet and so, as I started to re-invigorate old friendships and family relationships, more and more people became aware of my situation. This was a bittersweet and very difficult time in terms of my own mental health as the more I tried to dilute the mental load by talking about my problems, the more terrified I became that the whole thing was consuming me and the fear of others' judgement grew.

An application for Shared Residence is a serious step change from the access orders that I had previously been working under. Up until then, Victoria had been in total command of the frequency and nature of my contact with Grace. It was the increasingly volatile and combative use of that authority which led me to ask the court to review the arrangements. A Shared Residence order brings exactly that: a more balanced division of time and responsibility between both parents. Even at the time, it was more than I had hoped to achieve.

Victoria would still remain Grace's primary resident parent but I would be able to see her for more of the holidays and possibly even during the week. It's a position most separated parents aspire to, but few achieve, particularly because – in order to be awarded Shared Residence – the parents need to be able to actually work together and to share the work.

I was petrified where the logical conclusion of the current arrangement (full residence with Victoria and partial access for me) might lead. Looking ahead, what was to stop Victoria and Grace from moving away? Although Victoria worked in Milton Keynes and Grace went to school there, increasingly I was having to travel to collect Grace from Cambridgeshire. How easy would it be for Victoria just to up sticks and go? I had heard so many other men share their stories of the children they had lost contact with. They had lost contact because they hadn't managed to demonstrate the impact that losing their father would have on the children and I didn't want that to be me. I had come too far and invested too much to walk away without giving this hearing absolutely everything I had.

I wasn't looking to create a problem, in fact quite the opposite: I was trying to resolve one. If I could just get the chance to explain, I would be able to go through the constant wasting of police time, the doctors' reports showing that Victoria was asking for more and more potentially unnecessary medication, the school reports detailing her attempted segregation of Grace due to allergies that she didn't have, the CCTV footage and witness statements that would disprove her allegations of assault. Despite these individual actions being small and insufficient to tip the balance on their own, might their accumulation over the years finally demonstrate that Victoria was willing to lie to anyone she needed to in order to get what she wanted?

But I'm not a lawyer. If I lost here, I wouldn't be able to walk away, thinking that I had performed well. Like a child at sports day, I told myself that I could only do my best, but I didn't believe it. Instead, I could feel the doubt and uncertainty grip my chest like a vice and the potential consequences of my best not being good enough were all too real. I started to question everything. Was this actually what Grace needed? Would she really want me to keep pushing like this?

I re-focused on one simple thought: this wasn't about me. And not even about Victoria. It was about Grace. All I had to do is give her the voice she deserved. If I could put Grace in that room then I could be proud, no matter what happened. With a revitalised sense of purpose, I walked through the courtroom doors holding my daughter's hand in my mind's eye, ready to be the daddy she deserved.

Two hours passed while Jane sat patiently waiting outside. I came out of the courtroom with a back slick with ice-cold sweat and shaking uncontrollably from all the pent-up adrenaline.

'It's a lunch break, we're going back in after,' I panted, almost out of breath.

This was not supposed to happen; it was not in the plan. It was either going very well or very badly and I didn't know which. Jane and I sat in a pub next to the court, hovering over a lunch that neither of us ate, trying to work out what was going on. Magistrates courts use professional agencies such as CAFCASS to determine what is in a child's best interest and agencies like these have a vital yet impossibly difficult function. Their workers are tasked with compiling information from the parties involved and then base their recommendations on their experience and professional judgement. In all my research, I had come to know that courts rarely make a decision that runs contrary to their findings or recommendations.

But what if the information that their report was based on wasn't factual? CAFCASS wasn't the police. Many such council departments are often so woefully underfunded and understaffed. Often, CAFCASS simply don't have the ability or time to fact-check all the statements they are given; if someone tells you they're frightened, should you risk dismissing their claims and potentially ruin your career in the process? I suspect that you, just like me, probably wouldn't.

It's that human element which brings both reassurance and danger. Reassurance that the real world isn't always clear or defined and so the ability to bring context and understanding to what would inevitably be a very emotional situation is vital. Danger because that judgement could potentially be influenced, particularly by someone who has a talent for manipulating people.

As a point of non-professional, unauthorised and completely discretionary advice, I would suggest that if you are ever faced with any potential inaccuracies within an official report such as (but not limited to) a CAFCASS report, it is prudent to ensure at the earliest opportunity these are flagged and corrected. I would recommend that you ensure that you maintain a respectful tone while calmly and clearly highlighting that the team may have issued the report while working under certain misunderstandings such as:

- failure to undertake interviews with both parents;
- misrepresentation of key events;
- errors in documentation (including, but not limited to, inaccuracies around the names of the children involved);
- key documents marked as 'missing' with no justification requested;
- a lack of even the most cursory of fact-checks.

Just as a hypothetical example, remember.

When faced with these types of problems, they can feel daunting to the point of being overwhelming; trying not to 'cock it up' is a massive responsibility and I felt the weight of it very keenly. Unfortunately, the self-confidence to step forward and challenge the unchallengeable with people in authority is not something that can be borrowed from anyone: you must find it within yourself. But you *can* dig deep enough, because the alternative is to allow any potential mistakes to dictate the future for you and your children.

Another hour back in court and it was finished. Everything that could be said had been said. After I emerged from the courtroom, Jane and I waited outside on an uncomfortable steel bench for a further hour before the decision came. While relieved and calm now it was done, my sweaty palms betrayed my nervousness. I hardly ever know when Jane is nervous: she invariably manages to hold things together. Meanwhile, my resolve slowly dissipates and I start talking hysterical nonsense and filling the silence with nervous laughter.

There was a vending machine at the end of the corridor, so I went over to investigate. My hand hovered over the button, ready to deliver a cup of scalding-hot distraction, but I stopped: I could see my finger shaking. I hadn't noticed before but when I saw it, it looked really weird. I could feel it, but it looked oddly detached and I frowned, trying to understand what was going on. I looked back up at the tea machine and thought, *My finger is shaking, that means I might spill the tea. If I'm likely to spill the tea, that means I might spill it on my trousers. If I spill the tea on my trousers, that means that I'll have to go into court looking like I couldn't be trusted to go to the toilet by myself.*

And so I retracted my finger and walked stiffly back to sit next to Jane. She looked up at me, surprised: 'You were gone ages. Are you OK? Did you get your tea?'

'No,' I replied, 'I didn't want to piss myself.'

Jane frowned and as she opened her mouth to ask me what the hell I was talking about, the call we had been waiting for came over the tannoy. I was summoned back into the courtroom.

A magistrates' court is a daunting environment and very different to the family courts I was used to. Magistrates are volunteers, people who have other jobs but preside over criminal and civil cases, including difficult family cases such as ours. Where a family court is usually at pains to create a calm and non-combative environment, with everyone sat around large tables, the magistrates' court is a full-on, no-holds-barred courtroom. The magistrates sit at a large desk at the front of the room, usually on a raised platform or plinth, and in family cases the two parties sit at rows of desks separated only by their solicitors – and in our case, crackling animosity.

Three magistrates sat in judgment on the future of my relationship with my little girl that day and it was those three people who momentously decided that she deserved to have the time with her father protected. It was an incredible outcome, something that I barely allowed myself to dream of: every other Friday afternoon through to Monday morning, which gave us a proper, full weekend. An incredible Wednesday night every week and, most excitingly, half of all the school holidays. I didn't know where to look or what to do with myself: from snatching hours where I could between worrying about collecting or delivering Grace at Victoria's inclination every other weekend, suddenly I had some real time with my daughter to build on. It was the first time that the system had managed to see the real me. It had been hard, far too hard, to get there, but once I had been able to metaphorically put Grace in that room, they could all see what I saw.

In a monumental turning point, they had seen me, heard me but most crucially, they had *believed* me. Up until now, Victoria had been able to act with impunity and her view was strengthened, supported and even encouraged by the very institutions that were there to support the child rather than the parent. But here was the opportunity to pull back on that imbalance. Included in the order were even more specific details: 'medication prescribed as to be "taken as needed" means exactly that' and 'pick-up and drop-off times will be conducted from the school to avoid unnecessary conflict'.

That was manna from heaven. No longer would Grace have to run the emotionally draining gauntlet of the pick-ups and drop-offs from home. We could make the most of every second we had together from the moment I saw her on the Friday until I waved her off into school on the Monday morning. We had reached the dream, there was nothing else left to wish for; we could all move on and make the most of our lives.

A dream is how I considered it. A relaxing, comfortable dream. Respite from the constant micro-aggressions made, what was effectively a common-sense approach to a difficult relationship, euphoric in its promise. With a sense of what would turn out to be misplaced optimism, then and there I made what would become an annually recurring pledge to myself that this would be a fresh start built on mutual and collective happiness, a chance to reorganise our lives going forward and to make the best of my relationship with Grace.

Chapter 17

The outcome from the magistrates' court was such an extraordinary, watershed moment. As a result, Christmas 2012 was an overwhelmingly happy time. I genuinely believed things would settle down and finally return to some sense of normality.

Of course, there were the ongoing annoyances, such as Victoria refusing to allow me to pick Grace up from school at 3 p.m. (the end of the school day) and instead sending a friend of hers to sit in the playground between the two of us for an extra half-hour before every pick-up. (This was because the magistrates who made the judgment had assumed all schools finished at 3.30 p.m. Small details like that meant there was a thirty-minute window where I was forbidden from being alone with my daughter as her mother considered it wasn't 'my time'.) Even though it seemed to go against any and all common sense, it was thirty minutes that Victoria wasn't going to let go. With a revolving conveyor belt of friends and acquaintances seemingly willing to come and stand between the two of us for half an hour before passing our daughter ceremoniously to me at the gates of a – by then – deserted and empty playground.

One of Victoria's favourite strategies was to create then change the password that the school used to prevent Grace being collected by anyone other than those she had specified. This would happen so regularly that the staff simply told me that the password had changed as I would arrive at the school. We would all wait and chat as I tried to get hold of Victoria to organise Grace's release. Chasing Victoria around her work didn't seem like an exceptionally good use of time, but that didn't stop her from doing it every week for six months or so and was yet another chapter in Victoria's playbook that she used to brutal effect. But it was March 2013 before we realised not only was I wrong about the year being OK, but also just how hairy things were going to get.

To make the most of our newfound holiday allocation, I booked Disneyland Paris. It has castles, princesses, cartoon tomfoolery . . . everything a little girl could possibly want. I sent over the ferry details, accommodation and full activity itinerary to Victoria so she knew exactly where, when and how we would be spending the week. All I needed was Grace's passport to make sure it was still in date. I knew children's first passports lasted for five years and as Grace was six, I wasn't sure we'd be able to travel.

We were due to go in the Easter holidays: a one-week stretch long enough for Grace to relax with me and still spend quality time with her mum before going back to school. I mentioned that I needed to check Grace's passport several times in January, but Victoria didn't show any intention of handing it over. I wasn't worried though: we had gone through all the details of the holiday and the specifics of the hotel, travel and timings had been made clear. We were locked in, it was a guarantee. Plus, this was a holiday *for* Grace: what problem could she possibly have with that?

During our handovers in February, I asked Victoria when I could expect the passport again. Because of the order from the magistrates, I had presumed that she understood that she was under a legal obligation to comply. My mistake. Not my first mistake, obviously, but another in a long line all tracking back from the assumption that Victoria played by the rules.

I didn't get the passport, or indeed, any indication as to when (or even if) I ever would. By 4 March we had suffered through two further hearings, Victoria had picked up a conviction for contempt of court and I still didn't have the passport. There was no time left and so I went back to court to try to finally resolve the problem. As you might expect, the outcome was clear and unequivocal: Victoria had to give me the passport and I was allowed to take Grace on holiday. Job done.

Except it wasn't. To enable a smoother transition and keep potential conflict to a minimum, an additional clause was added: Victoria was to 'make the passport available' to me at a neutral location of her choosing. It was a compromise that I was more than happy with – I really didn't care how I got the passport, I just wanted to take my daughter on holiday. Victoria offered a location: a children's nursery that she worked with, staffed by some friends of hers. Even a date was confirmed.

The day came, I went to the nursery and . . . the door was locked.

I'll admit, I swore then: loudly and with a certain amount of vehemence. It was hard not to, being prevented yet *again* from taking my daughter on holiday at this very last hurdle. But I went back to the car and checked the date, the time and the address. Then I started to walk around the building, trying very hard not to appear like a weird crazy man stalking what was clearly a very closed nursery. I sat in the car and checked their website. It became apparent that the place was closed for building work and had been for a while.

So I called the number on the website but got an answering machine message confirming again that, yes, the facility was closed for the holiday period. I swore again and paused, trying to think. I must have looked pretty odd, just sitting in that car staring into space. I called Victoria. No answer, of course – she hadn't picked up or returned any of my calls for months.

Maybe she didn't do it on purpose? Maybe she had mistakenly put Grace's passport in a safe, inside a locked building where she worked, which she knew would be closed, empty and unattended for the next four weeks for building work? Maybe . . .

I asked the court for an emergency response and two days later, which was only a few days before we were due to leave, Victoria came to court supported physically, and I presume emotionally, by her current boyfriend. Andy was a new face but I had seen his name on various documentation and was interested to meet him. He didn't hang around though; after this hearing I never saw him again and he mysteriously vanished from all subsequent contacts.

This was now the third time we had attended court requesting Grace's passport and there was nothing else to do and no time left to do it. It was now just days before we were due to leave for the holiday and I had to mentally prepare to lose the lot.

This time things went a little differently, though. I walked out of that courtroom with the knowledge that I could go for lunch, perhaps browse through a shop or two before returning to the same courthouse approximately one hour later to collect Grace's passport. One way or another, I was going to get that passport or Victoria would be in prison for the night.

This was validation that my request was perfectly reasonable and Victoria's response to it had been anything but. She had been held in two counts of contempt of court and received a fine to pay. If obstruction had been her tactic, then she had eventually failed, but it had required the court to muster every power it had. And it had taken a whole lot of effort to get there. Effort, heartache and stress.

But in one last twist, with the ground shifting under me, the family court sent a shockwave through my life and the dynamic between Victoria and I: I was told to keep Grace's passport indefinitely after the holiday. Now Victoria had to ask *me* before she could take our daughter out of the country. This wasn't something I had requested or sought. And it wasn't something that I wanted to use like she had; Victoria wouldn't have to beg for my permission to take Grace away or even give me any confirmations past the obvious date and ticket details, but the decision meant so much more than a simple shift of privilege. The effort that had been put in to get this far, the emotional and physical cost of all the unnecessary conflict and argument was all justified by that one statement: I would never have to go through this struggle to take Grace on holiday again. Conflict removed, I knew this was another area of Grace's life that would benefit from stability. I was doing the right thing.

It wasn't all ice cream and wonderful memories, though. Grace came to that holiday nervously clutching a photo of her mum and sister, which she had been told was 'to remember them if she never saw them again'. That message, given by her mother to a six-year-old little girl, cut deeply. It was an information grenade that Victoria had pulled the pin on, watched explode and then expected me to pick up the pieces.

Understandably worried, hurt and confused, Grace was asking me why her mum thought she wasn't coming back. To alleviate her concerns, I drew up a 'Sleeps Until We Go

Home' calendar, which we stuck on the hotel room door and ticked off the days as we went. With Grace calmed, we could enjoy the holiday as best we could, but that simple action injected a completely unnecessary sense of loss into Grace and cemented Victoria as a victim in the mind of her own daughter.

The idea that Grace would never be allowed to see her mother again left her with a deep-seated sense of separation anxiety. She had already taken on a carer role to her little sister and to some extent her mother, but this manipulation succeeded in creating a sympathetic bond so strong that Grace tells me that she sometimes feels that she has to actively fight it, an admission that makes me sad in so many ways. Although as Grace has got older she has been able to appreciate various alternative perspectives with regards to Victoria and her actions/motivations, it remains one of the emotional anchors that she still carries with her now.

Despite all the emotional games and manipulation, Grace and I did everything possible to make the most of the time we had. We made so many special memories on that trip, from our first sighting of the fairy-tale castle to the parade and fireworks; we soaked up as much of the magic as we could. For Grace, lunch at the castle with the Disney princesses proved the highlight and is the one experience we all remember and still talk about a decade later. Grace got dressed up in her most sparkly, glitter-covered princess dress and we set off for the Disney castle. We were seated by uniformed guardsmen and as we ate, enjoying what had already been a brilliant day, in walked Cinderella. The *actual* Cinderella. Jane and I nudged each other because Grace was just turning around to see what was causing the hubbub in the corner as her jaw proverbially hit the table. That moment of pure, absolute and unadulterated joy flash-froze itself into my soul and will be with me until the day I die.

Was the holiday expensive? Yes. A literal and genuine nightmare to achieve? Completely. But was it worth it? Absolutely, and I would do it again in a heartbeat.

Chapter 18

All that I have described happened in March 2013: an exciting month if your idea of fun is bouncing around court trying to get hold of your daughter's passport from an impossible scenario dreamed up by your ex-wife, while also trying to hold down a full-time job to pay the back payments in child maintenance that your former wife is falsely claiming you owe. I'm being facetious, of course – none of this was exciting. It seemed like a self-perpetuating fever dream as Victoria searched for, and continued to find, new ways to demonstrate just how far she was willing to go to try to remove me from the life of our child. And then, just as I was getting a handle on March, along came April.

In April, I received a phone call from Victoria's ex-partner Russell. After I had managed to obtain the contact order for Grace, he had gone to court to get a similar order for his daughter (Grace's half-sister) and was, himself, suffering from the knock-on effects of my dealings with Victoria. It had been a simple enough process and he had managed to tread the path I had forged with different and thankfully less traumatic issues. However, he called me to say that Victoria had attended court with a new boyfriend, a man called Wayne.

Never one for small talk, especially with me, Russell cut straight to it: 'This bloke, Wayne . . . Do you know him?'

'No, this is the first I've heard of him, why?' Conversations with Russell had become amiable if not almost neighbourly since we both had a common topic of conversation.

'She said that they're all going to Germany to live with him. They're about to get married.'

'What?!' Genuine surprise and confusion overtook me. I had been conditioned to expect the unexpected when it came to Victoria – I had expected her to try to move at some point but not out of the country.

'Yeah, I wondered if you knew him from before.'

Did he mean Andy? I considered. *He was at the court just last month.*

'No, Russ, I've never heard of him. Wait . . . she wants to take the kids to *Germany*?' I had to double-check just to make sure I understood.

'That's what she said. She's making the application,' Russell told me in what I had come to recognise as his usual impassive tone. I, on the other hand, felt as panicked as a man standing on the edge of a cliff, feeling it give way beneath him.

Russell explained that Victoria had been granted permission to take the girls on a preliminary visit and while I'm usually the last person in the world to judge anyone's choice of partner or lifestyle, Grace and I had gone through too much and come too far to sit back and accept Victoria unilaterally deciding to take our daughter away to live in another country with a virtual stranger. But I knew that I didn't know what I didn't know: I didn't know who Wayne was, I didn't know anything about the relationship between them or more importantly, between him and Grace. Grace hadn't talked about him and I had no idea if she even liked him. I wanted to jump straight to the conclusion that it was just the calculated next step of a cold-hearted and cruel woman who had been stopped from getting her way. But I couldn't. This was such a big situation and the impact on the children's lives (and everyone else's) would be enormous.

I forced myself to consider if Victoria's relationship with Wayne was serious because while it could have even been invented just for Russell's court hearing, it might also have potentially been true. What if it was serious enough to move abroad for? I wanted to make sure that Grace's welfare was at the centre of any decision regarding whether it should be permitted to happen.

A couple of weeks later, I received my own copy of Victoria's application and it made for interesting reading. When separated parents receive a formal application for the other parent to remove the child from the country, it's called a 'Leave to Remove' application. Essentially, the parent making the request is asking the court for permission to take the child (or children in this case) far enough away to preclude access for the recipient parent. Usually that's out of the country, but it doesn't have to be, depending on the circumstances of the family in question.

Wayne was an army man. Stationed in Germany at the time, he claimed that he was a mechanic by trade, spending his days with the heavy machinery on the base – tanks or other vehicles in need of repair or maintenance. Victoria had decided that the opportunities afforded at the barracks outweighed any potential negative impact of uprooting her family and that she was going to relocate herself and both girls to Germany to be with him. It was a move that would also conveniently resolve all contact issues with me and Russell as we would be unable to follow them.

The Leave to Remove application is a long and complicated document full of long and complicated sections with long and complicated words. I had got used to the legal process by now but this was on another level and the stakes were so much higher that I decided the best thing to do was to take legal advice.

There have been several times in my life where the stars and planets aligned and this was one of them. As luck would have it, now I was married to Jane, my newly acquired sister-in-law just happened to be a barrister (though not practising family law). I was incredibly lucky that I could ask for free advice and work out what my next step should be. Thankfully, one of the best pieces of advice she ever gave me was how to create a half-decent impression in court and not make a total idiot of myself (the tea situation of earlier being a very clear case in point).

I spent the following months taking any advice I could, because, and I have to be honest here, I was scared stiff. Going into court on my own, asking for access to see my daughter at the weekend was one thing, but this was a whole different ball game. I figured I needed to bring in the big guns but I had no idea where to start, so as well as securing as much advice as a moderately-priced bottle of Sauvignon Blanc could buy me with my family members, and having been pointed in the direction of the Legal 500 (an annually updated league table of who's who in the legal profession in the UK and around the world), I hit up some google action.

Unsurprisingly, any family law firm advertises themselves to both parties in a couple's dispute, but what seemed strange was that there were very few law firms that seemed to talk about men who found themselves in my position. Perhaps because almost all family law practices consider themselves to be capable of representing a separated dad and maybe that's enough for most guys. But I needed something more: if the ruling fell in Victoria's favour then Grace would be gone, perhaps for years. For my own peace of mind, I had to know that I was going in as fully armed and knowledgeable as I could possibly be.

So I downloaded the guidance for the Leave to Remove form from the UK government website and started calling as many of the local firms in Milton Keynes and the surrounding area as I could (I reached forty-three before stopping), asking how many had fought a 'Leave to Remove' case on behalf of the father (four) and of those, how many had won (zero).

That was a reality check. While none of them said outright that the situation was impossible (no lawyer is going to tell you that while you carry on paying them), the implication was crystal clear. The few successful cases blocking a Leave to Remove application that I heard about were won on the basis of the move being a front for an arranged marriage, terrorist connection or some other form of illegal activity. The lawyers spelt out how my case would be perceived from Victoria's side: she was exploring the possibility of a stable family life with amenities on tap and an escape from an ex-husband against whom she had made multiple police complaints and who seemed intent on continuing to chase her with legal action. Moving to a military base in Germany (ostensibly, one of the safest places she could possibly get to) seemed the only choice of escape to protect herself and the children.

On paper, I didn't have a ghost of a chance.

Having paused to regroup, I decided that I needed to reach further afield. I couldn't speak to all the lawyers in London, so I narrowed down the search to find someone who had actually won a Leave to Remove case for a dad in circumstances that weren't connected to some form of illegal situation, drugs or physical abuse. After a few weeks searching, I couldn't find any at all. None.

I realise that my research was far from exhaustive and there could well have been other examples of comparable situations, but what I took from the exercise is that while it was unusual but not uncommon for a dad to fight a Leave to Remove application, it is incredibly rare for him to win. What I did find was one practice who said that we could consider things a bit differently. Their pitch was intriguing: I could approach the court not just from a legal but also a psychological perspective by highlighting Victoria's very vocal intention to estrange me from Grace, while also tracing her growing desire for conflict. The dual approach seemed to make so much sense, particularly because so many of the problems seemed to be born out of Victoria's fundamental desire to attack me.

I requested a consultation and after paying out my last £1,500 (hello, London lawyers!), I found myself sitting in a very nice office in a leafy part of the city. For over two hours we sat and talked through my case, the number of conflict points that fluctuated in frequency and intensity, and the realistic probability of success.

The message was clear and unequivocal: with the best will in the world, if I wanted to fight it (and the lawyer was more than willing to take my money if I did), then I had to be prepared to lose. My case was full of mitigating factors, subjective arguments and frustrating limitations, but there was no smoking gun. Every example I could give could either be explained away or, taken in isolation, didn't provide a good enough reason to disrupt the dynamic of a resident mother. Damage limitation would be the approach: aim low and be thankful for whatever we could get.

But you know what? I could lose all by myself and save the best part of fifteen grand in the process. There was nothing I heard in those two hours that I didn't already know. I didn't have the gravitas that came with a law degree, a lifetime of experience or even the time to deal with the monstrous volume of paperwork involved in dealing with a full-on legal case like this while simultaneously holding down a full-time job. But no one knew the facts and history between us better than I did and there was no one that would fight more voraciously and passionately for my daughter than me.

I took the responsibility seriously, perhaps a little *too* seriously, as for a period it overshadowed everything else in my life. At work and at home, it felt like every conversation, every interaction was about this. Every spare moment was filled with drafting and re-drafting documents, forms and replies. I couldn't afford to miss anything. How I managed to keep my job I will never know, but putting in anything less than 110 per cent would have been just a token effort and already I knew the odds of success here were absurdly small. If I had any chance of making an impact, it would take everything I had and that left so little room for anything as insignificant as an actual career.

My attention turned to the military base where Victoria had proposed they would live. While gathering details from the internet and Wikipedia pages gave an impression of the place, it raised many other questions. I wanted to know what the local childcare provision was like and how did families actually cope with the stresses and strains of being so far away from their extended support networks? I also had to consider what the practicalities of travelling for contact would be and how often could I realistically commit to it. If there was a legitimate possibility that this would be Grace's new life, I needed to understand just how they supported children with acclimatising to a new country and life on a military base. I knew much of this was part of the military process for moving families abroad, but given Victoria's past record regarding contact, I had serious concerns that Grace would be effectively locked away on a military base and that I wouldn't ever be able to regain access to her.

I got in touch with the base to try to get more information but unsurprisingly, no one was prepared to share much with a bloke who emails and calls out of the blue with an unconnected but suspiciously keen interest in the base and particularly the schools/childcare provisions that it offered. Even I had to admit objectively that if I were them, I wouldn't have given me the time of day either.

If we were to really present a robust response, I would need to travel to Germany and physically visit the base. I wanted to understand what the full impact of living there would be; I was also desperate to keep an open mind because I wanted – no *needed* – to find the positives, considering the very high likelihood of me losing the case and Grace actually living there permanently.

Gaining access was tricky for many of the same reasons that no one was keen to talk to me on the phone. Predictably, the ex-husband of a woman who was soon to be married to a serving soldier wasn't someone that could ask for many favours and so it took a while to get permission to visit. But after some time, effort and a lot of explanation, in the summer of 2013 I did get a green light and so Jane and I headed out to Germany.

The visit proved vital. First, I managed to speak to one of the headteachers in person and now that I had some idea about the quality of the schools, I could, if the need arose, make an informed recommendation about which would be better suited for Grace. Reassuringly, I learned all about the support that was in place for new arrivals but interestingly, she said that raising children in that environment post-infant age was hardly ever the families' first choice. As their children got older, most people decided to partly relocate back to the UK or their children were sent to boarding school, where they would have the one thing that touring with a regiment couldn't afford them: stability.

I also now knew that the British Army base at Bergen-Hohne was in the process of being decommissioned. By the end of the year, it was to be turned over to the German people and all military personnel would be redeployed. It was this news that filled me with dread. After Hohne Station closed, Wayne, Victoria and the girls would be shipped off somewhere else. There was no doubt in my mind that I would be the last to know where or when, if I would be ever told at all.

Once I knew the scope of the problem, I once again saw myself staring down the barrel of two distinct options. The first was to give up, tell Victoria that I wouldn't oppose the application and that she and the girls were welcome to find happiness in Germany. With a view that I could get her onside as best as I possibly could to try to secure some kind of limited access to Grace.

The second option was to fight tooth and nail. I reasoned that Victoria's decision wasn't based on what was best for the *girls*. She saw me as the problem and so all of this was aimed at removing me from the equation. Without me around, she would be free to do anything she wanted and Wayne was offering her a way to do that in Germany, where I couldn't follow.

Unlike all the other times when I thought about stopping, this time I thought very hard about option one. It was the closest I ever came and a lot of people who know me well will find that very difficult to hear, but it's true. This was the application that made it clear that Victoria simply would not stop. Unless I played her game, she would continue to find ways to make life more complicated, more difficult and more painful for us all. That was not the life that Grace needed and certainly not the life that I wanted for our family. Fighting Victoria's determined efforts to stop me from being a dad and cast me as the feckless, capitulating, deadbeat father was exhausting. She had invented a nemesis and was laser focused on taking me out of the picture any way she could.

But could I, in good conscience, refuse to even try to protect Grace from that? Why did I leave Victoria in the first place? Was it so easy to walk out of that door, knowing full well that I was providing her with the licence to falsely represent me as 'The Father Who Abandoned His Child'? No. How then was this any different? Just because it was hard, did that mean I shouldn't do it?

There was no question that, despite my successful experience the previous November with the magistrates' court in 2012, this would be on another level entirely. The previous year, I had beaten the odds and I understood that it is rare, but not unheard of, for magistrates to rule for the non-resident parent in the way that they had done for me. However, the anecdotal evidence I could find from parental support groups or individuals talking from personal experience suggested that this was different, as the overwhelming majority of Leave to Remove cases were ruled in favour of the applicant mother. It was, and remains, difficult to get any real numbers on this as family courts are closed, but the little information I did have available reinforced the magnitude of the mountain I faced.

So that left option two. I knew now that the chances of Grace staying in the UK were low. *Really* low. So low that I started to map my route to and from the base to understand how many times I could practically visit and went over the facts that were in front of me. On the one hand, Victoria was the biological mother due to marry a man who lived overseas, she didn't drink or didn't take drugs. OK, so she hadn't made any friends during her previous court appearances, but the threshold for any form of preventative action is incredibly high. She was difficult, but a bad attitude alone didn't warrant refusing her application.

I, on the other hand, was continuously fighting the ongoing untrue and malicious accusations that were presented to the police, claims made that I had stopped child support payments and other complaints with Grace's school and the NHS. I was eventually cleared of all these cases, but as soon as they had been closed, all Victoria needed to do was to make another 999 call and the whole circus would start over again. In fact, when all was said and done, all I had going for me was a little girl who loved her weekends and weeknights every other week and half her holidays with me. It was hardly a watertight case.

With that information swirling around my head and the clock ticking down, I tried to commit to this course of action. How long could I keep fighting for and at what point did it stop being about Grace? I realised the truth was that for Victoria, it had stopped being about our daughter some time ago. Grace needed me more than she ever had; I *couldn't* give up now.

Chapter 19

In May 2013, just as she had alluded to her former partner Russell, Victoria married Wayne. Grace and her sister were bridesmaids, which they loved. She came back raving about the beautiful dresses, 'grown-up' hair styling and lollipops the size of her face in place of a bouquet. By all accounts, it was an intimate but very happy day.

That positivity didn't last too long, however, as before Wayne returned to his post in Germany, he decided to pay me an unannounced visit at my home. It was a bright early summer's evening and coincidentally, we already had two people visiting that day: Tim, my brother, and another friend of ours. Unexpectedly, Wayne knocked at the door. In contrast to Russell, he was shorter than me. He wasn't as slim as Russell but sported a similar shaved haircut, which came with the hard-jawed confidence of an army man.

Somewhat taken aback, I invited him in but he stood, stiff and awkward by the door, breathing hard, his face and ears red with pent-up energy. Clearly, he had primed himself for a confrontation. His words came in short, hard bursts, like machine-gun fire. He informed me that Victoria didn't know he was there – she hadn't asked him to come – but he wanted to make sure that *I* knew that *he* knew what I had done to her. I asked him what he thought I had done.

'You know what you did,' he shot back, 'you hurt her. She told me everything, all the stuff you did to her. *I'm* with her now and you can't do nothing. I'm telling you, you need to know that.'

'OK,' I said, 'now you've told me.'

'Yeah, she told me what you did, but I'm not scared of you.'

'I can see that.' I sat on the arm of my sofa, flip-flops dangling from my crossed feet before a bemused audience of friends and family. I had no idea where this was going.

'I'm not threatening you,' he said, 'I'm *warning* you. I'm not scared of you or what you think you can do. She told me all about everything. You need to know that I'm taking care of her and the kids now.' His red face and neck practically throbbed with the adrenaline coursing through his veins.

'OK.' What else could I say? Wayne certainly wasn't inviting conversation or an opinion of any kind. He had come to deliver a message and had done so, mission complete. Primed for an argument as he was, there was nothing that I could have said that would have made any difference to his frame of mind.

And with that, he left. It was a short, barely coherent and one-sided conversation. To give him his dues, some people might consider that bravery. It's got to be tough to walk up to a person's house that they've never met, not to mention in front of a group of their allies, and threaten them by very specifically saying that you are not threatening them. He was in front of an unknown and potentially hostile audience but filled with righteous anger and outraged by a litany of crimes which he had been told I committed.

I was left with an impression of a man who had sadly fallen deeper down the rabbit hole than I ever did. Clearly, he believed that he was doing the 'right thing' and was trying to solve what he saw as the problem in the only way he knew how. I've always thought that Wayne saw himself as chivalrous, a gentleman, but his view of me was misguided and misdirected. Influenced by Victoria's constant verbal battering, he believed her – and why wouldn't he? He had married her and I knew how that worked.

After his visit, Wayne returned to Germany and things became quiet and settled. Suspiciously so. While I craved calmness between Victoria and I, when it happened, I ironically became more on edge because I was just waiting for the next absurdity. I had no idea what might happen next and I had to be ready for anything.

One of the positive aspects of this period was Victoria started to use solicitors. Up to this point, her legal representation had been a bit of a mixed bag, swinging from refusing to use them to refusing to do anything *except* through them. Despite her initial success at speaking for herself, she had approached several firms at different times and persuaded some of them to take her case. Even though I would invariably have to go over the same process of introducing myself and providing the same documentation each time, I almost looked forward to seeing a new legal contact pop into my inbox. It helpfully meant at least a short period of reliable communication with Victoria (through a proxy) before they inevitably parted ways.

Even though they changed unpredictably, having a legal firm involved usually made sure that Victoria (mostly) complied with the court orders as we had them. But if there was one thing I could rely on it was that, following the magistrates' order, collecting Grace in school holidays had become an infuriating process. During term time things were much better as Grace didn't have to worry about conflict between us: I collected her from school on the Friday and delivered her back on the Monday morning, which, as the magistrates had intended, circumnavigated most of the potential friction. But during the holidays, things became more complicated as Victoria's wider attempts to control the situation were condensed into these handful of times where she *could* legitimately ask me to comply. I could live with it, I told myself, these occasions were now infrequent and Grace and I still managed to enjoy the significant majority of our time together.

In mid-April 2013 (and after the March from hell), I saw a 'For Sale' sign go up outside the house and received an email from Victoria's latest solicitor stating that she had moved in with a friend. No longer naïve enough to think that this was unrelated to the Leave to Remove court application and her desire to go to Germany, my alarm bells reached sonic boom levels as the possible scenarios doom-scrolled at lightning speed through my imagination.

In what I had hoped was a way to support Grace, I had signed over the house and all our associated assets to Victoria when I left. But perversely, this meant that Grace was completely vulnerable, as my initial fears were realised when within that same week it became clear that without waiting for the court's permission to follow Wayne to Germany, Victoria had unexpectedly accepted an offer on the house, sold most of her and the girls' possessions and moved out, leaving behind an empty property well before the sale completed. Her gamble was that as a single parent of two children, appearing homeless but also able to present an alternative home (albeit six hundred miles away) would be justification enough for approval of the application in allowing her to move with them to Germany. However, she also needed an explanation for choosing to become homeless, which did present a problem because she didn't have one.

As a father, not knowing if Grace was being forced to share a bed or if she even had a bed to sleep in for much of the week, when I could provide her with her own room and toys, was very difficult. While I had learned not to underestimate the lengths Victoria would go to, removing the children from the only home they had ever known, taking them somewhere with no toys, not enough beds and with nothing except the suitcases they were carrying was beyond what I thought she was capable of. If I had done that when I left, I would have been utterly condemned.

Victoria had accused me of many things over the years, mainly on court applications but also in complaints to Grace's school, her doctors' surgery, as well as to family and friends. It was exhausting to have to disprove the same lies continuously and although these complaints would create incredibly frustrating and time-consuming problems for me in the short term, they could inevitably be resolved by producing factual evidence. However, there was one resource that Victoria hadn't used yet.

On 22 May, my six-year-old daughter walked into school and claimed that I had hurt her on purpose and my world went into free-fall. To their credit, the school, police and social care initiated child protection procedures incredibly quickly and those procedures were appropriately rigorous. Over the course of that day and early evening, Jane, Grace and myself were interviewed within an inch of our sanity. It was a Wednesday, so Grace was due to come home to me after school and while this was still allowed, I had to have supervised contact during my time with her that evening, so the police watched my relationship pending the outcome of the investigation.

By the next day, a couple of things had become clear. Because Grace didn't have any reason to lie, she was more than happy to explain to those who interviewed her, in the way that only a confused six-year-old can, that her mummy had told her that if she came to school and said to her teacher that I had hurt her then she would get a lollipop. Also, Grace had absolutely no understanding that what she said could impact her life or her family in any way. This is testament to the professionalism of the police and social workers who, despite speaking to her at length, kept her secure and calm in an incredibly child-centric way. Kudos and my thanks to them for that. The case was closed after a few weeks and the notes showed that no one had hurt Grace in any way (deliberate or accidental), but I was left completely stunned by Victoria's increasing willingness to act against me rather than try to find a way to work together.

That night we tried to bring the emotional levels down from the major panic setting which Grace had been living under for the past few months. Calm, slow and steady were the order of the day. Perhaps it was foolish of us to believe that this would be the point that things might settle down, at least until the Leave to Remove request had been resolved. But just as we had found at each of these turning points before, the next step always took us by surprise.

Having failed to gain the more permanent outcome that I think she was seeking by manipulating Grace into making a malicious disclosure, Victoria decided that now was the right time to put all her chips in. Having been living temporarily at a friend's flat, she obtained a placement at a women's refuge for herself and the children. I don't know exactly what she told them to get accepted but given the nature of the allegations she was already making, I can easily imagine threats of violence, physical mental and sexual abuse would have featured in her application to the refuge too. Such accusations have an incredibly powerful emotional pull and Victoria had plenty of practice in using them.

But my main concern was Grace. And from a child-centric point of view, things at this time were looking bad. My former confident, bubbly and giggly little girl had turned into a shell of herself. I knew from the contact I was having with her and from her school that she had started having issues: she had developed a nervous tic, become very withdrawn with unusual emotional outbursts and suffered from frequent nightmares. I was seriously concerned. Living in a single room in a refuge when there were clear risks with other very vulnerable people was a huge worry, but it was difficult to understand how I could ease the impact of the chaotic nature of her life when living with her mum.

Victoria's latest solicitor suggested that Victoria, Grace and Grace's sister would stay at the refuge for several weeks until the Leave to Remove hearing and during this time Victoria asked that I comply with drop-offs and pick-ups taking place at Bedford police station. I couldn't believe what was going on: was I living in some form of alternate reality? How could I possibly leave Grace in a police station alone until such time as Victoria decided to come and collect her? It was utter lunacy! Agreeing to legitimise Victoria's decision to act in this way would be a betrayal of Grace's trust in me and so, desperate, I went back to court in July to ask for the situation to be reviewed.

Victoria didn't attend the hearing but instead sent her new partner Wayne with excuses detailing protracted medical incapacitation. The outcome was short and to the point: Grace would now reside with me full-time until the Leave to Remove application had been decided, with the contact reversed so that she would be with her mum on Wednesdays after school and every other weekend. I was expected to make one concession: to facilitate a holiday for Grace to Germany in May of that year. It seemed a very small price to pay.

I didn't allow myself to consider this anything other than damage limitation, though. Don't get me wrong, swapping the polarity of care between Victoria and I was a huge deal. But I couldn't get excited. I had an essential role in giving my daughter some much-needed stability: her own bed, a routine to rely on and some time and space to help her make sense of things. Also, I knew with the threat of the Leave to Remove application hanging over our heads that she could still be taken away from me at any time and I didn't know how I would cope with that.

Being able to take Grace home with me, even though on a temporary basis (as was made very clear), proved a joy. A stressful, apprehensive, anxious joy. That evening, I thought of all the obstacles that Victoria had put in front of me and the court. All the lies, control, manipulation and accusations. All the friends and family that I had lost to my own self-imposed banishment over the years; the sideways glances, the whispered nodding indictments at the school gate and the waste of police time. All the emotional strings, hooks and handcuffs that held and tied me down, stopping me from feeling anything other than a dark pathetic apathy for the world and my place in it. And after that, all it took to make sure Grace was safe was for Victoria to make herself homeless, convince everyone she knew that I had screwed her out of all the money, a couple of other events so damning of her, I'm not even allowed to talk about them, and then sofa-surf with two young children for a couple of weeks before claiming a room in a refuge in Bedford. It's a wonder how anyone noticed the problem at all.

But in an ironically dark twist, soon after the dust had settled, I was informed by someone close to the situation that the refuge had asked Victoria to vacate her room. Not only had she not made expected use of the refuge, but I was also told that she had given the address to Wayne, her new husband, who had subsequently stopped by to visit her. If true, and I have no reason to believe otherwise, as you can imagine, disclosing the location of the refuge, particularly to an unknown, unauthorised man, is a clear betrayal of the trust required from those who sadly need to use such a sensitive service. This created a serious problem and set metaphorical as well as literal alarm bells ringing for everyone involved. Having spent so much time and effort demonstrating just how much she needed all of the extra support, to throw it all away so easily was testament to how little Victoria valued the services in the first place, unnecessarily taking a rarely available place of safety from another potentially desperate recipient.

So, Grace temporarily came to live with Jane and me. By 2013, we were renting a three-bed end terrace in a nice(er) part of Milton Keynes. We were still only a few minutes away from Grace's school but still far from a life free from police involvement.

By 23 May, Victoria announced that she had booked Grace's ticket to go to Germany for her pre-move visit. Just as I had had been expected to when Victoria held Grace's passport, her solicitor confirmed that she would provide all the travel details, including times, dates and tickets. Originally, Victoria had said she would be flying over, then the week before departure her solicitor advised that this had changed to driving via the Eurostar. Then, a few days beforehand, she was going to catch the ferry but still there were no tickets. The times and dates changed multiple times too, which was confusing and irritating, but nothing that would legitimately be a problem. Annoying certainly, but not suspicious.

Victoria was due to leave on the 30th but by the 29th, I had still not received any details of the trip. As she became more insistent about collecting Grace, my requests for confirmation of travel documents became more urgent. In light of all the problems we had been through and the efforts that I had had to accommodate in order to secure my own holiday with Grace, I simply repeated the requirement to provide a copy of tickets of the trip before the handover. It was a simple enough process and one that she had demanded of me many times. Her solicitors seemed to completely understand and were more than a little embarrassed with the situation as the inconsistencies continued throughout the day, across emails and phone calls. Again, the type of transport changed and then the times. When the tickets did finally make an appearance via a blurry camera phone photograph, I had to pull the plug: Grace's ticket was in a different surname.

No wonder Victoria didn't want me to see the travel details! I don't know any dad, or parent for that matter, who on being given their daughter's passport (on the basis that the mother *was unable to be responsible for it*), would then say, 'Oh, you want to take our daughter abroad under a different name? Sure, no problem – that sounds legit!'

So, I said no. Victoria did *not* have my permission to take the passport with those tickets and I would not let Grace leave under those circumstances, although she did still have time to change the tickets if she wanted to. Victoria didn't take the news well and within the hour she was standing outside my house. She had a friend with her and they were banging on the doors and windows until the frames shook. I took an executive decision once trapped in the house to take Grace upstairs and limit the damage by remaining out of sight.

I had no idea how to explain what was going on to Grace. Listening to your own mother trying to break down your door while screaming obscenities through the letterbox is a tough ask for anyone, let alone a six-year-old child. Unsurprisingly, it was a scene that would play out again and again in Grace's subsequent therapy sessions and the memory of sitting there on our bed, watching her pretending to play games while glancing over her shoulder and asking me why her mummy was so angry and saying all those nasty things, never fails to bring me to the verge of tears.

Victoria and her friend were gone by the time the police arrived to take a statement. The officers listened as we explained the incident, made a few notes, then left. I was left incredulous then, as I have been so many times over the years, at how supportive Jane had been that night during a period of almost insurmountable strain on our relationship. Her amazing sense of moral direction in the face of such horrific events has never allowed any compromise when it came to doing the right thing by Grace and in all our years together, the security that her presence is in our lives is beyond measure. As I put Grace down for the night, I started to dread the fight that I knew was heading my way in the morning.

Chapter 20

The knock on the door came a few hours earlier than I had expected; just after midnight, to be precise. Outside my house stood three uniformed officers with faces strobed blue by the lights of their flashing patrol car. They asked to come in and as they did so, I saw Victoria standing by her car, arms folded, staring grimly at me in the dark. They told me that she had come to them earlier that evening and shown them the court order that allowed her contact from 30 May to take Grace on holiday. She had informed them that I had refused to allow her to go on the 29th and so now they were attending the house to enforce that court order.

They stood in my lounge while I asked them to confirm a few points as I wasn't convinced that I had heard everything correctly. They had come to my house in the middle of the night to remove my daughter, a six-year-old girl, from her bed? Yes. They were willing to do this because Victoria had told them that court orders must be made effective from 12:01? Yes. Had they *ever* done *anything* like this before? No. Apparently, this was not a joke. How, how, *how* had Victoria managed to convince the police, the *actual* police, to agree to wake up and physically remove a child from her court-appointed resident parent, at a home that was not demonstrating any form of disruption or disturbance at all? *At midnight?!*

There was no danger, no imminent threat, yet here they were, telling us they were going to take my daughter away anyway. They started for the stairs and Jane, who was closest to the steps, just reacted. She blocked their path and refused to move like a cornered lioness with a cub at her back. Her eyes were wide and wild with disbelief and incredulity, the absolute lack of child-centred decision-making and nonsensical police action had her wound up tighter than a Jack-in-the-box. Where I grew ever calmer, needing to wrestle some sense of logic out of the situation, Jane became increasingly incensed. She was braced and ready; no one was getting past her and up those stairs without a significant battle. With that potential escalation, the police officers took a step back, figuratively and literally: they at least recognised that this situation needed to pause while everyone calmed down.

It was made crystal clear to us that the officers' task in this situation was to pass Grace to her mother in order for the two of them to get to their 'holiday' and they had the power to arrest us for obstruction if we didn't co-operate. Even if it was ultimately decided that they were doing the wrong thing, the earliest that all this could have been sorted out was the morning (by which time Grace would be long gone). We started to see the no-win position that we were in: if we backed off, Grace would be handed over to Victoria, in defiance of all common sense, but if we refused to co-operate then we would be arrested and Grace would be taken anyway.

We surrendered. It broke our hearts but it was the only thing we could realistically do. Jane went to wake Grace up and put her in her dressing gown while I got the details of the officers. It was correct, I told them, I had agreed to allow

Grace to go with Victoria on the 30th but morally, I couldn't think there is a single person who might suggest that should extend to forcibly removing a child from their bed at midnight under these circumstances. Well, maybe one person . . . and she was standing right outside.

I don't believe that the police who attended my house that night thought that they were doing the right thing, or that they agreed with the decision to take Grace that way and hand her over to a woman who had arrived at the police station at 5 p.m. that evening, having spent the previous half an hour screaming through my letterbox. However, she had somehow managed to persuade the officer in charge to send three uniformed officers to my house and the decision was made despite the fact that the travel documents were issued with the wrong name, wrong date and wrong destination. They had arrived at my house with a single job to do and they did it.

I don't hold it against them. When it comes to matters of child safety, I can understand that there could be circumstances where removing a child in the middle of the night might be necessary. I do wish, though, that they could have considered the context and handled it in a more child-friendly manner. But they didn't and so we had to deal with the situation at hand.

That night Victoria was more audacious, more daring than usual, pushing harder than I had ever seen her push before. Convincing the police to forcibly remove Grace from her own bed in the middle of the night, without evidence of a crime, is no mean feat (or so I would hope). Had I still been holding onto any possibility, however small, that we could come to some kind of at least workable solution, then the events of that night vaporised it.

Once again, Victoria had found my limit. I no longer had any idea of how to deal with someone who was willing to go to these extreme lengths in order to control me and my relationship with Grace. As my little girl was led out of the house by two uniformed policemen, dazed and confused, blinking at the dazzling blue strobe lights, Victoria looked up and I saw a flash of white teeth as she grinned at me over Grace's head. As hard as it was to stand and bear witness to something so wrong, this would prove a serious miscalculation on Victoria's part.

Victoria knew that she couldn't keep hold of Grace in the short term now. Grace was living with me semi-permanently until the Leave to Remove case was complete and during August of that year the court cases rumbled on through multiple hearings. Looking over the paperwork that Victoria submitted and even though I was battle-hardened to the accusations she was willing to throw at me, I was still surprised at the all-or-nothing approach that she took, as exemplified by that night.

Victoria wanted to move to Germany and away from the life that she and the girls had previously known. Many families manage this transition well, some even thrive in that kind of environment. In fact, I know multiple military families who have done exactly that and the military lifestyle can provide community and the opportunity to experience many more different cultures, languages and people than if you were staying in Blighty. But what it doesn't provide is stability and if there was one thing that Grace was desperate for at that time, I knew it was that. Surrounded by chaos and upheaval, she needed a reliable point of reference to anchor her. The day that I had left our family home was the day that I determined to be that anchor for her and here was my chance to prove it.

I was on my knees, mentally, physically and emotionally. But the single most important lesson I'd learned from the exhausting process of litigation as a non-professional was never to let an untrue allegation pass without challenge. It often took days or weeks to construct responses and to collect evidence against the countless baseless complaints and accusations that Victoria threw my way. But the claims she made grew ever more ridiculous and the allegations, responses and reactions more bizarre. Slowly, I felt the reality of the world I was dealing with creaking and shifting under my feet. As the suggestions of drug dealing, gang affiliation or extortion, paedophilia, assault and arson piled up, I started to imagine some of my own fevered possibilities. Every now and then a wild and preposterous thought started to tickle the back of my mind: if these petty absurdities were her best form of attack, might I possibly be making some progress towards the stability that Grace needed?

Chapter 21

I put down the piece of paper I was proofreading, collected the chocolate bar wrapper that I had thrown across the desk and put it in the bin with the remains of the other three I had nailed in the last few hours. I glanced at my watch: it was 4 a.m. and I was in my work office, at my desk. The hearing was only days away and the deadline for submitting my paperwork was in less than twelve hours; this was my last opportunity to prepare. Jane and I had worked through many nights to get the preparation done after I had got Grace into bed, but this night alone we had pulled together three four-inch thick folders of paperwork, each with hundreds of pages. It was my final defence against the onslaught which awaited me in the court-room. I had to have the facts at my fingertips, I had to know the details immediately. The pressure was almost too much. I sat, looking at the page in front of me as the lines blurred and the words swam in front of my eyes.

But as I scrubbed my face with my hands and took a deep breath, I drank in the silence of the room. It calmed my nerves and I remembered that time when I was sitting on the edge of the bed, willing myself to get up, get dressed and leave the house but just couldn't. I remembered how powerless I felt, how out of control I was and how the problems just stretched out into the never-ending distance. As I sat in the quiet of a place usually bustling with the ringing of phones and the chatter of colleagues, a thought occurred: *No matter how stressful this might be, no matter how hard it has been, I can only give my best. That's all. And that has to be enough. I don't know where my limit is yet, but if I do give this everything I've got, then at least I can live with the outcome, whatever it may be.*

That acceptance swelled inside me. I felt the drive spark and start to burn again. It may have been the lack of sleep or the nerves of the impending court showdown, but I was warm with confidence in the part I had to play. I was confident enough to go to war against every legal opinion I had heard or paid for. Confident enough to face a system that told men like me (sometimes discreetly and sometimes less so) that we should accept our position, walk away and be quiet.

I was confident because I had nothing to lose.

A few days later, I walked into the family court in my best suit and shiniest shoes. I had bought a new tie, even splashed out on some posh aftershave; this was my armour and I felt invincible. I also felt incredibly hysterical. Too nervous to eat properly for the previous three days, I had existed on packets of instant noodles and a side helping of clinical anxiety. This was it: time to put up or shut up, to put myself in the firing line and go head-to-head with whatever Victoria was going to throw at me. It would be messy and confusing, of that I had no doubt, but I was pumped, ready and prepared for anything.

Well, perhaps not *anything*. Because there was one thing that I hadn't counted on and as I sat on the bench outside getting all the paperwork ready, something became abundantly clear as Wayne, obviously back from Germany, walked into the waiting room alone: Victoria wasn't coming. Again. The decision on where her children were going to live and who they were going to live with for the rest of their lives . . . and she didn't show.

I looked over and tried to catch his eye. He couldn't hold eye contact with me. Nervously, he poured a glass of water with shaking hands and as he tugged at the collar of a shirt that he clearly wasn't used to wearing, I saw myself hauntingly reflected in his face. That was me. *I* used to be that guy who was about to go bat to defend someone who wasn't there. I would justify the actions, opinions and reasoning, using lines that had been conditioned into me. But the outcome he was there to secure was impossible: without Victoria present, we couldn't expect *any* kind of decision. Yet I knew that when Wayne returned to her empty-handed that afternoon, he would feel like he had failed. After all, she had always told me that a real man could deliver. That pressure had almost destroyed me and by the look of Wayne that day, he wasn't holding up too well either.

We were in court for less than half an hour before we were all sent away. Once again, life had been put on hold, so I went home. There was nothing else to do. I had moved beyond frustration; frustration required effort. This was a feeling of stasis, everything paused until the next time that something was supposed to happen but didn't. I collected my folders and packed them away.

The calendar ticked over to 10 February 2015 and I arrived at court, ready to go. But it was difficult to get fired up. Because at the same time, Victoria still controlled us all just as tightly as if she was already in Germany. Her request to leave was understandable if you considered her position objectively and her parental position as a mother untouchable. All she had to do was turn up and make her case.

My name was called over the loudspeaker and I looked around. I wasn't surprised (disappointed perhaps, but not surprised) to see Wayne walking towards the door alone. My heart sank a little when I thought that everything would be pushed back and we would have to go through this whole rigmarole yet again. Clearly, Victoria had set Wayne up, once more, to take the hit instead of her. Walking into court, his face was flushed with the strain but set hard as rock, his walk stiff and impatient. Perhaps he had some trepidation, but he clutched his papers like a protective shield as he pushed open the door and went inside.

I thought back to those days in Falmouth where I had dodged, blocked and postponed all the requests from Victoria's work. It wasn't a road to happiness then and I didn't see how things were different for Wayne now. I had hoped that he would learn that lesson faster than I did and I was sorry that I couldn't help him. Wearily, I stood up and smoothed down my tie. *She was going to get away with it again*, I thought. *She has no boundary, no limit and will go further, harder and stronger than anyone to get what she wants. This road will never end*, I whispered to myself.

If Victoria didn't have enough respect for the law to attend court in order to decide the future of her own children, she would never give up, never see reason and I would never, *ever* be able to relax. How could I possibly hope to protect Grace against someone who simply didn't care about anything or anyone else? If she could arrange for the police to take my daughter from me at midnight, she could do anything. I stepped forward and reached out my hand to take the steel door handle. The cool metal felt good in my palm and I realised that my hands were sweaty. My body was betraying my nerves despite myself. I took a deep breath, walked into the room and closed the door behind me.

When I opened it again, I stepped back out into a different world. The building, the people and the reality were all the same but it felt different. It *was* different. I floated, up and away from the floor; my arms and legs moved mechanically across the ground but I was a million miles away. I met Jane outside and the muted buzz of our conversation sounded like a recording of myself talking on the phone. I told her what had happened and she cried, then I cried. We hugged each other and held on tighter than we ever had before, not wanting to let each other go. Not wanting to believe the reality of the decision. Time was meaningless as we stayed there locked together until a single thought pulled me back down to earth: it was nearly three o'clock and I had to collect Grace from school. We straightened up, wiped away the tears and pulled ourselves together. As we made our way back to the car, we decided that we would treat ourselves to an ice cream on the way home to celebrate, because this time, for the first time, we didn't have to worry about the future.

Victoria's application to take the children to Germany had been denied and I would take full parental responsibility for Grace indefinitely. Grace had opened my eyes all those years ago; we had fought hard and paid a bitter price to get here but we would be going home together, finally safe in the knowledge that no one, not even Victoria, could stop us from being together.

For days, I couldn't stop looking at the sheet of paper. I had put it in the folder with all the other orders that I had kept through the years but this was the one that I would get out. I would hold it just to feel the texture of the paper, rub the words to make sure they weren't coming off and pick at the red stamp in the top corner to check that it was real.

This court orders that the mother's application be dismissed.
This court orders that the child shall live with Robin Parkes.

I must have read and re-read those words hundreds of times, but they still give me goosebumps. Back then, they didn't seem real, but the order went even further. Victoria was not allowed to make another application without first asking permission from the court. When I initially heard the words, I thought that it seemed like an overreaction, a knee-jerk response from a judge who was sick and tired of being played by someone who simply refused to even acknowledge any authority but her own. But then I realised: it was a firebreak, a protective buffer to allow Grace space to regain the balance and security that she so desperately needed. Victoria would have to learn to jump through the same hoops as everyone else.

The days that followed that afternoon were some of the happiest I've had, the lifting of uncertainty and worry palpable. Finally, someone had seen what I saw and was able to actually do something about it. They *understood*. Grace could stay with me now, no more questions and no more arguments. I could make plans for her future, for *our* future – or at least, that's what I thought would happen.

It's true that for about a week afterwards I was on top of the world. Friends and family called with congratulations and I was feeling energised, invigorated and victorious. However, the more I was asked if I was pleased to have won, the more I realised that Grace had lost so much more than I had gained. She had lost years of a stable family, years of security, years of reassurance that she was loved unconditionally from the two people who were supposed to protect her and she could never get that time back.

Was it worth it? When you look at the alternatives, I

believe I didn't have any other choice because Victoria was on a collision course with a destination that would have destroyed the kids way before she reached it. But I had to understand the cost of doing what I did. I had secured Grace's future outside of an unstable, manipulative and toxic relationship, but I also put them in a position that had forced – and would continue to force – them to confront some incredibly difficult questions.

That week I ate like you wouldn't believe. We bounced through all our favourites, from pizza to burger to steakhouse to sushi and more. I felt fantastic; I had managed to beat the odds. I had achieved something that I had been told was impossible, something that no one else I knew had done. Ultimately, I felt that my daughter would benefit immeasurably from the decision and as a result, we all ate like royalty, no expense spared. In front of Grace, I still tried to maintain some semblance of a responsible five-a-day fruit and veg equilibrium, but behind the scenes, I was a late-night, stuffed-crust-ordering, fried-chicken-eating madman. I had been released from all limits and my university vices were back with a vengeance and all too eager to fill the void (usually with extra chips).

Then I started to feel guilty. Grace was seeing me so delighted but for her, the contrast couldn't be starker: why was I so happy when her mum would be so sad? By 2015, she hadn't seen her mum for the best part of two years as Victoria simply stopped turning up for her contact. By the time we got the final verdict, there was a protective order in place for Grace, stopping Victoria from contacting her except by letter. But those letters never came. If I considered this a victory and continued to revel in it, then I felt that I would be exactly the man that Victoria was proclaiming me to be; I would be setting Grace the wrong example. Just as she had shocked me from the slumber of my toxic marriage, the thought of her disapproval at my celebrating this moment served exactly the same purpose.

Nobody 'won', I reminded myself. We all lost; it was just to varying degrees.

Part Two:

Criminal Intent

Chapter 22

At 14.32 on Tuesday, 5 November 2013, my phone buzzed as it received a text message:

Where are the drugs you promised me rob

It wasn't a number I recognised so I put it down to an unfortunate misdial or a joke from a friend with a new phone. I showed Jane and we both laughed as we contemplated which of our friends had come up with this funny prank. Seven minutes later, that text was followed up with another:

You've been supplyin me drugs for the last 3 years. Where are my drugs rob

Then again:

You need to sort out the drugs you owe me rob

Perhaps it's worth highlighting at this point that the most rock and roll thing I've ever done with any form of recreational drug was a weekend in Amsterdam when I was seventeen years old. I ate a cannabis-infused brownie and really pushed the boat out, spending the afternoon in the Van Gogh Museum. So, a narcotic connoisseur I am not and after establishing that none of our friends had recently purchased a new phone, I was fairly confident about where these messages were coming from. However, I didn't consider them any more than an amusing conversation piece. Then a few days later I got more:

Have you got my drugs rob

They didn't seem to be stopping, so I decided that the most sensible course of action was to inform the police and let them know the situation. They said the number belonged to a 'burner' phone that wasn't registered to anyone and although annoying for me, a few text messages didn't constitute the need for any additional investigation on their part. I asked if I should reply and was told that I could if I wanted to; if I found out who was sending the messages, I could let them know.

This was not the response I was expecting and getting this so far anonymous antagonist to volunteer their identity while attempting to frame me as a drug dealer seemed unlikely. Besides, it wasn't as if I didn't already know someone with a massive grudge against me and a proven track record of manipulation and coercion of others. But it was an unfortunate truth that even when they considered my 'history', the police couldn't or wouldn't take the subject any further. Eventually, impatience got the better of me and I replied:

Who are you?

Not the most imaginative of starts, I grant you, but I thought it best to get straight to the point. I soon received a reply:

Have you got my drugs you fucking shit cunt rob

Wow, that escalated quickly. I decided not to reply to this one and my mystery text assailant seemed to frighten themselves with the aggressive nature of this last message as things then went quiet for almost two weeks until 28 November, when the secret texter sent me their next masterful attempt at criminal persuasion (I should point out here that these text messages have been published exactly as I received them):

Rember rob. Ive paid you over £500 for the drugs that you promised me. And £500 more when you've got them ready for me

We had moved on to money, but while I may have been briefly tempted to confess to a life of lawlessness, I stopped short of admitting to crimes that I hadn't committed. As it was coming up to Christmas, I decided that buying a pair of slippers for my mum was a better use of my time. In the absence of a reply, and seemingly undeterred, my aspiring nemesis tried again just a few short hours later:

If you are not going to keep your side of the deal and get me my drugs, its been to long now, now what do you think when they see what you do to that little girl that loves with you? How young is she?

Just as when Victoria had told me about that night at my student house in Middlesbrough, I knew that sometimes even the suggestion of a crime could be enough to change a life. With insinuations of me being connected to first drug dealing and now paedophilia, my ex-wife would have the opportunity to once again become a victim and suddenly here was apparent 'proof' from an unknown apparent customer. This time, the police did start to look into the identity of the caller but despite my suspicions (or near certainties) about who was behind the messages, there seemed a frustrating lack of urgency. As the first Christmas Grace and I might finally be able to enjoy together in years closed in, I tried to put the false and nasty messages where they belonged: in the bin.

On 1 January 2014, I woke to the sound of someone banging on my door. Not something that you'd expect before seven in the morning on New Year's Day. Two baffled-looking policemen stood outside. Given my recent, dare I say, semi-regular dealings with the Thames Valley Police, I was not as surprised as they were.

'Are you Rob Parkes?' asked Policeman Number One.

'Yes, that's me,' I replied wearily, while mentally checking both my wife and child were safe in the house. 'What's happened?'

'Nothing,' said Policeman Number Two. 'To be honest, we're both a little confused. We had a report that you called 999 to say someone was trying to set fire to your car and we were sent to check. However, we can see that everything is fine. The car is OK and you look OK. Are you OK? Did you make that call?'

'What?! I called *you*?! I'm absolutely fine, officer, thank you. I didn't make any call, that wasn't me.'

Of all the weird twists and turns that I had considered, this was not one that had crossed my mind. While I had no proof or anything other than previous experience-led intuition, I had no doubt who I thought was behind the call: Victoria had upgraded from abusive texts and there was one clear candidate for the man who could be persuaded to call the police pretending to be me. All of my dealings with Wayne so far had shown me that he had fallen into the hole that I had left behind. All of the techniques that Victoria had used to persuade, influence and mould me had been expertly crafted and perfected until Wayne could be primed and prepped like a cruise missile.

But what was the point? Another ridiculous and annoying intrusion on our holiday morning, a reminder that 'we're not gonna leave you alone' or 'I can get the police to do whatever I want them to'? Whatever it was, we decided that it was just another incident to draw a line under and we'd all probably laugh about it in the years to come.

The following morning, I was woken up again, this time slightly earlier: 5.30 a.m. There was no banging on the door this time. A car alarm had gone off instead. I stirred and pulled the pillow from the floor, where I had pushed it the night before, to under my head, to prop myself up a little in bed. *Is that mine?* I thought drowsily in the way that most people do when they hear an unexpected car alarm. It was close, perhaps it *was* mine. It wasn't stopping and so, with the eerie thought of yesterday morning's visit in my head, I decided to pull on a dressing gown and padded out of the bedroom to take a look.

With our bedroom at the back of the house, I had to turn right out of the door and immediately right again to go downstairs in order to see outside. From the top, I could see over and through the open handrail down into the lounge. If you turned right at the bottom of the stairs, you would go into the kitchen and then out to the back garden. And if you turned left, you stood directly opposite the front door on the other side of the room with the window next to it looking out onto the driveway. At half past five in the morning in the middle of winter the room should have been dark, but there was a streetlight just outside the house which always kept things bathed in a soft yellowy orange glow.

The alarm was still going off. Louder and more insistent now that I was closer to the front of the house. As I came down the stairs, I noticed that the streetlight outside was bright and flickering. *That will annoy Grace if it doesn't get fixed, should I tell the council?* I wondered.

The driveway was paved with brick and relatively small: enough space for a car and a motorbike. I don't own a motorbike and so I had the luxury of parking right up to the front of the house, but pure laziness invariably dictated that I pulled in sideways over the driveway and stopped at a diagonal across the front door and windows. This is how I had left the car the night before.

It was only when I got to the front door that I really became aware of the noise: a roaring, popping, crackling noise. It was the sound of a bonfire except *angrier*. I put my hand on the door handle and glanced over to the window. The blinds were drawn but I now knew it was a fire from the way the flames moved the shadows across the inside of the room, brighter with each passing moment.

I have heard that Formula One drivers say when they are driving at speeds that should under any other circumstance prove to be utterly uncontrollable, their thought processes speed up enough to allow them to instinctively take rational actions. Their reactions are sharper and decisions aren't so much made but willed into existence, things just *happen*.

I opened the door.

My car was fully ablaze. The windows seemed to have turned into skylights through which I could see hell itself, filled with fire and rage. Flames covered the bonnet, sending sparks flying twelve feet into the air, and the heat hit me like a bat to the face. A million enraged bees roared alongside the continuing blasts from the horn; toxic, black smoke billowed off the roof and poured past me through the open door into the house. I turned, slamming the door behind me and moved back inside the house.

I remember shouting loudly, really loudly, for Jane to get Grace from her bed and then teleporting to the middle of the stairwell, watching Jane make her way down the stairs towards me just as the windows let out a short but distinct single clap. The sound sharply resonated through the room and stood out above the crackle of the fire and the (now distorting) regular sound of the horn. I had no idea what it was, but the neanderthal part of my brain knew it wasn't a good noise and we should hurry the hell up.

We rushed through the kitchen to the back of the house; Jane was in front of me, carrying Grace and shaking. She tried to open the back door but it was locked and the handle wouldn't move. I reached around her and unlocked the door with the key we always kept in the lock, turned the handle and flung open the door. The back patio reached out to a set of concrete steps, which led up to the grass and the garden fence came all the way around the edge of both the patio and the grass until it met the house with a gate on the right.

Behind that gate a group of people were shouting and trying very hard to get into the garden. The gate shuddered as they battered at it and tried to open the deadlock. Jane froze; she literally stopped as if the world had pressed the pause button on her remote control. I barrelled into her back, sheer momentum pushing her forward towards the gate, my mind still on the sound of the splintering glass echoing from the front room.

That's when I realised that there was someone on the other side of the fence. Someone who wanted to be on our side. Someone who wanted that very, very much. With no idea if they were a rescue party or something more threatening, I looked at Jane, who had now glued herself and Grace against the back wall of the house. Jane – absolutely terrified – was breathing in short, sharp gasps, eyes wide and white in the darkness. The words fell from her mouth as she backed up into my body: 'What if they're going to try and take her?' she whispered, clutching Grace even tighter. Turning towards the gate, I listened to the shouts, saw the gate rocking against its hinges as someone threw themselves at it from the other side. I looked around – I had nothing to protect us. Nothing to defend my family with and no way to get out.

What could I do? I reached out to the deadbolt that was keeping the gate closed, forming a hysterical plan to reclaim the element of surprise. If I waited until the person or persons stepped back before charging at the gate again, I could throw the gate open and instigate a wild dash out with Grace and Jane before they could expect us.

Just as I started to pull back the bolt, life chose that exact moment to remind me that I am not Bruce Willis and do not exist within an action movie. The cracks I had heard from the front of the house were the first panes in the windows' double glazing, fracturing as the heat from the fire expanded it beyond its capabilities. With the airtight seal in the window compromised, the vacuum between both sheets of glass had filled with air, which then heated and expanded until there was nowhere else for it to go. The front windows exploded with a sound quite unlike anything I've ever heard before or since. It wasn't just the chest-shaking crash or the high-pitched shattering of the movies, it was both of those mixed together with an added thunderous slam as the shockwave pushed straight through the house and out of the back doors behind us. Or at least that's how it felt. As the weight of the noise surrounded us, we all crouched involuntarily against the unexpected onslaught.

The gate opened on its own weight during that second and I grabbed Jane's arm, ready to go. But there was no need to fight as we recognised that the potential would-be attackers were in fact our neighbours trying to get in to reach us – and the relief was incredible. Jane, Grace and I ran round to the front of the house, out into the street and the gradual light of the morning.

The police and fire brigade arrived very quickly but it felt like hours as I stood in the street watching our car and house burn. Smoke spilled from the smashed windows and people poured out of nearby houses, rushing around with blankets and frightened faces. My pocket vibrated innocently. I must have collected my phone without thinking as we left the kitchen and it now buzzed with another text message:

Fucking pedo, shit dealer sucm you shit cunt robyn parks. When you show this ynu better show them the kids sex films that you've made and your in. You sick pedo robyn

I tried to read it without emotion but as the heat from the flames licked at and then covered the windows of the room where my daughter had been sleeping just minutes before, I looked down at this message and couldn't summon any emotion other than pure, unadulterated rage. I was so angry with this person who thought they could intimidate, threaten and terrorise me and my family. Angry at how easy it had been for them to endanger the life of my child and angry that Victoria was still trying to exploit not just my weaknesses, but seeking out and twisting other people with such potentially catastrophic results.

However, I knew that anger wouldn't help me. It was justifiable, understandable and completely legitimate, but it wouldn't solve anything. She was pushing other people in order to push me, to see just how much commitment I had. One misstep, one point of retaliation and I would lose everything I had gained. But just as she had before, Victoria underestimated me. If it meant keeping my daughter safe, I could cope with this. I was Grace's voice in the world when she didn't have one and I could be strong enough to say, 'You can't beat me.' I refused to give Victoria the ammunition she needed, I was stronger than that. I could – and would – be the father that my daughter needed me to be.

The police raided Wayne's parents' house, where Victoria and Wayne were staying, and arrested them but then bailed them after a few hours. I'll admit that for a brief moment I couldn't think of any International Human Rights laws that I wouldn't be prepared to break to get my hands on them. But I'm not King of the World and so I reluctantly decided to leave the investigation to the professionals. But the standard of evidence for a charge that serious is high and I was told there was insufficient cause to hold them. While there may have been a motive, acting on the impetus to commit arson is a big step up from an unpleasant divorce and bitter custody battle, which was, on paper, the only thing we had between us. Both Victoria and Wayne gave each other alibis for the night, which may have been suspicious but were certainly not the metaphorical smoking guns that were needed. Furthermore, they both seemed to be freely co-operating with the police and their inquiries. A few items were seized from the house to be checked over at a later date, but the couple seemingly posed 'no risk'.

No risk?! How much danger did my family have to be in to reach the threshold for protection? If trying to burn us alive in our own house wasn't enough, was someone going to have to actually try to *shoot* me before anything would be done?

After years of near-constant antagonism out of court and the stress of battling a system predisposed against me as a father and yet which defined what my family was allowed to be, I was sick and tired of it all. I could have coped with the constant text messages, the phone calls and complaints against me, the police knocking at my door, even being falsely accused of every crime imaginable. But being burned out of my own home and then seeing the perpetrators let go without any recognition of fault? I really struggled to understand that.

The hours that followed passed in a blurred haze. There were a lot of police questions and interviews but quite frankly, I can't remember any of them. How we even managed to walk ourselves around is a mystery. Stunned and exhausted, after borrowing some clothes from some shell-shocked friends and neighbours, we managed to drive to my mum's house (she had returned from Africa the year before) in order to have a bed to sleep in, but we struggled to make conversation. We all ate fish and chips with forced smiles and strained small talk before I spent an hour cuddling Grace until she fell asleep. She wouldn't let me go that night, holding me tight, just wanting the physical reassurance of my immovable presence, and I was more than happy to give it to her.

A day that I couldn't possibly have imagined was finally over, but how are you supposed to sleep after that? It's the bit you don't see in the films. After everything is finished and everyone has gone home, what do they do? I wasn't wired or agitated; I didn't feel any nervous energy or start pacing around. Instead, I reverted to the coping strategies ironically learned with Victoria all those years before. I mentally pulled the shutters down and locked out the world; I was awake, walking and talking, but it was all a front. There was no thought, just practical action; I did what I had to do to survive the day and nothing more. Looking back, I recognise that, in refusing to acknowledge the emotional impact of that day and pushing it all aside, I also stopped myself from processing those events. I didn't come to terms with what happened that morning for years afterwards. Sometimes in moments of quiet I wonder if, even now, I ever have.

Instead, I sat alone in the kitchen at two o'clock in the morning. The smell of my mum's perfume and the recently removed Christmas tree hung in the air. I stared at the empty glass that I held in shaking hands, unable to pull myself together enough to fill it from the bottle that stood on the table. I had tried as hard as I could, but still I couldn't keep my family safe. The more I fought against my feelings of inadequacy – trying to tell myself that I didn't have to take the role of the supposed man of the family, the protector, the hero – the more I felt that it was the only thing I should have been. I needed to be stronger, more powerful – all the things that Victoria used to tell me I had to be.

However, repeating the same routine meant that I was in real danger of making the same mistakes. It felt so easy to slip back into the role of the safe, unfeeling, cold machine that had allowed me to survive before. That Rob had depended on exclusion rather than inclusion, reaction rather than discussion, and masked terrified confusion with blinkered decision-making. But not this time. Now I knew that a man could be so much more than that. I had learned how to be a partner as well as a husband and this time there was a little girl upstairs who needed me to be more than just a robot: she needed her *dad* and there, at that table in the dark on my own, I started to cry as I tried to remember how to be one.

Chapter 23

So, what are you supposed to do the day after your house gets firebombed? I sat in my dressing gown and tried not to think too much. Unwashed, unshaven and uncaring, I had eventually given up trying to sleep and got up, then wandered back downstairs, easing myself out of bed and trying to tiptoe past the bedrooms of my thankfully slumbering family. I sat on the sofa watching as the morning TV programmes started and thought about the two police officers who had knocked on my door what seemed like both years but also seconds ago.

When I think back on it now, I understand that I was almost certainly in shock, but at the time I would never have admitted that. What was clearly apparent to anyone looking at what must have been a glassy-eyed, barely coherent, six-foot, half-naked human statue who appeared to be having difficulty trying not to dribble on himself was totally incomprehensible to me. Once again, I sank back into the comforting sanctuary that had protected and sheltered me from dealing with the horrors of what had happened and what might have been. I wrapped up my thoughts and emotions into a box and pushed it deep down inside myself.

I had probably been there for the better part of an hour before tell-tale floorboard creaks from upstairs broke me out of that early morning mental stupor. As Grace appeared on the stairs, my rational brain had no hesitation in seizing control and I physically shook myself before putting breakfast on the table and a smile on my face.

When I made that fateful decision to leave Victoria, I found myself starting from scratch. So just like then, I began to make lists. Lists of what we needed to do, what we needed to buy and who we needed to tell. Except this time, it wasn't from scratch: I had Grace, I had Jane and I had significantly more self-respect. I now had faith in my ability to pick myself and my family back up; I had done it before and I would make damn sure I would do it again.

The next day, I went back to the house accompanied by a police victim liaison officer. I wanted to see it for myself, to understand not just the devastation that had happened but also the implications of what might have been. The front door had a hole burned through the centre where the heat had melted the fire-resistant material that had kept the worst of the blaze at bay; the edges of the door were black, crisp and burned with soot. The wall around the ground-floor window was shadowed with smoke reaching up to the windowsill above and beyond to the roofline. Tiny shards of glass crunched underfoot as I walked past the burned-out shell of what was left of the car to the house. Police tape stretched across the yawning mouth of the door. It was closed at least and with the interior panel still intact, which, considering what was left of the rest of it, was testament to how quickly the fire brigade had managed to arrive. I walked past the window and around the side of the house to the gate. Left open, it swung in towards the garden in the morning breeze, creaking. Absent-mindedly, I wondered if I could remember where my can of WD-40 was so I could put some on the hinges.

Making my way inside, I stood in the blackened and burned debris of the living room before starting up the stairs, past the smoke-painted walls and into Grace's bedroom. I tried to get my head around the situation; the paintwork, furniture and Christmas presents that were either ruined or completely destroyed were just *things*. Just items that could be cleaned, washed or replaced. The biggest impact, though, was the smell and tar-like substance that coated everything within reach. It wasn't only a passing feature of the house but rather an omnipotent presence that attacked you. It had infused everything with its acrid, clawing stench, which attacked the back of my throat, trying to chase me out of the house. I wanted to turn away, to leave, but I forced myself to stand next to Grace's bed, the covers still thrown to the side in the rush, looked out of the window and instinctively tried to wipe away the black soot to see the green grass outside. It just seemed important that I could still see the colour through the gloom.

Alongside the practical considerations that this type of situation throws up (the insurance claims, the discussion about where you'll live and the all-pervasive stench of burning rage), there are also the emotional body blows, gut punches and uppercuts every time you see a ruined photo or singed teddy bear. *You can't keep them safe*, I would continue to tell myself for months afterwards. Jane and I both had problems sleeping after the fire and while she briefly resorted to medication to try to find some calm, I didn't want to. I couldn't: I didn't want to be calm, or sleep or be at anything other than DEFCON 1 at all times. A one-man human meerkat mob twenty-four hours a day, I was constantly on alert to ensure I could spot and prevent anything else from happening to my family.

And I *was* alert. At every dog bark, every door slam and every noisy motorbike, I was up, looking through the curtains.

For months, I was the ultimate curtain-twitcher, an entire Neighbourhood Watch and the local busybody all rolled into one. Even now, if I hear a car alarm then I'm up at the window; it's practically involuntary and I can't help it. Over the intervening years, the reaction has diminished from a startled jump to a wary but focused investigation every time I hear a nearby horn. But you know what? Even if it means getting out of bed for the third time and checking the window at 4 a.m., I'm OK with that because it means we can all sleep a little bit better that night.

After Christmas, Wayne had been due to travel back to Germany and Victoria went with him. Although shaken, Grace, Jane and I were otherwise physically safe and with Victoria and Wayne out of the country, it eased my mind to know that we were protected by the geographical distance as well as the active efforts of the police investigation. At this point we had plenty of suspicions and conjecture, but no proof that tied anyone to anything. What could we say to the police? 'It was almost definitely them . . . probably?' Hardly a cast-iron case so far and as much as the police continued to humour me, in listening to me reiterate my circumstances (which, in my mind at least, were proof enough), they continued to look for something more watertight that tied everything together.

But nothing happened. Wayne and Victoria were in Germany and going about their own business; they weren't held to account, there wasn't *anything*. I mean, what the hell? Someone tried to burn my house down with my child inside it and they get to *walk away*? Why wasn't anyone doing anything? It was tough, really tough, to think about that and keep calm. I had seen Victoria being granted a family court hearing within twenty-four hours because of her supposed fear of me but now, when I needed a reaction from the system, silence?!

However, there was something I could do. With the burden of proof less definitive in civil cases, I could petition a judge to see what could be done in terms of withholding any new address and better protection for the kids. With the sheer weight of circumstance in my favour, I appeared in court in an attempt to demonstrate that Victoria had, at the very least, pointed Wayne towards my house, even if she hadn't wielded the petrol can herself. But despite the implications, yet again she didn't attend court and to my continued confusion, she didn't even make any representation or attempt to confirm contact with Grace at all.

The judge granted me a No Contact order for a fixed period while the residence hearing was resolved and although it was the right thing, it felt awful. The result weighed heavily on me: not only did I question how and why the woman I met all those years ago was becoming this bitter black hole of fury, but also, where this would end? Of course, Grace would grow up and ask me what happened and what could I tell her? How far was her mum going to fall from the person that I used to know?

After the fire, the house that we moved to was only a few minutes' drive from our previous one. It was a conscious choice because I didn't want Grace to lose her roots in the area (we needed all the stability we could get for her at this time) and to be honest, I felt defiant that I wasn't going to be driven out of a place that I enjoyed living in by a bully. With the No Contact order, I thought we were safe and could start to, once again, recover what was left of our lives. It also kept our whereabouts a secret; any new addresses would be withheld from Victoria and anyone connected to her. This, we hoped, would give us a bit of breathing space, assuage our paranoia and allow us to begin to process the events of New Year, 2014.

By early February, we'd got to know Mark, the police liaison officer working on our arson case, quite well. He was an earnest, straightforward and open professional, qualities which always helped put us at ease. We were set to be his last major case before he was due to hang up his metaphorical truncheon and retire, so he told us that he wanted to make it count. He would usually ring to check we were at home before dropping by to give us an update, and he was sensitive enough to do so when Grace was at school, something that I will always give him credit for.

It was an unremarkable morning in early spring 2014 when the postman dropped the A4 manila envelope through the letterbox. We were used to receiving updates from social services, the police and the court system, so it wasn't a surprise to see the Thames Valley Police postmark. I ripped open the seal and pulled out the latest letter that accompanied the enclosed report.

It had only been a couple of months since the fire and Thames Valley Police were ensuring that we were kept up to date with the recent charge of arson. It looked to me like a fairly standard copy of an application to the court that they had made to gain access to some documentation from the family court. It's the sort of paperwork that gets sent out to everyone involved – all related parties, their solicitors and any other services to keep everyone aware of what's going on. I've been the unfortunate recipient of many of these through the years as police and social care investigations work their way through the system: it didn't seem particularly interesting and wouldn't say anything that I didn't already know, I thought.

After scanning the front page, I left the rest on the table while I went off to make a cup of tea. A few minutes later, Jane called out after me: 'Did you read this?' Her voice was puzzled, as if she was thinking something through.

'I read the front page but haven't gone through the rest of it yet,' I replied, squeezing the tea bag and pouring the milk. I like my tea to be the colour of He-Man: that's when you know you've got the right tea-to-milk ratio – I don't like being rushed as it takes time to achieve the perfect cup.

'You should read it,' she said, '*NOW*.'

I glanced up, a little annoyed: 'Why are you talking to me like that? What's up with you?' I pulled the papers over, opened the report, turned the page and stopped. Boiling-hot tea spilled over my hand as I fumbled the mug onto the table. Right there in black and white, just below Victoria's contact details, was my name and new address. My 'should-be-kept-secret' address. My 'I-had-to-get-a-court-order-to-stop-the-person-suspected-of-burning-my-house-down-from-finding-out-where-I'm-living' address.

'You don't think they've sent this to her, do you? They couldn't be that stupid,' I stuttered incredulously.

'That's the standard application, everyone gets a copy. There's a statement at the bottom saying documents copied to all parties. That's gone to them,' she said.

'Give me the phone . . .'

But I didn't get the chance to dial because Jane grabbed it and punched in the numbers of the Thames Valley victim support line, the very real fever of fear and agitation palpable between us. The receiver buzzed before being quickly picked up by the automated caller control system. Increasingly frustrated as we worked our way through the labyrinthine options and departments, we finally managed to get hold of Mark. Then Jane's previous coolness and professional exterior broke in a tidal wave of anxiety.

'Have you seen the application?' she demanded. No, he hadn't. 'Did you realise that our address was on there?' No, he didn't. 'Has that report been sent to Victoria?' Yes, it had. 'What the hell did Thames Valley Police service think they were playing at?!' Admittedly, that last question was me trying to shout at the phone through Jane's hand while simultaneously trying to listen to what Mark was saying.

There was a pause on the line before he said, 'I think I'd best come and see you.' Twenty minutes later, he was pulling up on the drive.

'First of all, I can confirm that the application has been sent to Victoria in Germany and I apologise on behalf of the Thames Valley Police force. It should never have happened.'

'Is that it? Is that all you can say?' I blasted into his face. 'We've got to move again. We've just arrived and now because of this, we've got to move *again!*'

'Not exactly.' Mark paused. Obviously there had been a more important reason to get over here as fast as he did other than an apology. 'We've also received credible intelligence that they have tried to source a gun with the intention of bringing it back into the UK and we don't know exactly where they are at this moment in time.'

'*What?!*' I must have looked ridiculous; my whole body froze with my hands up, fingers extended in a physical representation of shock. All of my indignation and exasperation suspended like I was playing musical statues. Of all the things that I was expecting Mark to tell me, this wasn't one of them.

'When did you know that? What else don't we know and what the bloody hell are we supposed to do now?!' The questions came thick and fast really without me needing to do any thinking. Pointless, needless questions but ones that came from a deep-seated need to understand everything about the situation we were facing.

'Listen, the timings aren't important, but since they might now have your address, I'm here to offer to take you and the family somewhere safe while we assess the risk properly. You don't have to, you can stay here if you prefer, and I'll go through all the details with you. But if you decide to come, then we need to go *now*.'

It was a moment that I'll never forget. I knew from the morning of the fire that time isn't always what I believed it was and this news triggered that same visceral 'kick': a call to action that lit up that instinctive part of my brain and the world slowed again. I looked over at Jane and she looked at me. We didn't speak, I just nodded and turned back to the house. Within half an hour all three of us had bags packed and were in the car, following Mark to an undisclosed location.

When you mention that you've been in protective custody, invariably it elicits similar reactions from people: 'What was it like?', 'That sounds exciting!', 'Could you tell anyone?' I haven't spoken to anyone else who has had a similar experience but I can't imagine it would be much different to what happened to us, which was essentially a small hotel room, a few new people hanging around a lot (that you are very careful *not* to call policemen in front of the kids) and loads of pretending that we are all on a very happy, big surprise holiday. If that appears to belittle the seriousness of the situation, then that's far from my aim. Even if our actual experience of police protective custody was fairly uneventful, we had to use that time to process the idea of me being at constant risk of being murdered.

It was a big weight to hold. It's something that happens to someone else, a soap opera plot, a TV drama or Hollywood movie. After the fire, I hadn't had time to think about my own mortality, there had been too much to do. Too much to arrange and organise, but here we were put into a situation where there was nothing else to do but think about it.

But I didn't – I couldn't. I poured myself into everything, *anything*, except thinking about it. And that was no easy task. We didn't have an armed guard outside the room or patrolling the grounds, there was no panic button, no code words. But we did have to check in every day, the hotel staff were briefed with photos of Victoria and Wayne, and we were stuck in a single room, relying on other people to tell us it was safe to leave. The days we were there were stressful, not because of what we knew, but because of what we *didn't*. Were we going to have to move house again? Where would we go? How could I keep everyone safe if these were the lengths that Victoria would go to? And the one question that seemed to keep coming round and round in every conversation: how on earth had she managed to get hold of a gun?

It seems like a particularly exceptional kind of cock-up to actually send the address of a victim to the partner of the very person pending trial for attempting to intimidate and kill them. That's ridiculous, it would never happen, surely? There are multiple processes and checks in place to prevent this exact circumstance. Yet here was Mark, standing in the foyer of a hotel that I was checked into by the police, under a different name, telling me how sorry he was that was exactly what had happened.

Thankfully the letter had been recovered, we were assured, *before* Victoria and Wayne received it. The process that followed should put any institution to shame, especially one whose primary function is, to coin a phrase from our overseas cousins, to 'protect and serve'. There had been days of uncertainty while the letter was being traced and the postmark was tracked from depot to depot. Did it travel by air freight or was it transported over land by truck? That alone took two days to discover. Once it was known that the letter had arrived in Germany and had been handed over to the German postal service, a whole other level of bureaucracy ensued: there was considerable confusion over whether the authorities were even *allowed* to open someone else's post box to retrieve an item, even if it contained life-threatening information.

I like to imagine that the process had involved military police surveying the house: a highly trained SAS 'black ops' team skulking in the bushes, waiting for the unsuspecting postman to deliver the package. Then, in a cacophony of walkie-talkie gibberish and crackling static, busting through the door, screaming, 'POLICE! EVERYBODY FREEZE!' . . . only to stop and very politely (these are British soldiers, don't forget) ask Wayne if he would be so kind as to retrieve his post and hand over the A4 envelope with 'Thames Valley Police' stamped across the back of it, without opening it if that wouldn't be too much trouble, thank you very much. Mind you, if it did go down like that, I wonder if they would have told me?

Once the details of what was happening in Germany became clearer (at least to the authorities, if not to us), things seemed to settle down. As we shifted our attention from dealing with the repercussions of our lives being turned upside down, to finding out why the hell it happened in the first place, the need to keep us in secure isolation diminished enough for us to be able to go back home. All we wanted was to stop this crazy merry-go-round and just pause for a minute.

The fire was still so very real and raw and Grace was suffering from horrible nightmares. Sleep was still something that proved very difficult for me, so I couldn't imagine what it must be like for her. I needed to make sure, as much as I was able, that this wasn't going to define her as she grew up into the beautiful, confident young lady that I knew she would be. She had always been so happy and outgoing – gregarious in nature – but now she was introverted, holding back. She didn't know who or what was going to come round the corner and whether that meant we would have to leave again. I had no idea what to do or how to help her.

Grace still had to go to school, and we still had to go to work, because life doesn't pause just because things get tough. As much as we wanted to, we just couldn't afford to take a break. I had had quite enough of Victoria dictating my life and would be damned if I was going to let her carry on doing it after working so hard to free myself and Grace from her influence.

Talking to Grace's school and my work was a lot harder than I thought it would be. I still wasn't comfortable in showing weakness and asking for help. But when I did, the genuine concern and sympathy that I received were almost overwhelming. The relief at being able to reduce part of the pressure was immense and I started to feel like I had a better grip on what was an impossible situation. We changed Grace's school and found a child therapist who worked with her for the next few years, rebuilding her natural confidence. But Grace has never lost that sense of questioning scepticism that those early experiences gave her. It's no surprise, her whole world view had first been skewed and then her life thrown into complete chaos. She had seen her mother display distrust, even outright hostility towards the very people who were supposed to help her; first me, then her teachers, and through it all were all too many encounters with the police. She had been forced to follow her mother in moving out of her home and sleeping where she was told without knowing when or if she would get a bed; before experiencing an all-too-brief few months of stability with me, only for our family home to be attacked and, consequently, forced to run from the only safe place she felt she had had.

We logged our new address and the address of Grace's school with the police to ensure that anything that could be used to trace our whereabouts was withheld from anyone who didn't have permission from the court. Grace's school had photographs of both Victoria and Wayne in case they should ever unexpectedly materialise at the gates. We had to trust the system – we had no other choice.

Slowly, with no sign of Victoria or Wayne, we started to breathe again. Incredibly difficult as it was, Grace started to understand that she couldn't see her mum. That is an alien concept for most people, let alone a seven-year-old child who had lived her whole life believing that she needed to look after her mum because no one else was going to. I'm not sure if I can ever forgive Victoria for imposing that twisted world view on our daughter. It's a perspective that, once implanted, cannot easily be taken away.

Already Grace had had more than enough childhood trauma to last a lifetime and I didn't really know what else I could do about that. The therapy sessions she received seemed to help a lot: they gave her a safe place to talk about her mum with someone other than me, they made her feel calm. She also started karate lessons, which gave her the opportunity to focus and use the growing frustration she had inside her. It's something that I wholeheartedly recommend to anyone struggling with events that might threaten to overwhelm them, no matter what their age.

They say time heals, but our problem was finding that time. Making the space to deal with and then process Victoria's legal, emotional and physical attacks was proving impossible. Even though I had gained sole responsibility for Grace, Victoria had ensured that *she* was the one that Grace constantly thought and worried about. With the fire and everything that came afterwards, whatever time we *did* have was spent preparing ourselves for the next assault. Going to work each day wondering where the next attack would come from was a terrible, purgatorial way to live. Slowly, I was stumbling my way through life, knowing that I was paddling in a pond filled with hungry crocodiles, a rotting chunk of meat tied to my leg.

Would my next step be the one where I would lose a limb – or worse?

Chapter 24

So, we waited. As the months passed and nothing happened, there was less and less information coming from the police. And as Victoria maintained her boycott of communication and contact, another thought floated to the surface: *what if they get away with it? What if they are able to literally walk away?* How could I explain that to Grace? Was that really the system that we were supposed to rely on? Victoria had shown such contempt for the institutions that had brought us here and sought to take advantage of their opaque processes, but maybe she had finally beaten them into submission. I had to believe that there would be some kind of consequence for such a sustained campaign of destruction, endangering the lives of two adults and a child, which could bring Grace some answers to the questions that she will inevitably one day have.

I felt constantly charged with adrenaline, reacting to life like a punch bag, taking hit after hit. There was no control, no way to manage or regulate what was happening to us. Jane and I tried to talk as much as possible – it didn't matter what we talked about, it could have been anything. We just needed to hold on to a sense of normality; we read books to each other, if only to have a shared experience that didn't include police involvement.

Thankfully, Mark, our police liaison officer, continued to work on the case with the same dedication and passion that it held for me. He explained that the key to the investigation, and any subsequent charge or hope of conviction, lay with the 999 call that had been made the day before the fire. The caller had a very distinctive accent and tone of voice. Of course, having a memorable accent in and of itself should not, and thankfully does not, make anybody suspicious or prosecutable. But the circumstances in which this particular call was made (as well as its contents) were, it's safe to say, pretty unique.

First, the male caller, despite attempting to identify themselves as me, got the spelling of my name, my date of birth and address wrong. Then, they considered the differences in accent, tone, rhythm and overall speech patterns between us. That was enough to establish that it wasn't me who dialled 999 and so all that was left to do was to identify the actual caller. I thought this could potentially be problematic as a muffled mumble or cheap vocal voice-changer would make the call very difficult to identify. Or at least it would have been that difficult if Wayne had used any attempt to disguise himself or had a convenient twin brother with an identically distinctive vocal register. But he didn't.

The police interviewed Wayne fairly quickly but he immediately denied any involvement. They arrested him and searched his room at his parents' house. With a recording of a voice without a name, or rather the wrong name, the police needed to either match that voice to a suspect or use it to discount suspects. They put it to him that they had a recording from the day before the fire of someone who sounded *exactly* like him claiming to be me, but who was *definitely not* me, saying my car was on fire. He denied making the call and so the time dragged on.

With little else to do in the weeks and months that it took for the police to complete the investigation, I started to read up on the subject of voice analysis and identification in police investigations. Experts in recorded voice analysis are approached, employed, provided with recordings of the original call and the suspect's voice to analyse before being given time to report. That process is surprisingly expensive and so it's only done when all other avenues of investigation are exhausted. In my case, despite the clear circumstantial evidence and motive behind the events, there was no signed confession, video or live stream of anyone making the call. Therefore, without expert corroboration, the hoax call which pre-empted a genuine attack on me and my family would be considered nothing more than a circumstantial sidenote.

Wayne may have had motive and opportunity, but he also had an alibi. He shared that room in his parents' house with his now-wife, Victoria, with whom he had gone to bed the night before. He may have got out of bed, she didn't know. He may have got dressed and made the uncharacteristic decision to leave the house at 3 a.m., she didn't know. He may have driven forty minutes across country roads to specifically avoid any number-plate recognition cameras to set fire to my car in a frenzied attack, she didn't know.

She also didn't know why the police had found a mobile phone in her bedroom. A mobile phone that had been used to send the same horrendous text messages that I had received. That phone wasn't hers, she said. She had never seen it before. Victoria had no awareness, understanding or knowledge of any potential action Wayne may (or may not) have made against me. As far as she was concerned, the whole situation was a total mystery.

The air of frustration was tangible, as without the ability to directly place Victoria or Wayne at the scene of the crime or even connect them to it, past a burner phone which they both denied was theirs, reality just didn't seem to reach the thresholds of proof that would be needed to deliver justice. The professional evaluation of that hoax 999 call became crucial, but only once the police had eliminated *every* other circumstance, *every* possible connection and *any* other possibility. Eventually they were given the budget and green light to compare that recording against the recording of Wayne's police interview. The year had come and gone, a bailed Victoria and Wayne permanently returned from Germany and finally the report came back: it was a positive match. The truth I already knew was confirmed in stark, uncompromising focus and I had to confront the reality that it was Wayne who had made the move from words to action.

However, even though the police had initially charged both Victoria and Wayne with arson, the charge against Victoria was dropped due to lack of evidence. This was disappointing, but certainly not surprising. It had been clear that there was nothing directly connecting Victoria to the fire, phone call or text messages other than Wayne. Without doubt, she was the one with the stronger motive, that much was clear, but while both had the means and the opportunity, he was the one on the recording.

By this point, Wayne was the only viable suspect. Victoria had been careful, but it was clear that she was the only source of information about me – after all, Wayne and I had no history. No prior association or connection to each other, other than her. But it wasn't enough. Establishing and exploiting such intense emotions as anger within a vulnerable but very capable man wasn't enough. Fostering a relationship with such a deep and toxic dependency that equipped that man with the motivation and mindset to endanger the life of others wasn't enough. Wayne was in the frame for this on his own, which only deepened my pity for him. He seemed set to be the next fall guy to add to Victoria's growing list. The details of the charge were explained to him, the consequences laid out and the potential outcome covered in no uncertain terms . . . and still he pleaded 'not guilty'. So, in December 2015, we went to trial.

Although I had been in and out of court so many times by then that it had long lost its mystique, I think it's fair to say that a criminal trial is *nothing* like a family court. There is a judge, lawyers and a very imposing building with po-faced clerks running around shuffling papers, but there the similarities end. As I walked into court, the air became almost physically heavier, more charged, as if the weight of expectation could become corporal. All around me were men and women in suits, a few were expensive, others not so much. Nervous defendants, maybe realising for the first time that today could be a day that changed their entire life. Interested or nervous witnesses here in court for the first time, not really knowing what to expect. Angry or upset victims who have been waiting for their chance to see justice. And solicitors going about their business, having just another day in the office. It all had a feeling of potential action, an energy that brought the anticipation that *something* was going to happen, but I had no idea what.

Once again, I put on my best suit, nicest shoes, favourite tie and stepped willingly into a world that I hadn't experienced before. I sat in the witness waiting room at the back of the court, wondering why my legs were trying to shake their way out of my trousers of their own volition. As I held them tight with both hands, I tried to calm the jitters passing from my belly down into my feet. I sat, squeezed into an uncomfortable office chair. The small, high, frosted windows with dirty glass and dark panelled walls made the empty room feel small despite being twice the size of my living room at home. It smelled of professional cleaning products and anxiety.

As I waited, other witnesses came and sat but one by one they were called away by the court staff as their cases were heard. As I found myself alone, I got up and paced around, trying to work out some of the tingles that were in my toes. I pushed aside a PVC cushion-covered wooden chair and tried to peer through the window into the car park outside. I was thinking about Wayne and if he had any doubts, any questions or uncertainty about what he was doing. Was he even questioning the difference between the truth and his misplaced sense of duty?

Someone came to the doorway and called my name. I stood and took a deep breath, trying to remember the tips that my barrister sister-in-law had given me: confidently answer the question, disagree if anyone says something that is wrong and always, *always* look at the jury. I stood in the witness box and looked out across the room. The judge sat above me at the bar to my right and beyond him sat the jury. Having already listened to the opening remarks from both lawyers, twelve men and women looked back at me, all trying to understand what kind of person I was to warrant this attack. I looked across their faces and tried to take in each one. However, now, as I think back, my memory is just filled with blurred faces and colours as they merged into one entity without distinction. That is except for one man. He sat on the top row of the far left as I looked at him; he was perhaps in his early to mid-fifties, with brown hair peppered with a sprinkling of grey and a beard plus moustache combination that brought a proportion to his face which suited his large frame. He sat hunched in his chair, implacable and stony faced. Of course, all of the jury were looking at me but he was the one that I remember, this nameless man. He only ever seemed to glance down to take a few notes; otherwise he just sat and looked, deciding if he believed me.

In front of me the prosecution stood and asked me to read my statement. I spoke about the events of that morning and the impact that it had had on me and my family. I talked about not being able to sleep and how car alarms continue to fill me with an instant sense of dread. I spoke of seeing the rising flames outside Grace's bedroom window and the acrid smell of burning rubber as the car's tyres melted into the driveway. I said that the impact was larger than a personal attack, it was an assault on my whole family. Grace's nightmares went on for months and the thought of what might be waiting for us in the dark had stopped Jane from being able to go out at night at all. The fire, the text messages and the persecution were all, in my opinion, co-ordinated strikes designed specifically to punish and hurt me.

The defence didn't ask me to offer much else in the way of commentary; what else could they say? It was clear what had happened, what the result had been, but more importantly what it *could* have been. I stuck to the facts and was careful not to specifically associate Wayne with the fire. That was to be decided by the jury and I didn't want to play the role of a spiteful ex who was out for blood, so after I had said my piece, I took my seat in the public gallery and watched. Separating myself from the trial in that way and not giving in to the temptation of vengeance gave me a calm that bolstered my resilience. By not demanding any one particular outcome (be that a prison sentence, fine or anything else), I knew I could more readily accept the result, whatever it might be.

That's not to say I couldn't be disappointed with what did happen, but we'll come on to that.

Several factors suggested things were not going well for Wayne. First, his counsel did not call any witnesses in support of his version of events, i.e. to explain why it was impossible for him to have attacked my house and car. This was because Wayne had presented a particularly problematic defence. He hadn't volunteered much information or anything to corroborate his version of events and so the police had looked to the other people in the house to get an understanding of his movements. Victoria wasn't much help as she stated she had been asleep throughout the early hours of the morning. However, Wayne's mother had a few other details to share with the police and the jury.

I had, and continue to have, a deep sense of sympathy for the position in which Wayne's mother found herself. She was asked to provide evidence in court related to the actions of her own son, purporting that he had the ability and opportunity to do what he had been accused of doing. Her testimony of how he was connected to a petrol can on the previous afternoon was crucial. I can't begin to imagine what that must have felt like for her, knowing that the details she had could potentially convict him.

She knew that Wayne had been out very early in the morning. She was just getting up herself, ready for breakfast as he walked in through the front door, and she realised that he wasn't wearing a coat. Second, she also saw him carrying a petrol can that had been full the day before but was subsequently empty on his return. Leaving the house in the early hours of the night, during the depths of winter without a coat or jumper and returning with a recently emptied petrol can: circumstantial, coincidental and inconclusive? Absolutely. This testimony was hardly a smoking gun but it was certainly pretty suspicious and started to set the scene for Wayne's own evidence.

Wayne wasn't obliged to take the stand and give evidence in his defence. Even now at this, the eleventh minute of the eleventh hour, he could have chosen not to and as he stepped up to the witness box I thought that I could clearly see a man who had found himself in an impossible situation and knew this was a terrible plan. Conversely, if he *didn't* stand up and defend himself, the jury would be asked to decide if that made him look more guilty because he didn't want his voice to be compared against the recording of the 999 call. He was damned if he did, damned if he didn't, and the tension as he took the stand was palpable.

As he stood in the dock, he looked out across the room. He didn't seem concerned, nervous certainly as his flushed neck betrayed an internal anxiety, but perhaps his military training gave him the ability to control those nerves. Another fresh haircut, pressed suit and glossed black shoes; I think that we had both gone through the same routine to get ready for the day and felt we were too far down the rabbit hole to turn back.

The prosecution played the audio recording of the 999 call. A disembodied voice claiming to be me played out of the speakers. That voice didn't know my address and couldn't spell my name. This was what the jury had been waiting for, it was the one thing that the whole case revolved around. If they believed that it was Wayne on this recording then that connected him to everything: the fire, the text messages, the lot. If not, then there would be nothing left for the prosecution to hang their hat on.

In rejecting any potential opportunity to change his plea, perhaps the final decision to go all-in had given Wayne a welcome sense of serenity. I believe that he knew what was going to happen and accepted it as 'the price of love'. It may have been a misguided, misplaced and mistaken love, but to him it was real and that's all that mattered. He stood and listened to that recording in silence – chin up, shoulders back and chest out. His commanding officer would have been proud. As it played out across the court and the jurors heard a voice claiming to be me, asking the police to attend my house the day before the fire (in order, I believe, to measure the response time of the emergency services), the final nail of the case was hammered into the coffin of his defence.

The recording ended and the prosecution asked Wayne if he had just heard himself speaking. No, he replied, he had not made that phone call. Even before he finished the sentence, an audible murmur ran through the jury. They didn't need a voice matching expert to tell them what the rest of us already knew. The remainder of his evidence then attempted to describe his alibi and as I sat in that courtroom, I became even more incredulous.

His defence team asked him why had he gone out in the early hours of the morning on 2 January 2014 and where had he gone? Taking a deep breath, and being very careful not to look at me, Wayne explained that he hadn't been able to sleep and so he got up in the early hours of the morning, drove to a nearby boating lake and walked around it for two hours in the dark without his coat before driving home, where he met his mother, who had risen early for the day as he came in.

With Wayne's explanation for leaving the house in the middle of the night, in winter, without a coat providing less than a crumb of credibility, his defence team then took up their arguments on a more solid footing: the mobile phone that had been found in his room, a phone which contained the abusive text messages, wasn't his. In fact, he had never seen it before and had no idea how it got there. Now, given the fact that he was already clearly on the hook for the 999 call, connecting him with the discovery of a mystery mobile phone containing the fabricated threats and details of drug deals that he had sent to me being found in his bedroom was fairly simple. But still the decisions that Wayne made were his and his alone. After listening to the weight of the evidence against him, he could have chosen to tell the truth, but he swore under oath again and again that the person making that phone call or sending those text messages was not him.

It's easy to see in retrospect but I firmly believe once the recording had been played in the open court, the identity of the caller was never in doubt. That solidified the connection between Wayne and the fire and from there it was an easy step to apportion the act and intention behind it to him. There was no one else there, no one else who had been so intensely primed and thoroughly prepared to take the action that he took before and afterwards.

Wayne received a sentence of nine years' imprisonment on the charge of Arson with Intent to Endanger Life, which was reduced to seven after mitigation from the defence. The jury was split and the judge accepted a majority decision. It was a ten-to-two majority, with two jurors believing that the evidence hadn't been presented beyond a reasonable doubt.

Over the years, many people have asked me if I felt this was a suitable punishment, or if I felt that Wayne had received the punishment meant for Victoria. There is no doubt in my mind that Wayne perpetrated the act. He intentionally and deliberately attacked my home with my wife and child inside. However, there was no smoking gun, no autographed selfie or signed confession with which to try to understand his motivation. Personally (and I hope I'm wrong), I think that Wayne received two sentences: one that sent him to prison and one that damaged every relationship he'll ever have. I hope he's stronger than I would be in those circumstances, but I think that while it was the judge that took away his freedom for seven years, Victoria tried to take away his trust forever and I wouldn't wish that on anyone, even Wayne.

Do I, could I, or even *should* I forgive him? Although I can empathise with him and his position, my capacity for forgiveness as a commodity available for him is in short supply. That may seem contradictory, but before jumping to any conclusions it would be remiss of me not to give you the full picture, because there's still more that he has to give to our story.

In order to bring that into a clearer perspective, we have to shuffle back eighteen months before the arson trial. Wayne and Victoria had been arrested, then released by the police in the UK and subsequently moved out of Wayne's parents' house to a narrowboat on a local marina in Bedford. From there, Wayne returned to his station in Germany and Victoria followed him. That was where, if you recall, they attempted to secure a firearm. Following that incident, Wayne had been dismissed from his position in the army and they both returned home to their narrowboat.

We can rejoin them then licking their metaphorical wounds, with Wayne discharged out of the only career he had ever wanted and with nothing waiting for him other than a pending trial for firebombing his wife's ex-husband's car. Victoria, meanwhile, still unsatisfied and, hell-bent on wringing every last drop of usefulness out of the man, was steering us all into yet another new court application. Direct action had failed to get me out of the picture and so a new application (interestingly signed by Wayne on her behalf, rather than by Victoria directly) was issued.

It was the summer of 2014 and despite the pending criminal trial and regardless of the previous court orders made against her, Victoria was going all-in. This document, which was ultimately unsuccessful in its goal of requesting sole custody of Grace, contained an utterly absurd depiction of me that amounted to the most complete character assassination I had faced to date. Gang membership, fraud, drug dealing, ironically even arson featured, as well as the ever-growing baseless allegations of paedophilia and child abuse.

I could only shake my head. Although I didn't know it at the time, this document would be the last thing that Victoria would use to communicate with me directly. There was no longer any connection to a reality that I recognised; the hate, anger and venom practically dripped from the pages in every lie and untrue, unfounded and fictitious allegation. But so too did the confusion, fear and deep-seated trauma. I couldn't pretend to imagine what kind of person they believed me to be. Had Victoria finally started to believe her own lies? How else could I believe she would be willing to maintain and even continue to escalate the pressure on those around her to champion her cause, despite the ever-increasing demands she would place on them to protect her.

During those months, I would often sit on the edge of my bed in the silence before sleep, thinking about the years gone by. The early times that Victoria and I had laughed ourselves sick over terrible jokes that neither of us could remember properly, how we had gone on road trips in the middle of the night for no better reason than to search out somewhere, *anywhere*, selling a box of Krispy Kreme doughnuts (this was well before they were stocked in the local supermarket) and the shared experiences that were once part of a loving relationship. Then I would get up and go to stand in Grace's room just to listen to her breathing. I would tuck her in, even if she didn't need me to, and kiss her head. I asked myself how the creation of such a beautiful little girl led to a situation that I would never have imagined was possible. Where I would have to defend my very integrity as a man and human being in the face of a dehumanising onslaught of accusations that had, over the intervening years, unfortunately proved to be so devastatingly effective in their outcome.

But, ridiculous as it may seem, I can understand Wayne and Victoria putting in that application. Had I given up and accepted what seemed inevitable in the face of overwhelming odds, then things would be very different now. So, I do have to ask myself if I can really claim the moral high ground and consider Victoria's actions in pursuing legal contact and parental control of Grace to be different in nature and intent to mine. Well, after many hours of deliberation and consideration of the evidence and facts to this point, I have concluded that actually, yes.

Yes, I can.

Considering the gravity of the situation, my prior experience of her actions and knowledge of Victoria's not inconsiderable level of education and intelligence, I had to assume that she had directed and approved the direction of travel that she was pushing us towards. The baseless, horrifying lies being levelled at me seemed ridiculous. The demands were absurd and the conclusions utterly non-child centred. But any consideration of a possible alternative to the source of this new application were just as worrying, whichever way I thought about it: either she had told Wayne what to write and had therefore deliberately orchestrated the mistakes, abuse and lies, or he was so convinced by them already that he didn't need her prompts.

At first, it was almost a joke – funny that Victoria thought that such a document was in any way acceptable to be put to a court. I *knew* her: she couldn't have thought this would persuade anyone of anything and as I fought my way through the pages deciphering the requests and details, I started to understand more and more. She had accepted this. Victoria had intentionally placed Wayne in a position so unbelievably alien to him that she was, I believed, consciously setting him up to fail. Her hold on him was so complete that, as we would see a year or so later, he would do whatever he could to fulfil her requests, despite knowing he was out of his depth; to do otherwise was unthinkable. He had no choice but to take every single scrap of capacity he had to the breaking point in order to try to deliver what she was asking.

Just like the darkness that I had fallen into, I was seeing him willingly take on the responsibilities that she asked of him. Wayne was being consumed and it must have been excruciating for him. I imagined him sitting at home at a desk, looking through these papers. They must have seemed totally incomprehensible and written in a completely different language. Staring at those forms, aware that he was going to trial for an arson attack, not knowing if he would face prison for attempting to smuggle a gun into the country, but certainly about to lose the only career he had ever known and she *still* wanted more.

I could relate to that man hunched over the application. Not because of the things he had done or his intentions in doing them, but in trying to please a wife who asked for the impossible and blamed him when he couldn't deliver it. I felt sorry for him because I had been him. But I had got out; plenty of others, including Russell, had too. Were we the exceptions, or was Wayne under such absolute control that he had lost any form of individual choice whatsoever? What Victoria wanted, he wanted. His refusal to plead guilty at the trial that would follow this application suggested that he would still value what he believed was her love to such an extent that he was even willing to go to prison. She truly had found someone who would do anything for her.

It was Victoria whispering in rage and resentment that I heard behind Wayne's words. The shadowed murmuring of blame that gave her reason and direction. *I* was the reason why she was unhappy. *I* was stopping them from having a good married life and therefore by removing me, I was also the solution. It could even seem logical in an absurd kind of way. The conclusions she reached if I considered them from her perspective might even be understandable; with Wayne she had a physical representation of all the emotion and vitriol that she felt. Here was someone willing to follow through and act on her every whim and desire; the feeling of power must have been incredible. If you had the ability to hurt someone you hated and get away with it, would you do it? I'm not sure how many people would be able to hold themselves back.

But here is where I give myself a figurative shake to try to pull myself together. Then another, and another, until I wake from whatever daydream allowed me any kind of empathy with Victoria's actions. *Nothing* about what she and Wayne said about me was true, save the fact that I was Grace's father. The disinformation and untruths she laced into their relationship were frightening in their cruelty. Her desire to remove me from Grace's life was absolute and also the fuel she used to control Wayne, while simultaneously fighting the contradictory part of our relationship that she seemingly couldn't let go.

Wayne's total subservience and subsequent incarceration marked a dramatic and clear turning point. Victoria had seen just how powerful these tools she had developed could be: she had been able to convince a man to take a metaphorical bullet for her. He had gone to prison for her because he *wanted* to save her. For her the rush must have been intoxicating. To paraphrase a saying that I believe is attributed to Lord Acton, the problem with this kind of absolute power is that it corrupts absolutely, and unfortunately, Victoria hadn't exactly found this out by accident. With Wayne now in prison and his usefulness at an end, she filed for divorce, moved away and started again; with Wayne claiming that she left behind baseless accusations against him, just as with me, of assault and abuse.

Chapter 25

By 2018 it had been ten years since Victoria and I had separated but every few months during that time, there had been a text message, DM or other kind of communication from someone asking about or referring to her in some way or another. Some, I had taken seriously (the text messages received after the arson attack are my point of reference here) and others hadn't amounted to more than random attempts to establish if I really was the drug-dealing, child-abducting, low-life scum the sender had been led to believe I was.

For the first few years, between 2008 and 2012 or so, I had occasionally responded. It was sometimes just too difficult not to, particularly when the accusations became personal. I would on occasion give an erudite answer, explaining that I had no wish to spend any more of my time in defending myself against further malicious lies. On other occasions (often after a few glasses of wine) when yet another unknown number would once again pop up on my phone asking if I was indeed the same Rob Parkes that they had been reliably informed was a wife-beating, cannabis-dealing rapist, I would simply ask the sender to do one in no uncertain terms. Eventually I simply wrote the sources of these messages off as current or ex-boyfriends, testing the more gratuitously blatant lies for their own morbid curiosity, or perhaps from Victoria herself to see if I would either entrap myself or bizarrely start to admit to the perceived crimes that she had unilaterally convicted me of. Either way, I saw all of these messages leading up to the fire in 2014 as bait and I had had more than enough drama in my life to want to stir up any more problems than I already had. I didn't want to enter into the significant effort, time and further discussion in proving why and how they had been lied to, so I stopped responding and tried to separate myself from the growing stresses of that time. But then Graham Wall came along and changed my life.

I first met Graham in 2020 in the witness waiting room at Chelmsford Crown Court and I could see that he recognised me straight away. I had no idea who he was or why he kept looking over. We sat on different sides of the room, stealing glances for very different reasons. I was trying to situate this man within the wider context of everything that was happening and he'd finally come face to face with *me:* the man who had seemingly brought his entire life crashing down around him – but we'll come back to that later.

Graham had actually first contacted me in late 2018. He sent me a very short direct message on social media, asking if I knew Victoria. I didn't reply; I figured that he was just another of Victoria's manipulated boyfriends who felt he had to take control of the situation on her behalf. But Graham had a quite different motive and in February 2019 he got in touch again, this time through my wife, Jane. It was the first time she had been approached, as before now Victoria's partners had focused on me. He apologised for disturbing us and asked again if we knew Victoria. Jane also didn't reply.

Graham continued to message Jane through 2019: two, three and further messages followed, each more urgent than the last.

They never received a response, but still they continued to come. Over the course of these messages, Graham tried to express why he was concerned:

> I have been going out with Victoria Breeden for 4+ months . . .
> I am having major worries concerning her and her behaviour.
>   I realise that you don't want to rake up the past but need to talk to someone who understands, please.
>   I think she is a bad person but need confirmation. I need to talk to Rob, please.

These were not the usual unsolicited communications that we had come to expect from anyone in a current or former relationship with Victoria, but as suspiciously jaded and tired as we were of the relentless drama and turmoil of anything or anyone connected to Victoria, we continued to ignore them. Then we received a message that really made us sit up and take notice:

> I reported her to the police but no one is interested.

Jane and I read this in September 2019, a month or so before we would hear the name Graham Wall. We asked ourselves the obvious questions: was he real, or was this whole set-up really Victoria herself trying to catfish us into conversation and find out where we were? Sadly, even if we didn't know why, we understood that was an all-too-real possibility that we had to be cautious of. Against all my intentions not to get involved, I started to reply, but even as I typed, I was having doubts. If I was making a mistake and it really was Victoria on the other end of this screen, had I really recovered as much as I thought? If she could hook me again so easily, had anything actually changed? Would I ever be free of her if all she had to do was press the right emotional buttons? I decided not to let her have that satisfaction, so I turned the phone off and steadied my nerves while congratulating myself on being stronger than I used to be. An impenetrable fortress of emotional intransigence, I would not allow myself to be suckered in to yet another cheap sentimental trick.

Then I turned my phone back on again. If it was Victoria, then so be it; for such a long time I hadn't been able to talk about or ask for the help that I needed to make sense of what was happening to me. Destructive and coercive relationships had been terms that simply weren't available to me, but if this *was* real then here was a guy reaching out and asking for the support that I hadn't been able to admit to myself that I needed. He was already stronger than I had been, and he was asking for my help – I couldn't walk away from that. I knew I was a different man now, stronger emotionally and psychologically. I didn't have all the answers, but just as I knew that I was in danger of losing myself, had I chosen to stay with Victoria, so too I knew that I wouldn't abandon this man who had managed to recognise that something wasn't right, even if he didn't know what it was. But I also wasn't about to expose my entire life to this stranger. I told him that, yes, he had found the right person and if he had concerns, he should go to the police and ensure that the authorities knew what was going on. I didn't know it at the time, but that decision led to a train of events, culminating in the day I finally met him a year later in the witness waiting room of Chelmsford Crown Court.

But before I jump ahead, we need to stay in 2019. Autumn 2019 to be exact and Hope, my second daughter, had been born just a few weeks before. Since Grace had come to live with me in 2012 and after the fire in 2014, our focus had been entirely on creating a rock-solid base of normality. We moved house and school for Grace in order to find that fresh start and it had been working. Managing the school run, sleepovers and the imminent onset of teenage hormones were the biggest problems in our lives and they were more than enough, thank you. However, 2019 was already shaping up to be a year to remember, even before we began ignoring Graham's increasingly insistent messages. I had changed jobs and after years of Grace begging for a sibling, Jane was pregnant. We had moved hell and high water to complete some building work on our house by the time Hope was born at the end of September of 2019 and, while technically a success, personally I would prefer more than a five-day gap between the exit of builders and the entrance of a new baby into the family home if I were to do it again.

When she did arrive, Hope brought with her more than her fair share of problems. Some very nasty jaundice, tongue-tie feeding-related issues and an undiagnosed cows' milk protein allergy ratcheted up the pressure and as she started to drop weight far too quickly, this led to the need for overnight stays in hospital. Medical support followed and even when we did manage to come home, outpatient trips in and out of hospital were scheduled alongside home visits.

Seeing a child of mine back in hospital, having tests and treatment, was far more difficult to process than I was expecting, even after so many years. This time, though, I had Grace next to me, as well as a partner who also considered me to be exactly that, so the circumstances were completely different and, needless to say, far more positive.

It is not the same, I told myself in a comforting whisper, *don't worry*.

Of course, such things are easier said than done and I worried constantly, both rationally (will Hope be OK?) and irrationally (are they going to take her away from me?). I know that Jane matched my level of anxiety for different reasons. New mums are hardwired to worry about everything, so I'm still in awe that despite the hormones and emotions raging through her, the mental load, worries and demands that a new baby brings, she remained calm and measured as we juggled everyday life, all while hospital staff, health visitors, family and well-meaning friends came and went. Thankfully, Hope recovered well and remains blissfully unaware of the concern she caused us.

Autumn 2019 was also the same time that my brother Adam died. Cancer took hold of him frighteningly fast and within just a few short months, the lively, upbeat, funny, sarcastic, grumpy, neurotic, helpful, loving man that I grew up with wasn't there anymore. His last days spent in a hospice were made as easy as they could be, as he knew that time was short and every second counted. It was not what I would consider perfect timing then, when I received an unexpected call from the police on the very day that I said goodbye to my big brother. I was sitting on the kerb in the car park, having stepped outside to try to get some air, when the phone rang and a disembodied voice asked if I was available to give a statement.

'I'm not in a great place right now, to be honest,' I mumbled, exhausted from the emotion of the day and replying through bleary eyes. 'Can it wait a few days?'

'Not really,' came the reply. 'It's a very time-sensitive situation, we need to talk to you about your ex-wife, Victoria.' Well, of course they did. There has never been another reason why the police have wanted to talk to me. 'We will come to you so it can be done as soon as possible. Are you at home?'

On that initial call they didn't go into much further detail. I got a vague impression that the police had received plausible information about Victoria approaching certain people with the intention of finding me. There was a possibility that these people knew where I lived, the police considered the threat to be serious and Victoria was currently in custody, although they wouldn't tell me exactly what she had been accused of. They now had a fixed time frame to charge or release her and considering the nature of the conversation they wanted to have with me, I got the feeling that they really didn't want to let her go.

By now, it didn't seem too unusual to have this kind of contact from the police, although it had been some considerable time since we'd heard anything, so it did intrigue me. As part of our last court hearings, Victoria had been prevented from knowing where Grace was going to school or from contacting any of us at all. Naïvely, I assumed the call must have something to do with this. In hindsight, perhaps I wanted to find a reason to block out the emotion of that day. Certainly, my internal protective mechanisms kicked in and didn't allow me to initially take the call that seriously. My mind and eyes cleared and I focused on dealing with whatever new crap Victoria had in store for me this time. I turned my attention away from my brother and focused on getting through dealing with the next instalment of Victoria's attack.

As I made my way back on autopilot across bleak, winding countryside roads, on the newly familiar route between the hospice and my home, I started to mentally pack away all the emotion of the day. I had half an hour to pull myself together before I got back to the house and so I called Jane from the car to let her know to expect more visitors. She took the news with characteristic calm. On top of recovering from giving birth to our daughter, coping with a healthcare professional sent to assess the declining health of our newborn baby and me clearing off to try to manage my own issues, I was now asking her to brace herself once again for whatever potential disruption and abuse Victoria was throwing our way. I've said it before and I'll say it again, my wife is amazing. We spoke about calling the police back and telling them that I would come to the police station instead, but with the limited information that they gave me over the phone, decided against it because we had no idea how long it would take. Besides, I needed to get back to support my family at the hospice as quickly as possible.

I returned home only moments before the police car pulled into the drive. I greeted the health visitor, with whom Jane was deep in discussion, checked in on my two-week-old baby daughter and put the kettle on just in time before the doorbell rang. When I opened the door, I was faced with three people standing on the doorstep. Two of them introduced themselves as officers from the local Thames Valley Police force who, in the interest of time, had been asked by the Cambridgeshire force to take a statement from me. The third person was not a police officer, she was from a TV production company who were making a documentary series called *24 Hours in Police Custody* – I was not expecting that.

As it was the only thing I could think of to do, I invited everyone in and offered them tea. Introductions were made and everything remained quiet while I checked the identity tags of the police officers. I was then asked a question that has unquestionably altered the direction of my life: Would I be happy for my statement to be filmed?

We took up residence in the lounge, pivoting around Jane, Hope and the health visitor as we made our way through the house. I can't see how it did us any favours to introduce the person tasked with gauging our ability to care for our struggling newborn to two police officers and a film crew but we seemed to have escaped further repercussions, for which I am not a little grateful. I sat on the sofa and waited as the officers checked their notes. I had again robotically offered everyone tea or a chocolate biscuit despite the fact that we had no biscuits, chocolate or otherwise. As the uncomfortable quiet of a group of strangers waiting for someone else to break the silence descended, I found myself clutching my mug and zoning out while the room busied itself either in notebook preparation or camera set-up. My body may have been physically present but my mind was pulled back to the hospice with my brother, where I had been just an hour before and running over the many vivid memories of happier times together.

I found myself thinking about all the many things he had given me: my niece and nephew, an exemplary dedication to family and a stone-cold fear of ever riding a motorbike again. Once, when I was seven, he pulled up at the house on his brand-new motorbike. I can't remember the type but I do remember the colour: mainly white, but with blue detailing. It looked like a streak of lightning and was the coolest thing I had *ever* seen. Mum had taken one look and stipulated that he was not to allow me anywhere near it. I was not even supposed to touch it for fear that I might be caught with the go-faster bug that had swallowed my brother whole and brought her to cold sweats whenever she thought about him out on the roads.

Just like any responsible older sibling, though, Adam had at least waited until she had gone out before asking if I wanted a ride. I eagerly agreed – *my big brother loved it*, I reasoned, *so why wouldn't I?* Back in the late-eighties, there were no major bypasses or motorways around the Northamptonshire village where I grew up. Islip, a little village on the edge of a small town, Thrapston, which in turn was identified only by its relative proximity to a slightly larger town, Kettering, which was (at the time) still at least an hour away by car. In other words, it was in the middle of nowhere, surrounded by B-roads and dirt tracks, dangerously exciting gravel pits and ruined barn buildings.

Over the following thirty minutes, my big brother proceeded to give me a lesson in speed that was so visceral, so intense, that it still stays with me over thirty years later. After half an hour of eye-watering, vomit-inducing and (I'm not ashamed to admit) bowel-loosening speeds, often at what felt like no more than a hair's width from the ground, I swore that I would never, *ever*, get on the back of another motorbike as long as I have breath in my body. With that memory still fresh in my mind after more than thirty years, I have kept that promise. Over time, I have come to believe that this was an intentional act; a gift from brother to brother, always making sure that he followed Mum's request in looking out for me, but choosing to do so on his own terms and never passing up the opportunity to have a bit of fun in the process.

After pushing him away for so many years, I felt enormously guilty for not making the most of the time that we had. I cycled through the usual rhetoric: if only we had had more time. If only he had told me sooner, if only I had known just how serious it was going to be. But none of that really helped; it had been his solidity and permanence that had held us together as a family and with him gone, I had lost the chance to tell him that those were the lessons that I brought with me through my own dark days with Victoria but now had developed a ferocious determination never to lose again.

I managed to spend some time with him in the hospice, holding his hand towards the end. He never was one for deep or meaningful chats, even during his final days, and while he told me that he was glad I was there with him, I knew that his time here with us was not something I could selfishly keep as his pain continued to grow. I continue to remember him now as I think he would want me to: laughing and joking with his family and friends. That big, easy grin of his and relaxed sense of humour was always a huge presence in my life whether he was in the room or not.

I learned a lot about life from him, mostly positive, a few things not so much, but everything worthwhile. I don't think I'll ever forget the afternoon he picked me up from school and gave me a heat-and-eat dinner before sitting me down and showing me horror films before Mum came to collect me. The Phantasm series were his particular favourites at the time and his VHS machine whirred and crackled in the corner of his living room as I watched a weird old man with a murderous semi-autonomous flying sphere terrorise a young boy and his older brother. I was only twelve and had nightmares for weeks before Mum found out what had happened. He got into a bit of trouble for that, but once again I think he saw the whole thing as a part of his brotherly duties. The legacy still lives on too as I haven't touched cans of pre-mixed beans with sausages since and still can't watch horror films without the uncomfortable leaden dread bringing me out in goosebumps.

Of course, my brother had his own demons to manage like the rest of us, but with him next to me, they would seem a lot more manageable. When I was in trouble, he was always able to make me feel stronger when the time came to face up to my mistakes. Through his attitudes and actions, he showed me that, when it comes to the crunch, family is whoever and whatever you want it to be. The last thing he ever said to me, in a croaking whisper, was how proud he was of me for never giving up and I've been doing my best to live up to his example every day since.

These days, I can recognise that I still haven't come to terms with my brother's death. I can talk about him and go through the motions of acceptance, which is all very important, but I also know that there is a reason why I can't stop myself from sometimes inexplicably bursting into tears when I'm alone in the car. My mum has a picture of him in her flat that I see each time I go to visit her. Of course, she has lots of them, but that's the one that I always look at. She put it on his coffin at the funeral. If I'm honest (he won't mind), I've never felt that it's an especially flattering picture of him; he's sunburned and sweaty, squinting towards the camera and leaning forward to give a thumbs up in a way that creates a weird perspective. But he's also got that grin on his face that he always had when he was having the absolute time of his life. Whatever he was doing that day, he was loving it and it shines out of the photo like a Supernova. That's the man I remember when I sit down last thing at night on his birthday and pour out two glasses of whisky: one for me and one for him. I toast another year without him, then drink his glass for him because that's what he would have wanted – he was never one to let a glass of anything go to waste.

For so many reasons (the need to be an emotionally strong 'man', the feeling that I didn't have enough time and that it was simply just too painful among several others), I ignored what Adam's death meant to me for such a long time. I suppose I've only just started on that road now, all these years later. In part, that recognition has allowed me to see that in many ways DS Barnshaw, or Mike, the police officer I met the month that Adam died and who was in charge of the 2019 criminal case against Victoria, reminded me of my brother – I'm sure that's why I liked him.

Both men were physically similar in age and stature – shorter than me with closely cropped haircuts, broad shoulders, heavy boxer's hands and a sense of purpose behind their eyes. They had the tangible weight of responsibility hanging about them and neither ever seemed very comfortable wearing a suit. Both were intense decision-makers who didn't like to spend much time on the phone because there was always something more important to get done, but invariably when I spoke to either one of them, they always found some way to bring the conversation back to family – mine or theirs. Coincidentally, both seemed to have a penchant for wearing great shoes too, timeless light brown or black Italian leather and immaculately polished. Their jobs couldn't have been more different, but I got the feeling that they would have liked each other had they ever met and that gave me a strange sense of comfort.

It was Mike's personal dedication, and that of his whole team, which brought the case against Victoria to trial. His team, and specifically DC Louisa Abbott who I would meet later on, was tasked with uncovering the story behind the circumstances presented to them. But I'm getting ahead of myself because, if I were you, I would have a few unanswered questions, like: what happened to Graham Wall? Who is Mike and why did he get involved? And is the reason that I feel the need to tell you all about my dead brother simply an attempt at a cathartic expression of otherwise repressed and unexpressed grief? Well, don't worry, while I thank you for your patience during this little bit of self-diagnosed therapy session, I can assure you all will become clear.

Chapter 26

'No, thank you,' said the police officer sat on my sofa as he looked up at me, clearly waiting for an acknowledgement of his statement.

'Sorry?' I blinked and shook my head, slightly confused.

'No, thank you, I don't want a biscuit or tea. That's very kind but it's not necessary.'

'OK, no problem.'

OK, biscuits. No biscuits needed, understood. Come on, Rob . . . I gave myself a mental slap round the face to get back in the room.

The policeman got straight to the point: 'Essentially, we've had someone attend the police station with a recording of Victoria and another person conspiring to murder someone.'

I wasn't sure where this was going, but I was fairly confident by this point that it wasn't anywhere good.

'The content of that recording is directed towards yourself.'

Yep, that was it. That was the point where I hit my mental buffer limit. On the recording, you can see me nod and pause for a couple of seconds. I look calm, composed and in control, if a little shocked. What no one else realised, though, was that my brain had decided right then would be a good time to check out and have a brief holiday. I wasn't calm, I was vacant. My conscious decision-making process had gone AWOL and any resemblance to self-control was mistaken for the reality that was effectively mental eviction. I found myself with only a very limited ability to nod and drink tea. Luckily, and unlike the last two times this had happened, when my body had taken evasive manoeuvres in order to prevent a complete mental disintegration, this time my psyche at least managed to keep me awake as it brought down my cerebral shutters and nailed boards over the windows of my mind to buy me some time to process what I had just been told.

I could see the policeman's mouth moving and I knew he was still talking, but I wasn't paying attention. The whole situation just didn't seem real. Not remotely real. The words being said to me just weren't registering and, like an old-fashioned split-flap railway noticeboard, I imagined a checklist of things I needed to do next:

Clackclackclack . . . Move house.
Clackclackclack . . . Move Grace's school.
Clackclackclack . . . Leave my job.
Clackclackclack . . . Ask Jane to leave her job.
Clackclackclack . . . Install security cameras – a lot of security cameras.

The mental strain was just too immense and overwhelming for me to cope with. Again, I saw Victoria forcing me to uproot my family and change our entire lives due to her attempts to get to me in any way she could. And for what? What was it all for? It had been seven years since I had even seen her. *Seven years* and she was still trying to drag me back in or seemingly eliminate me if she couldn't.

Objectively, I can also recognise that – at that moment – I was still reeling from the immediacy of my brother's death.

Any therapist would have been more than willing to book me in for a decade's worth of sessions to just deal with that. I understand that it was a simple coincidence that Victoria had been detained at the same time that I would lose my brother, but subjectively it was, and continues to be, incredibly hard to separate that loss from my former wife's second major attempt at ending my life. More than the emotional dissonance and lack of closure, what I felt most was confusion. The more my mind whirled around the events of the day, the more confused I became. As the world came back to me, I realised that:

1. I would have to tell Grace at some point and so a lot more information was needed, and
2. I had been drinking tea from an empty cup for an unknown period of time, which must have looked really weird.

I raced through some potential justifications for any possible mistake to have happened. From the tenuously plausible (was Victoria actually describing what had happened with Wayne?) to the downright absurd (does she know someone else called Rob Parkes that she's also trying to kill?). What could she possibly hope to gain? Did she think that she could take Grace if I was dead? Surely, she must realise that her actions over the past ten years had rendered that impossible.

Perhaps it was about money, but I couldn't see that either – she knew she couldn't get any more money from me. When we divorced she got the savings and the house and now with Grace in my custody, she was no longer eligible for any kind of child support payments.

Could it be as obvious and simple as revenge? Retribution against the man whom she blamed for leaving, for walking away from the life that she felt she deserved and the life he took from her? It's possible but seemed almost too simplistic a motivation for the woman I knew – it would just be too 'neat'. Victoria had never wanted me gone, quite the opposite. Even when she was doing everything she could to destroy the possibility of a positive outcome between us, she couldn't bring herself to let me go. Whether it was creeping into my room while I slept alongside another woman or demanding that I present myself at her house to drop Grace off, while simultaneously claiming to anyone who would listen that she was terrified of me doing exactly that. No, revenge couldn't be the whole story either. Clearly, I wasn't going to get anywhere near understanding what was going on by myself. The initial information had been shared and so now I had to give the police the details which had required such urgent action that day. What they were after was the history of my connection to Victoria and if I could provide the context to support or contradict their theory that she was not only capable but, most importantly, willing to arrange for an attempt on my life to be made.

This interview with the police, including my commentary on the history of my relationship with Victoria, was recorded and shown as part of the Channel 4 documentary that covered the case and subsequent trial. A permanent record of what had happened to Grace and I, as well as an insight into the previous seven years and the relationships that had been touched. The relationship that I thought I had left behind me was being brought back in the most brutal way, reminding me that this woman was reaching out from hundreds of miles away and able to rekindle emotions so visceral that I feel their consequences in what I expect of myself to this day.

In the documentary you can see my reaction in real time as I try to process the information that I was given. 'Riiiiight,'

I managed to say, trying to buy time to figure out what was going on. There is always a question with regards to these types of programmes: was it exploitative of the production team to film the exact moment that I was given the news? No, I don't think so. I knew what was happening and had chosen to put myself in that position. Was it an interesting example of the human response? Unequivocally, yes. If I was watching that instead of being a part of it, I would have been totally fascinated.

Watching the subsequent documentary was not going to be a comfortable experience – what I saw on the screen was to be a long-forgotten microcosm of my relationship with Victoria played out in stark, uncompromising detail. All the most horrific parts of a ten-year relationship condensed into two hours and like any substance that has been boiled down to a concentrated essence, it was emotionally sticky and all too intense. The idea of having an everlasting record of that relationship broadcast to the world for all to see seemed, at first, to be the very last thing I would ever want to be a part of. So, despite agreeing to being recorded, after this initial police interview I refused to take any further part in the programme.

There are many people who would disagree with my change of heart but I reasoned that it was pride that had played such a large part in stopping me from leaving Victoria, pride that made me feel inadequate during my subsequent relationships and pride that had held me back in asking for help. The more I thought about it, the stronger I was convinced that it was pride that was stopping me now. The more details I learned of the other men that Victoria had targeted, the more I was forced to look at myself. I was the first and so had a responsibility not only to Grace, but also to all of these men to acknowledge and legitimise the experiences that I understood they had had.

It wasn't their fault just as it wasn't mine. I couldn't let my pride hold them accountable and be judged in the same way that I had been. This story was no longer just about me and if I was prepared to stand up to be counted for Grace, then I should be prepared to do it for them.

When I finally got to see the recording of what had happened on the day before the police came knocking on my door and supported by Jane at my side, I was horrified, fascinated and concerned in equal measure. On the screen in front of us I saw Mike answer a phone call, the silence of his office punctuated by his broken responses as he listened to the voice on the line.

'DS Barnshaw. What's she come into the inquiry office for? Taking the phone? We can't really let her go now that we've got hold of her. She can come here and we can ask her the questions that we need to.'

And it was with that conversation, Victoria lost her freedom.

Graham had told Victoria that he had taken his mobile to the police because it contained a recording of her talking about murdering me and there she was, trying to collect that phone as if that was the most normal thing in the world, presumably before anyone could review the recording.

Bodycam footage from the officers then showed Victoria attending Ely police station, relaxed and nonchalant. To see her was a body blow of a memory. She remained just as I remembered her from all those years ago, but also different. Seven years had passed and she clearly wasn't the same woman I had known but she still looked so very familiar. Her hair that she was once so proud of was still straight, long and brown, but this time pulled back and held up in a clip. Her face filled me with memories – her eyes, cheeks and mouth all fit into my mental space so comfortably it was as if they never left. It was an intensely contradictory uncomfortable yet intimate feeling. I watched as she walked with ease into the police station but then awkwardly stumbled into an interview room ahead of the officer, grimacing in pain as she sat down, casually mentioning a procedure on her back for which she was in recovery.

Suddenly I could smell TCP. It was so distinctive and unexpected that I looked around my lounge to see where it was coming from. Then I got a whiff of hospital food, that unmistakable scent of hundreds of plates of barely-warm gravy, and it all came flooding over me in a wave; I felt the material of surgical gowns between my fingers, heard the squeak of PVC chair covers. I could see the waiting rooms, the wards, and the lies and manipulation as clear as day. Watching Victoria in that police interview directly injected the memory of the hundreds of depressing, institutional and clinically bland rooms where I had seen that exact same expression. I was there, holding her, helping her down onto that chair. Her slow, deliberate movements, the way she winced at each touch before getting up and walking off without a care in the world when it suited her. It made me shiver.

'The time is a quarter past three on the ninth of October. At this moment in time, I am placing you under arrest for the offence of Conspiracy to Commit Murder.' The officer was matter of fact. 'At this moment in time, you are now in custody,' he said calmly.

If you have seen any of the *24 Hours in Police Custody* programmes before then you might have observed similar reactions to Victoria's in the moment that the officer told her that she was under arrest. Genuine or otherwise, Victoria is not a lifelong career criminal and so being arrested, even though this was not the first time she had experienced it (she had also been arrested on the morning of the arson but released with no further action), the experience must have been difficult. However, I reminded myself of two specific facts:

1. Victoria had lied to the police with the express aim of retrieving a phone that wasn't hers.
2. That phone contained a recording of her discussing when, where and how would be best to kill me.

As difficult as she may have wanted getting arrested to appear, my sympathies didn't last long. I didn't have time to think any more about it, though, as the camera cut back to her: 'I need to go and pick up my son.' Victoria's disbelief was extreme, her eyes bulging, mouth hanging open in incredulity.

The conversation continued: 'We will sort out any arrangements you've got for childcare,' reassured the police officer. 'Where is the nearest person who can take care of your son?'

'My mum, I don't know . . . I don't know her details because I haven't got my phone. My ex took my things. He's got my keys, he's got my phone. He's got everything, he took everything.'

Woah, stop the bus! Stop it right there. Now I could hear something else: alarm bells. This was the Victoria I knew, dialling the emotional pressure up to eleven.

With the arrest details issued, the police officer made a swift exit, presumably to arrange Victoria's transfer to Cambridge as Mike had requested. The bodycam footage was then interspersed with Mike, again on the phone: 'Is she all right? How did she take being arrested?'

Not very well, Mike, I thought, but it was all still the same; the same approach, the same pleas for help and the same masked objectives. To someone who didn't know any better, Victoria was presenting as someone who was understandably upset, distraught even. She had just been arrested for Conspiracy to Murder, an incredibly serious crime. Expressions of disbelief and incredulity would be a perfectly reasonable reaction in this, the most extreme of circumstances. Then again, other than being concerned about her son, there was only one other thing she was asking for. One small, seemingly insignificant thing: her phone. Except, it wasn't her phone and it coincidentally also happened to contain the only copy of the evidence relating to the very crime she was being accused of.

I shook my head, struggling to cope with my own level of disbelief in what I was seeing when the camera cut back to Victoria. Through the police officer's body cam, we now saw her lying on the floor, curled up, crying and rocking while the officer asked if she was OK. Once it had become clear that she was not going to be able to retrieve the phone or leave the police station, Victoria had collapsed. A memory grenade exploded in my head and I couldn't take any more. Through the camera I was once again looking down at Victoria, who was seemingly unable to move, speak or even communicate past moans of pain. For more times than I can count, if she had come up against a problem that couldn't be managed, cajoled or persuaded away, I had held her hand and stayed with her while this happened.

I had had enough and needed to take a break.

The documentary's portrayal of Victoria's arrest was heartbreaking. I knew that Grace would watch it at some point and see this version of her mum. It certainly wasn't rose-tinted and while I can't say I wanted Grace to remember her mum as perfect, I was so sad that she would have to endure this, just as she had had to endure so much else. Here was demonstrable proof that Victoria was still deploying the same kind of emotionally coercive manipulation that she had with me all those years ago. I didn't know if I should cry in vindication or pity.

But unlike the television programme, I couldn't pause my life. After I had washed my face and cleared my head, I had to come back into the room. And when I did, she was still there, waiting. But the documentary wasn't just about her. In fact, the more I watched, the more I started to really see the people she had discarded over the years. The people around and connected to us, the people that she hurt the most.

There was one face that caught my attention more than the rest. One man who, when he appeared on screen, sat on a beige sofa in the middle of police interview room in a baggy T-shirt and jeans. I couldn't believe it was the same man I knew all those years ago. Wayne had changed far more than I could have thought possible. Gone was the stiff-backed confidence, the steely self-respect and the well-deserved pride in his profession in the military. Prison had given him a different outlook. His cropped buzz cut had grown out and now with dreadlocked hair that stretched down to his shoulders, he started to give answers to the questions that I had wanted to hear for such a long time.

'She never really stopped, she was always telling me that Rob was hurting the girls, that he was a paedophile . . .'

Even as I heard the words, I could hardly believe them. I had always thought that some measure of consistent mental load and battery had been the siege that Victoria had waged against him, but to hear Wayne spell it out was still just as difficult. All these years later, he was seemingly still on edge, as if even by talking about her, she might be able to reach out and touch his life again. I knew how he felt.

My arms were heavy and numb, my fingers tingled. Even my hair felt electric. I blinked and flexed my fingers to get some normal feeling back into them. Wayne paused, took a breath and then continued: 'She [Victoria] asked me how easy it would be to get weapons from the Army.'

He was talking about the gun. The gun that my police liaison officer Mark had been so worried about. More questions that Grace and I may never get answers to, but which filled in gaps in our lives by opening up more questions: what gun was it? How many of them? How far did he manage to get? Perhaps it's nothing more than a morbid curiosity on my part by now, considering that the outcome was ultimately a failure, but understanding what exactly Wayne had been asked to do held an intense allure. I think that I'm not alone in wanting to know just how close Victoria had come to achieving her goal.

Wayne and Victoria's connection with Andrew gave me the closest indication that I'll ever get to any answer to that question. He wasn't part of Victoria's trial and hadn't been involved with anything or anyone that I had been aware of up to this point and so as the camera offered his name and face to me, I frowned and wondered how this stranger, a man my age with a giveaway short military haircut, had been caught up in what was the record of my life.

With a clear and confident voice, Andrew (Andy) Peebles started to tell his story. In 2013, Andy was driving towards the British military base in Belsen, Germany, where he was stationed when he spotted a broken-down car ahead. Even from a distance, he recognised that the vehicle had the distinctive number plate of a car registered in the UK. A man who had been taught to help where he could, whose profession was to protect and whose immediate reaction was to provide help to a stranger in need, on seeing the UK number plate, he decided to stop.

Now he was closer, he saw two people: a man and woman, standing beside the road. *Perhaps they were going to the military base, or maybe they were tourists in need of some local knowledge?* Victoria and Wayne both sat in the back seat of his car and by all accounts, seemed happy to chat. Well, *Victoria* was happy to chat. Andy considered that Wayne remained noticeably quiet, not exactly sullen but perhaps withdrawn and reserved.

'My ex-husband is a paedophile.' What was so odd to Andy was just how quickly Victoria cut to the chase. There are not many things that elicit as universal a response of sympathy as the willingness to share such seemingly intimately personal details. Her meaning was clear: he has taken my children, I am powerless, I am helpless. Victoria hadn't changed her approach and the modus operandi she employed had been consistently effective. Pulling on those emotional levers usually triggered a deep-rooted sympathy and, presumably due to the time constraints that being in that car created, she was left with little option than to be as subtle as a panda wearing lipstick.

Like Wayne, Andy seemed to represent an opportunity that couldn't be ignored, but she didn't have much time so the call to action needed to be immediate and compelling. Andy recalled Victoria chatting openly and at some length about 'how she wants her kid back'. As he sat and talked through his encounter with them, on a lonely road in the German countryside, one thing that Andy seemed to be certain about was that Wayne would do anything for Victoria. *Anything.* That put more than a little frisson of concern into my thoughts about Wayne. This was coming from a man who claimed he had only met him an hour or so earlier and already seemed to have reached a clear judgement about the desire of this couple sitting in his car. But, as I have been at pains to point out throughout this story, desire is one thing, intention and capability quite another.

'If I can get a gun, would you do it for me?' Andy's face looked out at me from the TV, mouth slightly open as if someone had hit pause. Or was that just me? Did he just say what I think he said? Was this the story behind our time in protective custody? Was it Andy who I have to thank for stopping Victoria and Wayne from making a second attempt? I had thought that I couldn't hear anything else about Victoria or this case that would surprise me, but I was proved wrong once again.

'Are you OK?' Jane looked back at me and I realised that my mouth was open and I must have looked like I was trying to communicate something but I had no idea what to say. I was counting the tally in my mind: that made at least three requests of three different men. I felt sick wondering what else I didn't know – it had started with Wayne, then Andy, as well as whatever and whoever was on that phone recording. I had to wonder what Wayne was thinking. Sitting there back in a police station, but this time feeling able to say the things that perhaps he had wanted to say before but didn't or couldn't. As if in perfect sync with what I was thinking, I noticed that the programme had cut back to Wayne.

'She told me that it would be a good idea . . . I wouldn't get caught and I saw red . . . Before I knew it, the car went up.'

In that sentence, I could see Wayne trying to express the conflicting demands of struggling to cope with the pressures and mental weight that Victoria expected of him in their relationship. In front of me, he shook his head slightly as if still trying to work it out himself.

Maybe he still doesn't understand it, I thought. It could well be that even now, he can't grasp why he did what he did, beyond knowing that his life with Victoria was all-encompassing, that it had obliterated every question and objection he might have had.

I've not been able to ask Wayne about what happened and why he made the decisions he did. I think that it would be difficult for him to speak to me; it wouldn't be comfortable for me either. But I think it might be something that could help both of us. Maybe. I hope that maybe one day he'll be willing to talk to me about it and I'll be able to find the answers to some of those questions, but in the meantime, Grace will have to make up her own mind about his part in what happened to us.

On the screen, Wayne wasn't finished. Before the camera cut away, he described one last experience with Victoria: 'After, she accused me of hurting her, raping her, stealing money. I never did any of that. I'm glad that I'm not with her no more and I feel sorry for anyone who is.'

In the end, even after all he had done for her, he received the same treatment from Victoria as I did. I can't say that I knew Wayne, I have already recounted almost all of the very limited interactions that I ever had with the man. He and I could not be more different and I would be prepared to bet a lot of money that he wishes that he had never heard my name, but I'm glad that I know his. Here is a man who has had his whole life taken away: his career, his freedom, his future. I haven't forgiven him for what he did to my family. Perhaps that will come more easily in time, but I hope that he knows that I don't blame him for it. He has paid for his actions with much more than three years of his liberty and learned a lesson in doing so that he didn't deserve. That is as much as I feel I can offer him.

Fundamentally, Victoria's ultimate intention or aim in bringing Wayne into Grace's life is inconsequential. Was this true love? A replacement father for Grace? An accomplice, co-conspirator or convenient and disposable fall guy? It really doesn't matter now. Events overtook us all and removed whatever the importance of that original desire may have been. Crucially, what's left for Grace is a face and a memory from the time they spent together of a good man. I hope he remembers that. Seeing him again, I realised that my feelings towards Wayne and Grace's connection with him are so much more complicated. Even now, so many years on, my reaction is part anger that someone had the audacity to attempt to intentionally intimidate and harm my family; part shame in the suggestion that perhaps I could have prevented the danger and part stone-cold fury that someone, who was capable of such a cold act of violence, was lucky enough to be in the privileged position of being a role model for my daughter, or any young child, and then wasted it.

Chapter 27

On Monday, 2 March 2020, the first day of the trial, I couldn't decide if the heady and confusing mix of apprehension, nervousness, excitement and trepidation that gripped me all at once was a good thing or not. It was a warm day, but a chilly breeze ran down the road and I hadn't worn a coat over my suit jacket. It froze the sweat that had secretly crept across my back and sides without me realising – I was obviously more nervous than I had thought.

Chelmsford Crown Court, a grim-faced fortress of concrete and brutalist design, was originally opened in May 1961. The imposing brickwork had been further darkened by traffic fumes over the years and a floating first floor looming outwards over the entrance gave the building a dirty, squat appearance. Ugly and brooding – I hoped this wasn't a reflection on how the trial was set to go. I squared my shoulders and stepped over the threshold. Only to be told I was in the wrong place. In contrast to the Crown Court, the trial itself had been moved across the road to the magistrates' court, which was a 2012-erected tower of polished stone, steel and glass. Maybe this would be a positive sign. Light poured into the reception through windows that reached all the way to the roof and if not for the enormous coat of arms proclaiming it as a court of law, it might easily have been mistaken for any other twenty-first century office building. The warmth of the sun through the windows felt like liquid gold in comparison to the mental chill of the Crown Court.

I was never really sure of the reason for the change in venue. Maybe the more modern building was considered to be suited to what was expected to be a well-attended trial, or perhaps in an inspired moment of prophecy, the clerks had predicted that wheelchair access might be required – who knows? I walked through the entrance hall to the reception desk and was thankfully shown into a nearby waiting room and told to sit until I was called.

The room felt full with five people in a space that could have easily accommodated thirty. Its occupants sat as far away from each other as possible. Nobody spoke; it had a forbidding air of tension like the worst doctor's waiting room ever, each person wondering why everyone else was there but no one wanting to ask. I took a seat in a square of four chairs right in front of the door. Having been through the process before, I knew just how long this could take, so I had brought a book with me. None of the witnesses were allowed to talk to each other, so I sat, read and pretended to mind my own business, while we all tried to steal glances at one another.

A man dressed in a smart blue-grey suit sat on the opposite side of the room, slightly to my right underneath the window. He had a quiet demeanour and his constant glances over to me that never quite met my gaze told me that he clearly recognised me, as did the young man sitting opposite me. *Just how many people are connected to this?* I asked myself.

Then Hamish came through the doors. He was a big guy – in personality as well as stature. Even though he was practically the same height as his police attendant, his presence was unmissable with his broad shoulders and heavy hands which hung by his side. We all looked up at the sound of his broad Glaswegian accent – 'Aye, I just wait here then?' he boomed. Nothing about Hamish was quiet and in the uncomfortable silence of a socially repressed British waiting room, he broke the nervous and awkward tension perfectly.

Hamish turned to look across the room, slowly assessing the space. He would tell me later that he was an ex-doorman and while I got the impression that he was nervous, his apprehension didn't manifest in a quiet separation or constant fidgeting like mine. Instead, he registered my face and paused for a moment, as if considering his next move. He was self-assured, confident in himself, which was almost certainly a consequence of his days on the door, and very different to the other occupants of the room.

It was so strange, I thought to myself, *to have these guys know who I was, to have them here in court to talk about me.* But it wasn't really me, it was the me that they had been told was me. They had been presented with an image calculated to make them want to hurt or even kill me and yet here we were: some of us quiet, some loud, but all nervously waiting to see what was going to happen. Where was the woman who connected us and what was she going to do next?

As I sat and waited, trying to avoid eye contact and not talking to anyone, I started to wonder what Victoria looked like now. I hadn't seen her for seven years and it had only just occurred to me that I might be about to. Of course, I had been told that she would be there, but it hadn't really computed that I would actually *see* her, in front of me, in the flesh. As soon as that thought appeared, the floodgates opened and I allowed myself to think the previously unthinkable: were her family going to be there? Her parents? We hadn't exactly been on the best of terms the last time we'd spoken. I closed my eyes and thought back through the years – everything that had happened, how I'd got here, how many times I'd wondered whether 'this' year would be different from the last? But it never was. All that time trying to find a way to take away Grace's pain and asking what else I would have to give up to put an end to the conflict. After the fire, I had given up looking for closure: I couldn't go on pretending that Victoria and I would ever find a compromise. But it had never occurred to me that what would eventually tip the scales would be a desperate bid for her ultimate endgame: my death.

I *was* nervous, I decided. More nervous that I had been for years. I didn't want a fight with her, or her family. I remembered standing in front of their house and I remembered the words that followed me as I got into the car that day. It had been the last thing that Michael, her dad, had said to me: 'The devil is coming for you, Mr Parkes.'

I sat up straight and opened my eyes. Several police officers had come through the door and were splitting off towards various corners to speak to people. Mike caught my eye and headed my way: 'How are you holding up?' His voice held genuine concern. I got the feeling that while this was still part and parcel of his day job, it was important to him that witnesses and victims were able to keep themselves together enough to get through the day. I appreciated that and I knew I wasn't going down this time.

'I'm OK,' I replied, glad that I sounded stronger than I felt. 'What time are we due to start?'

'That's great,' he nodded, 'they've already been at it this morning, sorting out the parts of the case that both sides agree on. The defence has chosen to accept your statement – that means you won't need to give evidence. Our barrister wants to have a chat with you about it, all right?'

'Sure, no problem.' I was probably more shocked than I should have been. I hadn't said anything that wasn't true but I had still anticipated a robust denial and/or counter-argument. It was a knee-jerk reaction but one that I had many years' previous examples to refer to – I certainly didn't think Victoria was going to accept my statement without any kind of response. Maybe unlike his client, her barrister knew that any kind of response should be one that didn't deny reality.

Mike led me out of the room and up to the court itself. There, in a small room with barely enough space for the solitary desk and two chairs, I sat with the prosecution barrister to talk through what had happened and what was going to happen.

'It means that the timeline and details of your relationship as you have described them are now presented to the jury as fact,' he told me.

The jury? Of course, I had completely forgotten about them. Questions rushed to the tip of my tongue: who were they? What were they thinking? What would they do? What questions did they have? It was all rhetorical, of course – they didn't know *anything* yet.

'There were a few things in your statement that haven't been included, though,' Mike added before I had a chance to speak. 'It was decided that they either weren't relevant or we're not able to tell the jury about them for different reasons.'

That all sounded reasonable. I hadn't realised that they could chop and choose which parts of statements to present, but OK, I could roll with that.

'Which parts are you leaving out?' I asked.

'We've kept almost all of it. It was strong and we really appreciated you being so clear and honest. We had to drop a few things, like what happened with the fire and the previous cases – they just weren't relevant.'

'Right, fine. That makes sen . . . Wait, *what*?!'

How could the fact that Victoria had been arrested in connection with an arson attack on my house and the perpetrator convicted of that crime was her husband *not* be relevant in a trial predicated on the notion that she wanted to kill me? It sounded like, through some unbelievable turn of events, Victoria was being given a chance to slip away without taking responsibility *again*. I could feel the ground shift away from under me and the room pulled back in a sudden rush. I felt like screaming, 'I know it was her that convinced Wayne to do it! What does this woman have to do in order to face the consequences of her actions? Please, for God's sake, explain to me how she is being allowed to get away with it?!'

My face must have advertised my internal diatribe rather well because the barrister was quick to jump in: 'I know it seems strange, but it was Wayne who was convicted, not Victoria. And even though there was all that circumstantial evidence, the reality is that at the time, Wayne didn't implicate her. What you *believe* happened is not strong enough to be presented to the jury as fact, I'm sorry.'

Sorry? He was *sorry*?! My fingers were numb and my mouth was dry. My stomach leadened as I sat and realised that the man in the black gown and white curly wig sat opposite me was not there to secure me the closure I was so desperately asking for but to present the best case possible in order to secure a conviction. He had decided not to let me speak and now he had decided not to offer the jury the possibility that Victoria had been arrested for a previous attempt at following through on the very thing that she was on trial for. But I was supposed to understand that?

'Why? How? If you can't say it, *I'll* say it!'

I couldn't help myself as the words came out of my mouth, while reeling from trying not to map out all the potential conspiracy theories: what was her game plan here? She always had an angle. Was she going to whip something out of the madness of the last twenty years to try to discredit me? There is no way she would accept what had actually happened between us without some form of scorched earth final play.

The barrister remained impressively calm under the weight of my impassioned outburst but his professionalism just enraged me all the more. 'You'll still have your victim impact statement, which you can say to the judge to make your points,' he said softly. 'The fact that the defence has accepted this statement means that they can't cross-examine you, you won't have to give evidence and they can't dispute anything you've said.'

'Yes, but the jury won't *know*. They won't know what she's capable of. I don't mind being cross-examined,' I said. 'Bring it on! I can tell them what she's done to us.'

I had started to sound desperate, I realised, and I knew that was the last thing I needed right then. Through all the years of struggling with courts, lawyers and clerks, judges, never-ending paperwork and the darkly opaque legal system itself, I had never lost my self-control . . . until now. I was desperate because this was the closest I had ever been to the peak of the Everest-sized mountain of crap that Victoria had thrown at me over the years. Desperate, because that final argument was being given by someone who wasn't me, to people who hadn't been there, so how could they possibly understand how important it was? And finally, I was desperate because I knew that the decision had already been made, it was all going wrong and this time there was nothing I could do to avoid yet another lifetime of dealing with this woman.

'Without a legal connection, we can't include it. I know that the police wanted to use it too, but we just can't.' The barrister's tone was soothing and his words were clear: this wasn't his first rodeo.

'But she was arrested, isn't that a legal connection?' I tried one last-ditch attempt to push the point, not willing to give up despite the inevitable.

'Yes, but she wasn't there and Wayne was convicted of the offence. That means that we can't accuse her of being connected to it in this trial.'

I knew he was right and in the bright sunlit world of hindsight, I'm glad our legal system has these checks and balances. It's completely fair that, under normal circumstances, a spouse shouldn't be convicted by proxy of a crime committed by their partner. But mine have never been normal circumstances and the injustice burns like hell in that moment when there is no opportunity for redress or even acknowledgement in the face of indisputable historical evidence.

The waiting room for the court itself was on the top floor, with windows on two sides flooding it with light. There were metal benches in four rows across the room and more along the sides to give plenty of space, because in this waiting room, unlike the witness room, anyone would be able to mix freely. I took a seat and waited for the court to restart. The quiet was comforting; I tried to relax into the cool metal uncushioned seat and waited, glancing up from time to time as court clerks and officials came and went.

I had taken out my book (an easy Lee Child novel that didn't require me to think about anything else except the words in front of me) and started to read. Then I saw Marie, Victoria's mother, take a seat on the other side of the room. We hadn't noticed each other as she came in through the doors but now we were sat directly opposite and she caught my eye for an eternally long split second. I had no idea what to say or do and very clearly neither did she, so after that blazingly hot second, we didn't do anything at all.

She was dressed smartly with a plain jacket and was clutching a large bag. She'd come in with Victoria's brother, who also hadn't seen me, but spoke to Marie and stole a look my way once he realised I was there. Matthew was dressed more casually than I had expected, with a polo shirt, trousers and trainers, but then he was not on trial. They spoke to each other and sat down to wait, just as I had. The air congealed around us and I couldn't stop gulping – my tongue was dry and sticky and I shivered as hot sweat trickled down the small of my back. They glanced at me, I looked away. I wished I could open a window to get some air but pressing myself against the cool metal frame of the bench was the best I could do.

The time dragged on for what seemed like hours as I read, re-read and then re-read again the same two paragraphs. Finally, the clerk announced that the trial would start and I lined up behind Matthew as we shuffled into the courtroom. He held the door open for me and we looked at each other, he raised his head in the barest nod of recognition and I returned the favour. I felt poised on a knife edge between fight or flight.

We walked into the room and looked around. I couldn't see Victoria. To my left, a few people, who I assumed were press, milled around a set of office tables with laptops; to their left was a raised dais where evidence would be given from any prospective witness. Turning a corner to the right and against the far wall, the judge and officials would sit on two levels and on the ground level between us a woman and man sat, one wearing robes while the other spent a few moments connecting wires to a computer screen.

Against the far wall, across from the door and straight ahead, past four rows of desks that ran across the middle of the room like a ploughed field, were two rows of raised chairs separated from the rest of the room: the jury bench. They had their own door and access to what I assume was their own waiting area. I've never been a juror and have always wondered what it would be like. I suspect now that, just like all my experiences in a courtroom, it would entail an awful lot of waiting around.

A chamber on the right-hand side of the room was walled off, cutting into the room at a right angle, creating a separate space to the public viewing gallery in front of me, its seats bolted to the floor. I couldn't see what was behind that wall. I walked up to it, pulled down one seat from a bank of spring-loaded, retractable chairs from its vertical position and sat down. The barristers (both prosecution and defence), along with the press, filled the rows in front of me. Mike and the other police officers filed into the room and took their allocated seats in the row in front and slightly to the left of where I sat. As I watched, one after the other glanced across the chamber to the room on the other side of the wall beside me, some with curiosity, others with concern.

Realisation dawned. I suddenly felt hot and cold at the same time. My ears burned; my head felt like it was popping and crackling like a firework . . . Victoria was on the other side of that wall. Perhaps it was a defence mechanism to stop me from evaluating my own thoughts and emotions, but I found myself wondering what she was feeling. How was she coping with the pressure of the day? Did she know I was there? Did it worry or concern her? Did she even care?

What I came to learn that day was that 'Opening Statements' take a long time. Both the prosecution and defence sides spent hours wading through what they were going to talk about and what they were expecting the witnesses to talk about. The prosecution's case revolved around persuading the jury that Victoria had been making active and persistent attempts to seek out, recruit and persuade multiple men in order to kill me either directly or to facilitate others who could be persuaded and/or paid to do so. It was an aggressive, engaged and determined series of actions whose sole purpose was to eliminate me. Quite frankly, that all scared the shit out of me.

Even after all this time, even after everything that I had lived through, I hadn't seen or wanted to believe the stark, naked truth. *She wanted me dead. Gone, erased, deceased – actually, physically and entirely dead.*

The defence, for their part, didn't try to deny any of what the prosecution had put forward, which wasn't exactly reassuring. Their approach was to suggest that Victoria didn't *really* mean it. People say things they don't mean all the time, especially about their ex-partners. Particularly ex-partners who have unexpectedly and unusually gained sole custody of the children. And as the defence set out their approach, I found myself saying, *Yes, it's true, they do. People say horrible, spiteful and hurtful things that they don't mean. If that is what happened, should Victoria really go to prison for that?*

My uncertainty about the possible outcome and the logical questions that led from the arguments presented by both sides was an emotional rollercoaster in the truest sense of the phrase. By the time that the judge called the end of the day, I was completely and utterly knackered despite having done nothing except sit down for six hours. As the rest of the room stood and stretched, I waited until I was the last to leave, trying to give myself some space to take stock. I paused at the door and took a deep breath: why was leaving the room as hard as coming in?

Outside stood Marie; it seemed she had been waiting for me.

We left the court building and walked away towards the town centre. The awkward conversation ended almost as soon as it started as there were photographers waiting outside who followed us down the street, taking pictures. It seemed like a ridiculous end to what had been such a confusing day; dodging photographers like some kind of absurd celebrity with the second-to-last person whom I thought I would ever want to talk to. Splitting away from Marie, I turned suddenly down a side street to regroup my thoughts and avoid a photographer standing fifty yards down the road with a telephoto lens.

I tried to consider that this habit, need (or whatever you want to call it) to bend relationships to breaking point, just to benefit herself, clearly wasn't something that Victoria was going to simply stop doing. There would be more relationships and more victims.

The next time I had the opportunity to, I moved away from that wall. I still sat on the front row of the public gallery, but a few seats closer to the door. It sounds strange but it felt too close, being able to reach out and touch the wall, knowing that Victoria was just on the other side. It made my hands tingle as I pictured the connection between me on one side and her on the other. Both of us reaching out and touching the wall at the same time but with, I suspect, very different reactions. It was utterly irrational and there was no way she could have known where I was, but it was still uncomfortable.

Tuesday, 3 March 2020

Anyone who's ever worked in an office and found themselves clock-watching will understand that you can't maintain such an enforced period of nothing for more than a few hours before finding yourself pulled into a perpetual cycle of revolving tea or toilet breaks. Arriving at court the following morning, nothing seemed to be going on, so I waited. And waited.

I waited outside the courtroom as officials came and went, carrying important-looking files and books. I waited inside the courtroom with the police and barristers as they busied themselves on laptops and complained about the timing of their next case. I waited outside the building in the cold March sun, but mostly I just stopped and remembered the years that had gone by. I did it slowly so as not to miss anything. Not one sad smile or one cold cuddle.

Marie and Matthew waited with me. Not talking, just waiting. The hours stretched out beyond imagination, but eventually, the door opened and a group of people had a hushed conversation between the barristers, police and court officials until something was decided and they broke off in different directions: the defence to Marie and Matthew, the prosecution into the courtroom proper and Mike in my direction.

'She's not here,' he said bluntly. Not maliciously, just with an obvious directness that was refreshing when I consider my own innate tendency to attempt diplomacy whenever I am asked difficult questions. 'She's in a wheelchair and so it took them hours to arrange an ambulance to collect her. Then when they did manage to get her en route, she told them that she had stomach pain but didn't have the right medication. They've diverted to a local hospital but even if they can see and assess her, I don't expect us to get anywhere today.'

I shook my head, smiled ruefully and watched the disorientation run across Mike's face. 'This isn't good,' he said, 'she's managed to delay the whole trial. She's trying to pull the strings and it's another day to get the jury on-side. This time it's her pain and medication, but tomorrow, who knows what she's going to do?'

'I know,' I said, realising the irony of my calm acceptance versus Mike's agitation, 'it's the same thing all over again.'

It was the same modus operandi, the same performance and the same delaying tactics that had been so devastatingly effective over all those years back in family court and in the police cell, time after time after time. But *surely* she didn't think it would work here? She couldn't just pretend none of this was happening.

Mike's phone went off and he apologised silently before walking off, muttering into the receiver.

'I told her you came yesterday.' Marie's words came from over my shoulder and I turned to look at her. 'She asked me if you had come to court and I told her you had.'

What was I supposed to say to that? Part of me wanted to give it a puffed-up, 'Well, no wonder she didn't bloody turn up then.' Or maybe, 'What did she expect? Did she really think I wouldn't come?' accompanied by a melodramatic roll of the eyes. But I didn't – I didn't want to acknowledge that I might be the very reason that she was evading the consequences of what she had done for even one more minute. Hours ticked by and I stayed because there was nowhere else for me to be. Then, just before the time of no return when the whole day would have to be cancelled, and with an eruption of energy and excitement, Mike burst open the door and came to find me.

'We're going in,' he said. 'The judge doesn't want to waste more time with the jury and we're going to start on the witnesses anyway.'

I rushed into the courtroom, fascinated to see who would be called. Desperate to start getting the detail that I had been missing for all these years. Looking over to the doors on my left-hand side next to the press table, the man whom I would come to know as Hamish stepped out of the doors at the far end of the courtroom and leaned over the dock. Like a giant suited bear, he was imposing by virtue of his sheer presence. With a confidence born of the knowledge that he was the biggest (and probably most dangerous man) in the room, Hamish rested his heavy, calloused hands on top of the wooden plinth. Was he nervous? I couldn't tell. He didn't give me the impression of the kind of guy who got nervous, but then again, it seemed I didn't really know anyone involved in this situation, including my ex-wife.

Chapter 28

'Mr Lowry-Martin, is it right that you lived on a boat in the marina in Bedford and came into contact with a couple, Wayne Wood and his partner, Victoria Wood?'

'Yes. We moved on in November of 2013. It would've been probably four and six months after that. So, I would say early May, June or July of 2014.' Hamish's broad Scottish accent filled the room. He stood, plain suit fresh and pressed. Clean-shaven, he leaned heavily on the dock for support and his tie hung out of his open jacket. Relaxed but uncomfortable, his shoulders shifted under his jacket and the sleeves pulled up as he tried to adjust his suit. It was clear that this wasn't exactly Hamish's natural environment. He shifted his weight on his feet and the judge asked if he would prefer to sit down.

No, Hamish assured him, he didn't.

He continued, 'Whenever I get to meet new friends, I always tell them a little bit about my past . . .'

I could see several members of the jury sit up straighter to pay attention. It was an intriguing start and Hamish seemed very open in explaining his own story.

'I had a bit of a chequered past and I explained to her about that and how I'd changed my lifestyle around. When I lived in Scotland, I'd got in quite a bad crowd and I'd committed a number of assaults where I went to prison.'

If he didn't before, Hamish had the attention of everyone in the room now.

'I came out of that and realised that the people in Scotland weren't people to be around; I moved down south and changed my life. The people I know in Scotland aren't little guys who beat people up, they're guys who do seriously wrong things. At the time I had a friend who was "going through" for abducting and chopping somebody up, it's quite a tough area.'

There are times when people say things for effect, to 'sex-up' certain facts or impressions. Perhaps give themselves a bit more credibility. This didn't feel like it was one of those times – if anything, I thought Hamish was underplaying the situation. Mr Paxon, the prosecution QC, paused and looked a little shocked, trying to think of his next question. It seemed like he was as taken aback as the rest of us. 'Did you mention that? Did Victoria say anything to you?'

Hamish nodded enthusiastically. 'Yes,' he said, 'she'd asked me what sort of people I knew in Scotland. I said, "You wouldn't believe some of the people I know," and there was, at that time, a woman from Glasgow who'd been abducted, held hostage for three days. She was disposed of and a guy that I was good friends with was one of the people involved in it.'

I don't know if anyone else believed him, but I did – I definitely did. I didn't know what to think any more. The self-determination to leave a life like that and still have the confidence to talk so openly about it was incredible to see. Later, in a moment of morbid fascination, I tried to look up the story that Hamish had been talking about. After trawling through page after page of murder, kidnap and dismember-ment, I decided that I probably didn't need to know which of the ten or so names I found was the specific guy that he had a direct personal relationship with.

Hamish continued: 'I said, "I don't get involved in that," but she quickly moved on: "Well, do you know anybody who would?" and I said, "Look, I know loads of people like that in Scotland but that's why I don't get involved with them."' Hamish held his hands out in front of him, palms up as if trying to distance himself from even the memory of telling someone else about his past.

'You told her about the chopping-up incident?' Mr Paxton, the prosecution barrister, pressed. Hearing him repeat it just seemed to make the whole thing seem even more unbelievable.

'Yeah. I thought it would scare her off a little bit.' Hamish shrugged. 'She said, "If you know somebody, there's some money in it."'

Mr Paxton paused to make sure his next question hit the mark, 'And what was the figure that was mentioned?'

'Five thousand pounds.' Hamish looked over at me and I tried to understand what he was thinking, but I had no idea. It was a statement, a matter of fact. Was that a lot or not enough? He would tell me over a coffee later on that day that he had known 'agreements' made for much less. But (and I'm still not sure why) I trusted Hamish implicitly when he said that it didn't even cross his mind to consider taking the money to make that kind of introduction. This was a guy whom you wanted on your side and I was just glad that he had decided to be on mine.

Hamish went on to explain that the rest of the conversation seemed to go nowhere, as he became so uncomfortable at the thought of being drawn back into a life that he had tried so hard to escape from that he diverted the topic of discussion elsewhere. But there was more that he wanted to share with the court: 'Shortly afterwards, she showed me a picture of her ex.' He gestured towards me without even realising it. 'And said, "That's my ex, that's who I was talking about." It was unusual because for somebody who has got children, there was no pictures on walls or anything like that.'

Hamish's testimony was as compelling as it was incredible. This trial had clearly brought a clarity of hindsight that hadn't been available to him back then and I wondered about the similarities and differences between my life and his. What kind of strength had it taken for him to walk away from everything he had known? Just like my decision to leave Grace, he knew that he'd had to leave Scotland in order to survive. I didn't blame him for not going to the police at the time and reporting his concerns and I still don't. Like so many of the other men in this story, he was fighting his own demons and Victoria saw that. His strength in walking away from his old life, as well as resisting her emotional manipulation, was, and remains, an inspiration.

But even after all of that, something ticked in the back of my brain, dimly flickering there until suddenly it flashed bright in my consciousness. I gasped out loud and blinked as some of the press and police officers closest to me turned to check what the noise was. Red-hot realisation shot through my mind with something that I had previously missed: the timing of Hamish's account meant that Victoria had offered Hamish money to kill me just weeks after the arson. She had already moved on from Wayne after he had failed, gathered some money together and was trying to find her next option.

Just as I thought about it, frustration that the fire wasn't going to even be mentioned assaulted me again with a barbed heat. My fingers and cheeks burned as blood rushed through them with such intensity that I could hear my heart pounding in my ears.

Hamish's evidence ended and the court closed for the day. I rushed outside to find Mike to let him know what I had discovered.

'I hear you,' he told me, calmly and reassuringly. 'But . . .' His lips were moving and I could see him talking but his body language told me everything I needed to know. My revelation didn't matter: it didn't matter to the police, to the court, to anyone except me. The bare facts were the same, regardless of the timing of Victoria's conversations with Hamish.

'Sorry,' Mike was telling me, 'it doesn't make any material difference to the nature of the case.'

I had to let it go. Chalk it up as another example of the way that Victoria seemed to be given permission to operate outside the boundaries of acceptable society.

Wednesday, 4 March 2020

The next morning, Mike found me waiting outside the court-room as he came through the doors. 'She's done it again,' he said, not wasting any time. 'She's claiming she's not fit enough to sit up all day so is trying to be excused, but we're not going to let it go this time. We've asked for a medical assessment to know if there is anything wrong that can't be controlled with her medication.'

I tried to let it wash over me. I had found as much peace with Victoria's ability to manipulate her environment as I would ever achieve but still there was a layer of frustration bubbling just below the surface of my calm exterior. After a second of quiet contemplation, I just couldn't help myself and the words burst out from my mouth uncontrollably: 'It's ridiculous, Victoria can't keep dictating the pace of our lives. How long can this be allowed to go on for? A week? *Two*?'

My level of annoyance at the impotence of the system to enforce its own rules was nothing, however, compared to the potentially volcanic irritation that I could glimpse just under the bullet-proof shield of Mike's professionalism. 'I know,' he said after taking a long, deep breath. 'Go for a coffee. I'll call you as soon as I know anything else.'

I thought about wandering the streets, finding some green space in the sun to try to take my mind off the day, but instead, I said: 'I'll wait. I haven't come this far to miss anything because I'm on the other side of town. Besides, what else am I going to be thinking about?'

A few hours later, Mike came to find me. 'She's here,' he stated bluntly. 'She's in a wheelchair and not speaking, but at least she's here with all her medication and a medical green light. We're back on.'

Walking into the room, screens dominated the far end where Hamish had given his evidence the day before. Three fabric-covered boards that each stood about eight feet high and five feet wide ran from the door of the court over to the stand and a few feet beyond. The judge and jury could still see the person giving evidence, but it was a huge cocoon protecting the witness from the press, public gallery and everyone else including the defence dock.

Judge Chamberlain looked up from his notes and paused as he considered the room in front of him. His gaze moved up and slightly to his left, into the open room where Victoria sat. I couldn't read any reaction on his face but I was suddenly filled with an inexplicable desire to jump over the barrier in front of me, dash into the courtroom proper to find out what he was looking at.

A door at the side of the room behind the witness stand opened and closed. There were the muffled footsteps of trainers on carpet and then the prosecution asked the witness to state his name for the record.

'Daniel Proctor.' The voice was young and thin, the speaker beyond nervous as he struggled to be heard even in an otherwise silent room. Mr Paxton, the prosecution barrister, directed Daniel to please speak up, even shout if he needed to, and Daniel started his testimony, in as shaky and anxious a tone as I have ever heard.

He had met Victoria in 2015 while working as a handyman at a local dog rescue charity. Victoria volunteered at the same facility and they struck up a relationship. Daniel didn't talk about why Victoria started volunteering at this charity or how long she had worked there. She seemed to be interested in owning or adopting a dog. When Victoria and I lived together, we had adopted a cat, but when it came to dogs, she had explicitly recoiled at the thought of it. Of course, she was more than entitled to change her mind, but I wondered if there might be another reason why she was showing so much enthusiasm in this place at this time.

Daniel's description of the nature and extent of their relationship was limited but his anxiety on the stand was real. Whatever had happened between them had very clearly left an indelible mark on him.

'I want someone killed.' Daniel said that Victoria's words had left him unsettled. Even more so when she repeated them again later. But Daniel couldn't tell the court who she was talking about or why Victoria had told him this, and their friendship had ended as abruptly as it had begun. Looking from the outside, it seemed incongruous that Daniel would be called as a witness if it was only to repeat these two statements. Was there more that he wasn't sharing? He was certainly nervous and very shaken; the screens hid his face from the rest of us and compared to Hamish, Daniel couldn't (or wouldn't) identify me as the target of Victoria's request.

It seems to me, looking at the way she had moved through Wayne and Hamish, that Victoria's disappearance from Daniel's life as well as her volunteering at the centre happened just months after Hamish had knocked her back and she realised that Daniel was not going to be able to move her forward. Her time and effort were better spent elsewhere and she had quickly moved on.

We had a short break and coming back to the court after Daniel's testimony, I made my way up the stairs slowly. I pushed through the doors, entered the room and saw that the screens had been removed. As I sat in my chair, I could only wonder what was coming up next. I didn't have to wait too long as the man who I had seen surreptitiously assessing me at the beginning of the week stepped up to the witness box, slowly and deliberately. He looked sad but determined. His eyes were dark and I wondered how much sleep he had been getting over the past few weeks. He lifted his head slowly when asked to state his full name.

'Graham Wall.' Graham's voice was clear and deliberate; he did not wish to be misunderstood. Mr Paxton asked him if he had been in a relationship with Victoria. 'Correct.' When did they meet? 'Nineteenth October 2018.' How long did that relationship last? 'Until October of 2019.'

Looking at Graham, I couldn't help but think back to my memories of seeing Wayne on trial. Of course, Graham was here for the exact opposite reason – to testify *against* Victoria – but the physical similarities seemed oddly coincidental, as history appeared to repeat itself in front of me. Both were about the same height, the same build; both had cropped or shaved haircuts. Unlike Wayne, Graham had an aura of resigned acceptance about him. I felt that he had started to question if the life that he had expected had not only been snatched away just when it had promised him the most but was potentially never real in the first place.

'Were you aware that [Victoria] had been married to somebody called Rob?' Mr Paxton asked gently. 'Did you know what Rob looked like?'

'I was,' Graham admitted, although 'only through looking at his Facebook account'.

I thought back to those initial increasingly urgent messages Graham had sent me. Had I responded earlier, or not responded at all, would we be here now?

'She didn't really have anything nice to say about Rob.' Graham was addressing Mr Paxton directly, but his eyes flickered to the woman sat behind the wall next to me. My imagination conjured a picture of her sitting in a wheelchair, watching the courtroom in front of her. I realised that the woman in my mind was still the woman I married, ageless and suspended in time. I wondered how she had changed.

'Was [Victoria] favourable or hostile towards Rob?' A seemingly obvious question but one that Graham considered carefully.

'Hostile,' he stated after a moment, 'she referred to him as a paedophile.'

Yep, I thought, *that's pretty hostile.*

'Had she spoken to you in similar or different terms before?'

I understood that Mr Paxton wanted to establish a continued and persistent timeline and process from Victoria.

'She'd asked me in February if I could find somebody to get rid of Rob.' This time Graham responded without pause. He glanced to the other side of the wall again and then back to me. What was he feeling? Guilt? He had nothing to feel guilty for, but that's exactly why Victoria had chosen him. Just a few months after they met he was asked to help her kill someone. That was longer than the others, maybe she had felt something more for Graham. Perhaps that could be comforting for him in a weird kind of way.

'What was the conversation that you had with Victoria?'

Graham shifted uncomfortably on his feet when pressed to give the detail: 'I had her in my arms and she began to cry. I said, "What's the matter?" "I'm happy and my girls are not," she said.'

Graham's expression of how Victoria had expressed her concern to him brought obvious emotional difficulties for him and I felt the mood in the court almost soften along with his conflicted testimony. Even the implication that a child was suffering was difficult to hear. Solicitors are expensive, but he had been resolute and told the jury that he had offered to help Victoria get some money together to pay to go back to court. He emphasised his point and gesticulated with some animation. In that moment he was reliving his frustration and it was palpable and undeniable. He had wanted to help. He had *tried* to help. The anguish radiated out from him – the connection he thought he had made and his helplessness at Victoria not allowing him to even try to 'fix the problem' was almost incomprehensible. It was agonising to see it played out here in court, before a room full of strangers.

'And then?' Mr Paxton's question hung in the air. He knew the answer but wanted Graham's own words. Out of the corner of my eye I could see some of the jurors shift in their seats, waiting for the response.

'She became quite angry and said, "Well, you must know somebody. You must know somebody who can get rid of him."'

'And what did you say in response to her?'

'I said, "I don't know anybody."' Graham seemed almost heartbroken, as if he had somehow let Victoria down by refusing her request. The court paused, but he wasn't finished: 'She was very angry . . . she said to me, "Well, if you can't do that, then you're no use to me."'

It was like an electric shock had run through the courtroom. I glanced over to the jury: what were they thinking? I tried not to guess, as I had no way of knowing if that simple statement meant as much to them as it did to me. Graham was describing the same methods as I recognised to manipulate and control this relationship. I knew the power of those demands, particularly when mixed with the constant disapproval and criticism that he was describing.

Counterintuitively, though, I still couldn't help but feel a little bit envious of Graham: he was there to be counted and to make his voice heard, something I hadn't been able to do. After all these years, a part of me wanted to stand up and have my side validated and there he was, doing exactly that. I willed him on vicariously; this was a man who had been so much stronger than I ever was.

Mr Paxton continued, 'Is it right that on the Tuesday, the first of October, you went off to work and put your phone down to record any conversations that were had in the house?'

'I'd left it because I thought she was having sexual relations with somebody else,' Graham replied.

Apprehensive of what might be about to happen, and before going out that day, Graham had left his mobile phone underneath the stairs with a voice recorder app running. When he came back later that night, Victoria was asleep so he collected the phone and played back the audio file. But it was hours and hours long and he fell asleep.

The next day he woke, finished listening to the recording and then challenged Victoria. 'I couldn't believe my ears,' he told Mr Paxton. 'She told me to keep my voice down in case the neighbours heard.'

As I listened to him relate the course of their conversation, the scene was brought to life in my mind. I imagined the two of them in the kitchen, Graham red-faced and full of confused indignation while Victoria responded with an urgent need to diminish his understanding. Hands raised, she might have advanced on him to try to calm him down, distract him from the topic. Of course, if you were being accused of planning a murder, you wouldn't want the neighbours to know, but for someone so adamant that that's not what she meant, perhaps she was throwing out the gaslighting defence too early.

Graham went on, 'We went out for breakfast.'

Here was proof, if even more proof was necessary, just how easy it was to underestimate Victoria's power of persuasion. Even here, being accused of infidelity and planning a murder, she convinced Graham to take her to breakfast; somewhere public, where it would be difficult to talk though such a challenging subject. Graham shook his head as he remembered the morning: they had gone to a café and he had tried to ask her directly what she had meant by what he had heard on the recording.

Mr Paxton hooked into this account and asked the question that was on the tip of my tongue: 'Did she say anything back to you?'

Now it was me that was leaning forward – I wanted to know how Victoria was going to explain this away.

'She didn't really, she didn't want to talk about it. She said she didn't feel well.'

Graham described how they then went home and I sat back, hoping the techniques of deflection and distraction that he had described Victoria using were as clear to the jury as they looked over at her, sat in her wheelchair, as I had come to see them to be. He continued to give more detail: 'I said, "If anything happens to Rob, I should imagine the police will be knocking on your door." She said, "Well, if he's gone, I'll get my daughter back."'

I felt sick, flushed and cold and angry all at the same time. Was that honestly what she thought? I pulled at the collar of my shirt, feeling it suddenly tight against my neck as I swallowed to try to get some moisture back into my mouth. I looked at the wall separating us with around a foot of breeze-block and plaster. More than ever, I wanted to see her then, to look into her eyes, to find out who she was. What had happened to the woman that I had met all those years ago? This all seemed so alien.

Graham's tone dropped: 'I wanted her to listen to it [the recording], I thought it might actually make her see sense. She told me to get rid of it.' The sadness that we had seen earlier drifted across his face again. The memory of the realisation of an inevitability; he couldn't help her, she wouldn't let him because he wasn't what she needed. 'I tried to talk to her, she just wouldn't listen to me at all.'

'And in the days that followed, did you end the relationship?' Mr Paxton's tone had softened again, perhaps trying to give as much of a compassionate touch as was possible in the circumstances.

'It finished on the following Sunday,' Graham clarified.

'You said you didn't want any more contact with her. Did she come to your flat again?'

He replied, 'She came on the Tuesday, the eighth.'

A week after the recording, a quiet voice in the back of my head whispered to me, *he waited a week*.

'I looked out of the front window and saw her car,' he continued.

'And then what did you hear?'

'Banging on the door,' Graham gesticulated in the air to demonstrate, his suit riding up in his frenetic movements. 'I thought she was coming to get my mobile phone because that recording was on it.'

'Did you stay in the flat?' Mr Paxton questioned, while turning to the jury.

'No. She went round to the patio door and was trying to get in there. I legged it out of the front.'

'And you reported the matter to the police?'

'That is correct.'

'Mr Wall, I don't have any more questions.'

The thirty or so people in the room seemed to take a collective breath. The truth might have felt like it was the only thing he had left, but beneath it all, I think that I could see Graham still cared for Victoria. And because he still cared, this was all directed towards actually trying to protect her in the only way he knew how. Like staging an intervention with an alcoholic who can no longer be trusted to control themselves. I saw Graham as he looked at Victoria while she not so much pressed the button marked 'self-destruct', but smashed her fist down on it.

And as he drove to the police station that day, Graham had started the ball rolling on what became this latest whirlwind of experiences that Grace and I would have to endure. I can only thank him but I know those thanks are tinged with regret. *Maybe*, I sometimes ask myself in the darkest moments of the early hours of the morning, *I would have been happier never knowing?*

CHAPTER 28

The judge called an end to the day and I didn't disagree. I dashed out of the room and the building as quickly as possible. I was running away from Graham as much as anything else. Had I been as brave as him, then I was quite certain that both Victoria and I would have led very different lives.

Chapter 29

The speakers on the walls hissed and crackled as the recording was played. It was the following morning – Thursday, 5 March 2020 – and the jury shuffled the papers in front of them and followed a transcript as the disembodied words were piped into the room.

'So, who do you want disappeared?' A man's voice came through slightly muffled and I imagined the phone sat under the stairs, secretly accumulating minute after minute of priceless acoustic cargo.

'If I told you that, I would have to tell you everything.' It was the first time I had heard Victoria speak in over seven years. She sounded so familiar and it instantly brought back her face from all those years ago. Her long brown hair framing her pretty, round face, welcoming eyes and easy smile. It's funny, even now as I write her description and see her again in my mind, I can't think of her in any other way than smiling.

These were the edited highlights, the showreel of the much longer meeting between Victoria and Earl Gernon. By now, they had already engaged in small talk and chatted about life, relationships, what they regretted and what they wanted. Specifically, they had talked about both Graham and me.

In his interviews with both the police and the Channel 4 documentary team, Earl had always maintained that he had come to the house in search of a personal connection that might grow into a relationship and, through all his bravado and macho front, I can see how that might well be true. He clearly knew that Victoria was in a relationship as she made no attempt to hide that, but whatever *he* thought he was going to get out of the connection, what I believe is that he, just like so many men before him, was chosen for his susceptibility and suggestibility.

I pictured them sitting on a sofa in her house: mugs of tea on the table, the scent of a freshly bleached kitchen floor hanging in the air. Physically, Earl looked to be in his early to mid-forties, average height, average build, grey eyes and receding dark hair. Their body language relaxed. Earl believed he was on course for a quickie, but Victoria's plans were far more involved: she needed to see if he was the man for the job, the man to do what she needed to be done.

To avoid any doubt, my view on how impressionable Earl was or wasn't has absolutely no connection to whether he is a nice person. Being impressionable in and of itself is no justification for criminality. But impressionable or not, this man was clearly willing to contemplate murdering someone he had never met. Not only willing, in fact, but potentially ready to accommodate it for someone he had either known for just a handful of weeks or did know but hadn't seen for thirty-odd years (depending on which version of the story you believe), based on nothing more than Victoria's description of me. As clever as she was, and as suggestible as Earl may have been, the fact remains that at some point, he made the conscious decision that he was going to at least provide options to do what she wanted. The point is, whether it was created by vulnerable suggestion, bravado or machismo, Earl had actively entered into the exploration of ending my life without much (if any) hesitation.

'Yeah, I know people. Pikeys. They'll do whatever you want . . . take him into Thetford Forest and kick him to death.'

The man had never met me, never even heard of me before speaking to Victoria, yet he was able to put aside any qualms and arrange the murder of someone based on a simple, unsubstantiated and otherwise incredibly suspicious conversation. Was he the consummate professional, or was he so poisoned by toxic masculinity that he had to impress this woman, save her and solve her problems? Be her knight in shining armour. Be *me* (albeit twenty years ago).

Like it or not, I saw parts of myself in Earl, just as I could see parts of myself in Graham, Wayne, Andy, Daniel, Hamish and Russell. They had all tried to help Victoria; they had all invested to greater or lesser extents and I saw that they wanted to be The Guy. But they were also, like me, fooling themselves. Victoria bled us all dry and by the time she got to Earl, she was really good at it. In him, she saw an opportunity and grabbed it.

As things got more specific on the recording, I started to feel my connection with the man dissolve more and more.

'Is it expensive?' Victoria asked nonchalantly.

'Depends what you want done.' Earl seemed almost blasé, apathetic in his description: 'Thetford Forest is a couple of grand, but other things are very expensive.' A warning there that she would have to have some significant cash reserves.

'Like what?' Victoria seemed genuinely interested. She was asking for a shopping list to choose from.

'A classic is you smash his car window outside his house, and when he comes rushing out to check on it, you put a brick through his head on the doorstep.' They both laughed at the thought. Laughed at what Victoria's defence later claimed to be a 'silly joke' – 'A poorly judged, insensitive and poor joke.'

They laughed, but I remembered the sound of my car alarm on that January morning, seven years earlier. I remembered how I had opened my front door and looked out at my car on fire and what I now realised could have happened.

A classic.

Maybe she had thought of the same incident because right then, Victoria asked: 'But it can all be traced, right? How can you get away with it?' Her tone was casual, but intent. I remembered the nuances, I could hear the tension. Ten years of listening out for clues and subtle differences in what she said versus what she meant came flooding back. I could tell she was eager to finalise a commitment and I wondered how many times she had had this conversation. How many times had she got this far? She sounded so comfortable in discussing the options that she must have been going over this for a long time. I flushed again, hot and icy cold all at the same time. Then I shivered and felt the goosebumps prickle the back of my neck.

'How can you be sure it's safe?' she asked.

Earl paused for a moment; there was a sizzle of static and I could imagine him contemplating the question. 'Well, all I really need is a picture and rough location. You're not involved, I can get all that stuff from Facebook.'

Facebook. I had tried to lock down my social media presence and generally keep away from it after Wayne's botched arson attack and the subsequent text messages. I didn't want him, or anyone else, following me. But then Graham had reached out to me using the same platform so clearly controlling these preferences was an achievement beyond me. Who had seen what? And what had I posted that could give away any personal details? A careless road sign, a house number, or a post box in the background of a photo could take anyone straight to my work, my house or maybe even, God forbid, Grace's school.

But where does all of this stop in the modern world? My head still spinning from the inescapable inevitability of being traced in today's interconnected digital environment, I wondered just how many attacks had been facilitated by careless Facebook privacy settings. I decided that any social media check-ins and proud parent displays of affection would stop as of now. Admittedly, perhaps it was already six months too late, but I was out: Facebook could do one.

'I know where he lives.'

That got my attention. My eyes snapped back into focus as Victoria's voice breathlessly uttered those five words and they cut through my head like a knife. After moving three times, as well as being in and out of witness protection, I had been sure that my home was safe. Petrified, I stared at the speaker on the wall and the picture in my mind became real. I looked up and looked straight into the room where the two of them sat facing each other in my imagination. I saw the faded curtains, the second-hand sofa and the old carpet, well trodden and frayed at the corners of the room. I could smell the musty scent of an unfamiliar house with the morning's breakfast dishes piled in the sink, waiting to be put into the dishwasher. I could hear her breathing in the silence.

She was excited. Nervous and excited. This was the crunch point. In my mind's eye, I could see her barely concealing a tremble, managing to hide her excitement from Earl but not from me. I was a phantom observer of this recorded conversation but I *knew* her. Earl had passed all her tests up to now, but here was where it got real. I could feel her buzz over the recording. I was scaring myself with just how tuned in to her I was, even after all this time. 'What was he going to do?' I could almost hear her asking herself. Would he back off or was she in play?

'Let me have it then.' That's it, Earl was in. *She had him.*

'Give me your phone,' she responded quickly and in the scene playing out in front of me, she stretched out her hand to take it. He reached into his pocket automatically before some deep-seated sense of self-preservation and innate caution kicked in.

'Why do you need my phone?' The recording caught a slight pause before Victoria replied with a tone that I knew only too well. The lift at the end implied it was a question, but the note of annoyance was that of a particularly severe teacher chastising an inattentive pupil for an idiotic question.

'Well, I'm not going to write it down, am I?'

The figures in my head froze as the speakers fell abruptly silent: Victoria's hand outstretched; Earl clutching his phone, intuiting that something wasn't quite right.

'If I could just pause the recording here, ladies and gentlemen of the jury,' Mr Paxton announced to the now otherwise silent room. 'I must explain to you that Victoria was asking for Earl's phone because she knew that if the details of the "arrangement" were in Earl's possession, it couldn't be traced back to her. He had already told her that he could retrieve the information from Facebook, but she has offered and even potentially written the address in his phone herself.'

I nearly stood up and shouted, 'Of course she's writing it on his phone! Look, she's bloody there doing it!' but I didn't. No one else could see the scene in that living room except for me; no one else was looking at it because to them it wasn't real. Instead, I gripped the metallic edges of my seat through the thin foam padding and gritted my teeth. Someone pressed play on an unseen control panel and the tap-tapping of text being typed on Earl's phone was the only sound in both the real-life court and the imaginary living room as the figures unfroze.

And so, it was done: was there a plan, expectation or implicit agreement? That was for the jury to decide, but for now, Victoria needed to confirm more logistic details.

'So how much?'

'It's expensive, you're probably looking at fifteen grand or maybe more.' Earl seemed confident in the figure, as if he knew what the going rate was. In my head Victoria nodded thoughtfully and glanced around, while the courtroom remained silent.

'And you're sure it's safe?' she asked. The irony of that question gave me a wry smile as I sat, alive and well, in court at Victoria's trial. Safe for *whom*? Victoria? Safe for Earl? I'm quite sure she wasn't making sure that this exercise would be safe for *me*.

'He is a clever man. *Very* clever.' She was talking about me but it wasn't meant as a compliment. 'He can talk his way out of *anything*.' Again, it's a nice thing to say if you look at it sideways and with a very big spoonful of optimism.

'Be careful – he's incredibly manipulative and will confuse you. That's what he does. He hangs around Bletchley. I think he's been in trouble for fraud and I know he's been hanging around, trying to pick up kids over there.'

Ah, and there it was: the killer blow. If there's any crime that charges the emotional batteries and justifies violence, it's *that*. If Victoria hadn't got Earl before, she absolutely had him now. This murder was legitimised, it was righteous, and Earl was the *only* man who could do it.

We took a break and I stepped out into the spring sunshine. I walked along the street with my eyes closed, feeling the sun on my face. I stopped by a church and sat on a bench in the graveyard for a second. The seat was warm and it felt good; I had been sitting down all day but this felt different. I realised that I had been so tense – my shoulders hurt, my thighs hurt, my neck, back and even my fingers hurt where I had been poised, strained and tight with apprehension.

What was the thought process behind actually killing someone? Did Victoria really believe that I was the cause of all her problems? How did she reconcile that with consideration of Grace and *her* needs? I just couldn't understand it. During the years after our separation and leading up to the trial, Victoria had never written to her firstborn daughter. She had never sent a birthday card, Christmas card or made any kind of attempt to contact her since the last time they had seen each other all the way back in 2013, despite being given a court appointed PO box to write to. I wasn't just angry on my own behalf; Grace seemed to be the unseen and unheard collateral damage in Victoria's assault.

I sat there until the feeling came back into my limbs and moving them wasn't so much of an effort. I opened my eyes and took a deep breath. Then I took another one, and another, and another, recovering in the sun until I was ready to go back to court.

On reflection, I think that I would have preferred to have never heard the name Earl Gernon. When I saw his face on the Channel 4 documentary, he looked out of his police cell and straight into the lens of the camera. His was the face of Victoria's intentions for what was supposed to be the abbreviated version of my future made real. It's not that I didn't want to know who the man that had offered to do the things he did was, but as Victoria's 'boyfriend' he could have been an anonymised shadow who could disappear, never to be seen or heard of again. But now, I knew his name. I knew his face and I knew his voice and I'd never be able to forget him.

The truth is, I have no idea who Earl Gernon is. I know practically nothing about him, his life or what he has done or wants to do. Nor do I know the full extent of the circumstances under which he and Victoria connected and I'm not going to make a judgement about that. Perhaps the initial twist of fate that brought them together might have, under other circumstances, led to a romantic connection, a fulfilling relationship and a lifelong loving partnership, if that was what they wanted. Or maybe he was the career criminal that he claimed to be and simply looking to secure a new contract.

Earl had strutted into the police station, full of bluster and boast. I saw him listen to the recording. I looked at his face as the full weight of what happened when he met Victoria became painfully apparent and watched as he tried to verbally and physically ignore, then manoeuvre and twist away from the incriminating trainwreck of a conversation that she had set him up for. After all that bravado had evaporated and the reality of what was happening had started to sink in, I saw him pause and reflect on what could happen and then the cracks in his bombastic façade started to become more noticeable: 'No more dating sites for me,' he said mournfully, a self-deprecating smile playing across his lips.

Earl stood at the desk in his police-issue T-shirt and jogging bottoms. 'Mum? I'm in the police station.' He had the phone pressed tightly to his ear as he turned away from the CCTV camera at the sound of his mother's voice. 'They're trying to tell me it's Conspiracy to Murder.' It was a very different side to Earl than he had shown in the interview. The tone of his voice was pleading his innocence and full of the appalled horror that being falsely accused may bring. He purported to be an innocent bystander, sucked into a theoretical and jokey conversation in the hope of a casual hook-up. But, as shocked as he portrayed himself to be, that fault and blame could possibly be drawn from what he had said, there remained a layer of contradiction that jarred with me: 'No, they have audio, an actual recording,' he replied to the unheard question. 'It's serious, Mum.'

But still, I can't bring myself to condemn Earl. I might be doing him a disservice, but as I watched him on the documentary and listened to him first speaking in his police interview, then to the documentary team, I would like to believe that he wouldn't have followed through, that he couldn't have taken Victoria's money and facilitated contact with anyone that would be willing and able to end my life. But then again, I had thought the same thing about Wayne.

But Wayne, just like Earl and all the others, didn't have all the facts. None of them had known what I knew. Each had been told a small part of a story, a few facts laced with enough lies to sink a government, but as much as they all thought that they knew who she was, they had no idea what Victoria had done or was capable of.

Chapter 30

I used to describe how it would be impossible to understand the true extent of Victoria's actions without being the proverbial 'fly on the wall'. I have seen first-hand how any single individual action, choice or request, when taken in isolation, is often so understandable or reasonable. I thought it would be impossible to capture it and yet here I was, sitting through a trial and then watching a television programme detailing exactly that. Examining how each request she made built on the absurdity of the last and I could finally point to real concrete examples of just how unreasonable individually reasonable requests could be when someone is out to game and manipulate the system. I had needed this documentary team years ago to expose what she was really like, day in and day out, and finally here it was for all to see.

Until this trial, I hadn't realised just how long five days can be and I found myself with a new-found respect for those who sit on cases that last even longer than mine. Having sat through more than my fair share of unbearably long work presentations and attended a few conferences that seemed to sap the life from me after just a few minutes, I had thought being a juror must be an easy task, but these days I'm not so sure: even with the chaos (or perhaps because of it) that Victoria had managed to imbue to the proceedings, the consistent levels of energy and concentration needed to keep up, let alone understand what is required, were almost too much for me. Plus, I didn't have the burden of having to use the information I was being given to make any decisions.

My evidence had been agreed and we had heard more from Hamish, Daniel, Graham and even Earl/Victoria themselves. What I hadn't realised was that the police would also be called to give evidence, although I understand just how ridiculous and self-absorbed that sounds. When DC Louise Abbott was called to the stand I was initially surprised but then admonished myself for my own naïvety. The information she obtained might be the most crucial of all – after all, it was she who put the work into piecing all the parts of the puzzle together.

As the officer for the case, DC Abbott was responsible for obtaining the evidence and pursuing the inquiry contained in the bundle of notes that resulted in the decision to take Victoria to trial. While Mike had been my contact and was the officer who updated me on what had happened, he introduced DC Abbott as the real driving force behind the case. She had been the one who had collected all the evidence together and really seen the full extent of Victoria's manipulative ambitions. In court, DC Abbott was clear and self-assured, her voice ringing with certainty and integrity. She had waded through the layers of contradictions and inconsistencies that Victoria had presented as fact and it was from the transcripts of these interviews that Victoria had had with her that DC Abbott's evidence was taken.

Throughout the interview process, Victoria denied ever wanting to kill, murder, hurt or harm me in any way whatsoever. Her position under questioning was that she would never ever want anything bad to happen to me while I was caring for Grace, while simultaneously accusing me of being capable and guilty (in her eyes) of some of the most horrific crimes imaginable.

Those questions, and DC Abbot's testimony, were effectively unchallenged by the defence and as we entered the summing up, I started to feel at least some sense of closure. At the very least, I had seen the absurd dichotomy of Victoria's view of our relationship aired and tested.

Mr Paxton cleared his throat, stood and addressed the jury as he summed up the case for the prosecution to the judge and the court. From the prosecution's perspective, the persistent and planned nature of the actions that Victoria had taken was one of the most pertinent points. He reminded the jury that they had heard evidence that four men had been approached by Victoria to persuade them to help her kill me; for some the proposed motivation had been love, but others had needed a more financial incentive.

As I sat listening to the argument, I got more and more worried. I wanted to stand up, bang on the table and say, listen, *listen!* Just look at the connections: it wasn't just four, there were more of them, just follow the timeline. First, Wayne: he had been effective but unlucky, so she needed someone more reliable. Then she found Hamish and Andy. She had offered Hamish money but he didn't want to get back into that life, and Andy hadn't been able to come through either. She then tried her luck with Daniel before turning to Graham and moved back to the tried-and-tested emotional techniques that had worked so well with Wayne, before finally having enough money to find someone more professional.

By the time she was speaking to Earl and thanks to Hamish, Victoria knew that she needed some serious money to take any kind of plan forward. In conducting a search of her house, the police had found a significant amount of cash but there was a problem in terms of intent. Hiding £18,000 in baby milk tins sealed with gaffer tape in a cupboard is unusual but apparently, not a great cause for concern. But does lying to the police about the fact that she had hidden the cash – while at the same time entering into specific negotiation over how it might cost almost that exact amount of money to kill someone who she had openly described as being a paedophile and the root of all her problems – stretch the concept of coincidence past breaking point? Personally, I would argue that it does.

The defence was short but conducted and orchestrated with a huge amount of professional certainty. After all, they didn't have to prove anything, all they had to do was provide the possibility of doubt. They knew that unless there was absolute certainty in the minds of the jurors then it had to be a not guilty verdict. 'Well, she *probably* did it' just wouldn't be enough for a conviction and so the defence relied on the one thing that I knew could unravel everything: simple common sense.

How many times have you talked disparagingly about an ex-partner? Maybe you've muttered something in the heat of the moment that you didn't mean? How many times have you daydreamed about what it might be like to have a boss, neighbour or ex-partner 'disappear'? It's never anything that you would do or expect anyone else to do anything about, is it? You might even, after a few drinks, get a bit more enthusiastic about it, wonder how it could be done. Have a laugh with friends about how many of your problems it might solve and how much better your life could be if only you weren't being held back by your past problems. But it's not *real*, no one ever actually *intends* to do anything about it, do they?

It was as simple as it was effective. By the time the closing arguments were finished, I was a wreck. Even I, having personally gone through all of the years of Victoria's control and manipulation, followed by struggling to achieve the impossible and protect Grace, only to be pulled back into Victoria's world once again in the most graphic way possible, was tempted to say, 'Did she really mean it?' I mean, *really*? Then I thought about the fire, the gun and the brick. First, Wayne, then Hamish, Andy, Daniel and Graham. The way she had dropped each guy when they outlived their usefulness. And finally, Earl. She gave him my address and tried to set him loose just as she had Wayne. I believed that she knew what she was doing, 100 per cent – but would the jury?

Tuesday, 10 March 2020

The tension in the room was unpleasant, made all the worse by (what felt like) an almost oily layer of suspense. For this, the last day of the ordeal, I was sat with Jane at the back of the court, waiting for the verdict. It seemed like days after the jury had been sent out to conclude their deliberations. Then a note was passed to the judge to tell him that a decision had been reached. Graham was in court that day and sat behind me, patiently waiting to see what outcome his actions were going to have. The conflict was horribly real for him and he was obviously wrestling with what he had done to the woman that he loved.

An agreed verdict had been decided. I sat in my seat trying not to stare at the wall beside me, trying not to picture Victoria sat in her wheelchair on the other side of it. I didn't want to think about what she looked like or spend any more time considering what she was thinking. That time had passed. The decisions and choices that we had both made ever since I had left her were about to be weighed in the most brutal of ways.

Everyone stood as Judge Chamberlain walked in through the door at the other side of the room. The space between us seemed to yawn out as reality stretched. We all sat as he sat and waited while the jury filed in one at a time from their waiting area, and I held my breath. Was this going to be the vindication that I'd been denied for all those years? Would this be the time when the problems I had been screaming about for almost two decades were finally recognised? Victoria had slipped through the net for so many years; it had taken over half a decade with continued proof of unarguably extreme behaviour for the 'system' to even consider me a suitable caregiver for Grace. I tried to dull the intensity of emotion shooting across my body by concentrating on the fact that this decision was not being made by 'the system': this was twelve random people. And they were not expected to balance a threshold other than that of reasonable doubt and, at least in my opinion, there was nothing reasonable about Victoria anymore. It all came down to two simple questions: did they believe that Victoria had asked these men to kill me? And had she meant it? One or either would not be sufficient, it had to be both.

My fingers were numb and my knees were shaking. I gripped Jane's hand so tight that I had to make a conscious effort to stop myself from doing any damage. I couldn't stop shivering despite the sweat that was pouring down my back.

Count one (Hamish): *Guilty*.

Count two (Daniel): *Not Guilty*.

Count three (Graham): *Guilty*.

Count Four (Earl): *Guilty*.

My shoulders sagged and I let go of Jane's hand to scrub my face with my bare palms. Finally, there it was: incontrovertible proof that Victoria's campaign of gaslighting and coercive control of not just me, but also all the other men that she had brought into her life, *happened*. Not only that, it was calculated, morally reprehensible and she should be held to account for it.

Graham had let out an audible gasp as the tension he had been carrying was released. I glanced back to look at him and saw his relief at being believed turn to tears and deep sorrow on behalf of the lost love for the one whom even now, he still deeply cared. The world was filled with a phantom buzz and I closed my eyes and shook my head, trying to get rid of it.

'What's wrong? What's the matter?'

Jane's voice cut through the static and I opened my eyes, realising that I had tipped my head up to the ceiling.

'I . . .' I began, but I didn't know how to finish the sentence. I looked over to Marie, Victoria's mum, saw her jaw set and lips pressed tightly together in resolute accept-ance. As a parent, I knew that I could never stop loving my child, even in a situation as incomprehensible or unimagin-able as this. A picture of Grace as a baby sat with Victoria flashed through my mind, both laughing on what will be an eternally perfect summer's day. I could see Victoria's hair as it flicked up in the wind and reflected in the sun. I heard them giggle as they soaked up the warmth of the field we were picnicking in.

I appreciate that this incongruous memory, as it came to me at that time, might seem inappropriate, but remembering Grace's smile did bring with it a happiness that was reassuring in the moment. With the verdict delivering a final confirmation over the actions I took that I had always believed were right, I could at last feel free to be comforted by those memories without guilt or apprehension. Victoria and I might forever be at odds, but we did create a perfect little girl and we should be able to remember the good times we shared, as well as the bad.

I couldn't wait to get back to Grace and give her the biggest hug I could, but just as my thought process had moved from Marie to Grace, I was reminded that the connection between a mother and daughter couldn't be broken even in the most difficult of circumstances. Grace still had a mother, that hadn't changed, so who was I to celebrate the possibility that their connection might be, if not severed, at least incredibly complicated? I had based my whole parenting life with Grace on demonstrating how it was our responsibility to add more love and happiness to the world than we take. What kind of hypocrite would I be if I didn't take this opportunity to model that example? Surely no one would blame me for celebrating this hard-won victory, but what kind of person would that make me if I showboated the act of taking my own daughter away from her mother?

But even as I thought of all these new complications in my life, I couldn't wait to get out of that room.

Chapter 31

'Hello? Can you hear me? Is this working?'

Three months later and we were back for Victoria's sentencing. The same court, the same judge and the same uncertainty. Today would be the day that I would find out *why*.

Judge Chamberlain cleared his throat and the noise in the courtroom quietened. I looked back up at the screen and into the freeze-frame image of Victoria's eyes. She blinked and then with the slow but inevitable inertia of a breaking dam, she shifted in her seat. I wiped my hands clean of the clammy sweat on my palms.

'Before I confirm the nature and length of the sentence, Ms Breeden, it would be useful to confirm the result of the psychiatric assessment that was undertaken with regards to your mental health and the various medical concerns that you have cited before and during the course of your trial.'

After the trial and verdict, Covid-19 had brought the legal system to its knees and the backlog of cases was growing longer by the day. In all honesty, though, I was quite pleased for the delay: it had let me catch my breath and try to figure out what it all meant for me, for Grace, Jane and for Victoria. I didn't get very far, but I was able to start to think about the things I *didn't* know.

After all of the doubts, questions and speculation, Judge Chamberlain had finally been able to ask the question that I had wanted answered for years: was Victoria suffering from a clinically verifiable mental illness? Ever since that first consultant asked me about her mental health all those years ago, the question sat in the back of my mind: is all this *really* what she thinks? Did Victoria even *know* what she was doing? Was her perspective so skewed by a chemical imbalance that she couldn't control it, or did she simply hate me to such a degree that it had all been driven by pure, unadulterated vindictiveness?

Over the years, the sheer volume of medical intervention (or certainly the impression of that intervention) had been something that Victoria had been able to use to her advantage. She had been able to shape relationships with husbands, partners, friends and colleagues. It had been a consistently useful tool that never failed to elicit sympathy in others or at least in those who hadn't spent enough time with her to recognise the pattern. The question over whether the physical ailments were, are or perhaps have ever been connected to Victoria's mental health was something that I could never get to the bottom of.

Much of this book has sought to answer the question 'why?' Why did I find myself in an abusive relationship that I couldn't escape from? As a separated father, why was I trying so hard to be recognised and accepted as an appropriate parent? Why did I carry on fighting even when the risk of losing everything all over again was so high? But one question has followed me since the beginning and thrown an element of doubt into every scenario that may have unfurled. It is the ultimate abdication of responsibility, a metaphorical get-out-of-jail-free card (although the irony of being sent to prison while simultaneously being assessed for your need to be there is not lost on me). For a woman who had spent years claiming to be the victim of abusive relationships, of unfair discrimination and even of circumstance itself, I just needed to know: did she mean it or not?

Over the years, she had been asked, on multiple occasions, to undergo formal medical assessments to support her claims of illness and disability. Nearly twenty years ago, I had offered to go and register as her carer so we could both be reviewed, but Victoria always refused. During the custody hearings, when she stopped engaging with the court and was asked to provide proof as to why she had refused to attend so many hearings, no medical report or opinion ever materialised. Finally, during her time in custody and this trial, the judge had seen first-hand the desperate measures that Victoria was prepared to go to in using medical complaints without proof or a credible explanation.

Were all of the lies, deception, manipulation and attacks really and truly because she hated me, or was there, could there, be something else? A mental illness or disorder that she could point to and dodge responsibility for the damage she had caused? I was finally going to get an answer but as with so many other parts of this story, it was a lose/lose situation. Either Victoria did have some form of mental explanation for the mysterious ailments that she could use to blame as the root cause of her actions, or she didn't and the whole thing had been a cold, calculated effort to first control and then remove me from the lives of everyone I loved – I couldn't decide which was worse.

Judge Chamberlain looked at his papers and checked his notes. The pause must have been momentary but to my eyes we all moved in slow motion. He spoke loudly and clearly – I got the impression that he did not want anyone to misunderstand: 'Aside from a form of PTSD developed during her recent incarceration, Ms Breeden does not have any pre-existing conditions that would have contributed to the crimes of which she has been convicted.'

Well, that was clear. I had as definitive an answer as it was possible to get. Did I feel better knowing that she completely understood the implications of every single word she had uttered?

What I think is so sad about what has happened, and the thing that Victoria never really understood despite her single-minded obsession, is that none of this has been about me. It never has been. I made my peace with Victoria years ago; she stopped being able to hurt me the day that I ensured that Grace was safe. But with every new day that passes, our daughter grows up and understands more about her own history and story.

I am so sorry that Grace, and so many other children in her position, have to suffer like that. I have had an answer to my question, but I know that I am fortunate: I survived and overcame all the challenges of an abusive relationship – personal isolation, court bias, attempts on my life and the lives of my family. I survived and grew stronger thanks to their support and love, but there are so many other men and women who can't say the same. The fight for equity between separated parents shouldn't be this hard and I understand that this could be taken as a statement of male privilege, but I don't intend it that way and it is applicable to any parent. The power given to the 'resident' parent and the emotional stakes in those circumstances are so high that it is only ever the children who suffer.

I have worked so hard to ensure that Grace knows that her mum could still be a positive part of her life and I have tried to give her a perspective that allows her to see how that might be possible despite what she has done. I hope that knowing Victoria and my life together did hold some moments of light will go some way towards that, but I genuinely have no idea as to how things will all play out and I continue to try to be the best role model I can for her. As Grace grows up and learns more about what happened to us, each decision will be hers to make. All I have ever wanted is to give her the tools she needs to cope with the potential stress, pain, joy and love that there is in the world.

Victoria was sentenced to twelve years in prison before it was reduced to nine due to mitigation, but I can expect her to be released after serving about half of that sentence. I don't know exactly when that will happen, but what I do know is that as Victoria is released from prison, a whole new chapter of our lives will start. By that time Grace will be a young adult and have new choices, new opportunities and new decisions of her own to make. Whatever path she takes, I hope that she will continue to be as resilient as she has already shown herself to be.

I remind myself that there is no right or wrong way to deal with our situation. Every day I look at Grace, I see her strength and it's because of that strength that when the time comes, I know she will do what's right for her. Not for me, not for Victoria, but for her. It may not come for years, or perhaps it might only be a few months away, but I will forever remain true to the principle that I can't forget that it will be *she* who decides just how much of a part in her life she wants her mum to play.

Here, as I type these last few words on a Sunday afternoon, I'm sitting at my kitchen table, looking over at the sink piled up with the dirty dishes that Grace *promised* me that she would clean up hours ago but she is currently in the next room claiming to be practising her flute, while almost certainly scrolling through her phone. Jane is napping, cuddled up with a sleeping baby Hope, and I'm looking out of the window at a beautiful blue sky, thinking about all the things I've got to do next week. I look around at our lives and think to myself that if there is such a thing as 'normal', I really hope this is it.

I would like to believe it is precisely because of everything that has happened to us, that Grace's experiences have given her a specific and individual perspective on the world and her place in it. I hope she also knows that together, she and I can harness that perspective to bring more to the world than we have taken.

We are here for a reason and we are the lucky ones.

Dear Grace,

This book tells our story, yours and mine. When you were born, I held you in my arms, looked down and you awoke something inside of me that I didn't know was there: it was you who gave me the superpowers that I needed to protect you. I had no idea then what that was going to mean or where it was going to take the both of us. While this book might mark the end of my part in chronicling the events that happened, I hope it represents the start of your adventure.

I would like to tell you something that you perhaps hadn't realised. When I started writing this book, I was angry. I know I didn't look angry, but I was. Very angry. Angry with your mum for being so self-obsessed that she couldn't see how much she was hurting her beautiful baby girl, angry about the selfishness that came with expecting you to worry about her when it should have been the other way around. Angry with cancer for taking your Uncle Adam away and angry with Uncle Adam for dying. I was angry with myself for all the things I should have done differently and all the mistakes I made, angry that I couldn't go back and put them right, and angry with the whole world for being so bloody unfair.

I was also scared, frightened of what might happen and the future consequences of what already had happened. As your dad, I know I'm not meant to be angry or scared, I'm supposed to have all the answers and know exactly what to do all the time. But I don't, no one does really. Being angry or scared often looks like the same thing and while they are connected, believe me, it's all too easy to confuse the two.

I thought of you a lot during the trial – there were so many things that reminded me of the times when you were a baby and situations that I couldn't control or escape from. Back then, I didn't know how I could express that frustration or anger, so I took it and locked it down into a neat little box. Then I put that box away so I could go back to concentrating on being the best parent, husband, brother, son and man I could be.

But even all these years later, that box is still there: I can see it in my mind waiting for me. It is pale pastel blue in colour and I've tied the lid down with a purple ribbon crossed over, then held with a big bow on the top. I can imagine touching it and when I run my fingers over it, it has a smooth but textured finish, like wood or matte paint, and it smells of fresh cardboard.

It changes size from time to time and I catch it out of the corner of my eye expanding; the sides bulge out when we fight or when I'm on my own listening to music that reminds me of my brother. Sometimes, I start crying just at the fading memory of it all. Then it shrinks back to the same blue box with a ribbon on top. But each time, I worry that maybe it's just a little bit bigger than it was before.

And that's the scary bit; because I understand that one day I will have to pull the ribbon, lift the lid and look inside at what I've been putting in that box for all these years. When I do, I honestly don't know what I will find, but part of the reason to write this book was to make it easier for me to do that. To try to pin down the reality of what happened to us, identify why our lives turned out the way they did and recognise the mountains we climbed together to get here.

It has taken this book to make sense of it all. I understand now that I did need to do better, be better, but not in the way your mum thought I did. Not for her and not to prove to anyone what kind of a man I was. I needed to be better at realising that in my life with your mum, I had missed one fundamental principle: I should have understood that the importance of happiness, our collective happiness, should have been the very first lesson I taught you. Collective happiness is not just about you or me but also anybody who is important to us; it's about our family, friends and everyone we meet.

Finding and celebrating the joy in those other people will, I hope, in turn, bring you as much fulfilment as it does me. We can and should share the lessons we have learned and by virtue of that, we can then hope to share in the happiness of other people. Making sure we take ownership of the kind of emotional impact we bring to the world is a huge responsibility and I would much rather leave the world in a better place than how I found it. You make me prouder each and every time you choose to make decisions with the empathy, compassion and grace that are inside you.

So now you know that I know just how easy it is to be angry. Anger can legitimise your frustration as the injustice that you see builds all around you. It sits inside your chest and bubbles away, telling you that you are right, that you are being played, cheated or ignored. And you will inevitably be correct – anger is a valid response to all of those situations. But what I hope I've shown you in these pages is that you can be angry and calm at the same time; furious but focused. Even if you are mistaken (which, as you know, I often am), being angry shows how much something means to you, how important it is and so you can't ignore that. But anger should inform your decisions, rather than lead them, and then give you the perspective to make the next decision in order to fix that frustration. Listen to your anger but don't let it tell you what to do, because while it shows you what is important, it doesn't tell you why.

It is absolutely vital for you to know that even after everything that has happened to us, your mum remains an important part of my life, and our life too. When I started to understand that, for a while I was confused. Did it mean that I, in some (very, incredibly, cavernously) deep, recess of my heart still loved her? No, I don't think I ever really loved her in the way I now understand love to be. But she brought you to me and for that, I am grateful and so we will always be connected in some way.

As she went to prison, I realised that the actions she has taken and the decisions she has made will impact your life forever and that filled me with disappointment. She had broken the unspoken promise that people are supposed to make to each other when becoming parents, but, although she didn't live up to her responsibilities as your mum, there are also many positive things that I (and you) can and should thank her for.

Your mother is a strong, intelligent woman, you can be proud to count that as part of your heritage. Your musical ability is hers (it certainly isn't mine), along with your cheeky smile, beautiful long hair and stainless-steel-wrapped self-confidence.

But you are not her.

You are not destined to make the same mistakes or walk the same path; that is why we can count ourselves alongside the lucky ones. We have been given the opportunity to understand why family is so important and how we can make ours better. It's not been easy and there will be hard times again, but now you'll be able to see those times for what they are.

As you grow up, you can choose to look at all the things she has given you with righteous fury or resentment, but I hope you don't. You'll only ever have one biological mother and she is yours. That doesn't have to be something to run away from but facing the truth of your past will take courage and patience.

You don't have to accept or forgive her, God only knows I'm still trying to decide how or if I can do that myself, but you will need to recognise her if you are going to be able to let go of the weight of what has happened and live the life that you deserve.

I hope that all this painful, bitter and uncomfortable experience can show you that, with enough motivation (for me, that has been and always will be you) and some incredible support (look around you, your family and friends are amazing), we can accomplish anything. We have built a home from all our memories and experiences. We see them, we know them, and we use them to understand and surround ourselves with all the things that mean the most to us. Our home is not a house or even a building, it's a place where you can always feel safe, it's the people who love you unconditionally and it's a space in time when you need it the most. We should never forget that we are so privileged to have all those things and more.

My darling daughter, my lightning bolt and my little Tigger, let's go home.

With all the love in the world,

Dad

Acknowledgements

This book would not exist without the support, encouragement and enduring love and comfort of several people. They deserve far more than the recognition that I am able to give them here.

Mum and Dad, I have learned so much during this journey but never questioned your love and reassurance. I hope I made you proud.

Danny, the sentence 'this book wouldn't have happened without you' is literal in your case! Your dedication was unparalleled and I will never be able to repay the countless hours of mentoring that you poured into making my idea a reality.

Lu, you are the sister I didn't know I needed, you defend me with the passion of a tigress and love me regardless of how often I forget to message you.

Luce, the depth of your generosity is equalled only by the size of your heart. You are the most selfless human being I know.

Kate, you gave me the confidence to do things I never believed I could do and achieve the impossible. It was a gift that I can never repay you for.

Vicky, Sarah and Meryl and everyone at Orion for going all in with me, I'm still amazed that you have suffered through all my naïve questions to make this happen!

Charlie and the team at Brotherstone Creative Management, thank you for truly allowing me to believe that I could actually write something good enough to be published. Charlie, you are the consummate gentleman; diplomatic to a fault and critically supportive from the start, thank you.

Graham, Hamish, Dan and Andy, you didn't know me and yet you still put yourselves on the line for me. Your courage and selflessness in speaking out continues to inspire me to follow your example.

Timbo & Matt, you will always be by my side. Stand tall, we rise as one.

Ad, I know that you left things unfinished and didn't want to leave. You don't have to worry any more, we've got you. Rest easy, I love you bro.

Jane, you are my moral compass, my north star and my life map all in one. You have risked everything with me and asked for nothing in return; I didn't and don't deserve the love and kindness you continue to extend to me.

Grace, we've already lived a lifetime together and you'll never know just how you managed to save me. Maybe one day we could write a book about it...?!

Thank you all.

Credits

Seven Dials would like to thank everyone at Orion who worked on the publication of *Married to the Black Widow*.

Agent
Charlie Brotherstone

Editor
Vicky Eribo

Copy-editor
Jane Donovan

Proofreader
Sue Lascelles

Editorial Management
Sarah Fortune
Tierney Witty
Jane Hughes
Charlie Panayiotou
Lucy Bilton
Claire Boyle

Audio
Paul Stark
Jake Alderson
Georgina Cutler

Contracts
Dan Herron
Ellie Bowker
Alyx Hurst

Design
Nick Shah
Jessica Hart
Joanna Ridley
Helen Ewing

Finance
Nick Gibson
Jasdip Nandra
Sue Baker
Tom Costello

Inventory
Jo Jacobs
Dan Stevens

Production
Katie Horrocks

Marketing
Matthew Young

Publicity
Elizabeth Allen

Sales
Jen Wilson
Victoria Laws
Esther Waters
Tolu Ayo-Ajala
Group Sales teams across Digital, Field, International and Non-Trade

Operations
Group Sales Operations team

Rights
Rebecca Folland
Tara Hiatt
Ben Fowler
Alice Cottrell
Ruth Blakemore
Ayesha Kinley
Marie Henckel

Resources and Support

The first step is always the hardest. If the themes in this book have affected you (or someone you know), then I encourage you to reach out.

Campaign Against Living Miserably (CALM)
www.thecalmzone.net
0800 585 858

Dads Unlimited
www.dadsunltd.org.uk
Helpline: 01233 680150
Domestic Abuse Support: 01233 680160

Directions for Men
www.directionsformen.org.uk

Families Need Fathers
www.fnf.org.uk
Helpline: 0300 0300 365

Fortalice
www.fortalice.org.uk/support-for-men

Men's Advice Line
Helpline: 0808 8010 327
www.mensadviceline.org.uk

ManKind Initiative
www.mankind.org.uk
Helpline: 01823 334244

Male Domestic Abuse Network
www.mdan.org.uk

Men's Aid
www.mensaid.co.uk
Helpline: 0333 567 0556

Reducing the Risk
www.reducingtherisk.org.uk/male-victims

Refuge
www.refuge.org.uk/i-need-help-now/other-support-services/
support-for-men
Helpline: 0808 2000 247

Samaritans
www.samaritans.org.uk
020 8394 8300

SHOUT
www.giveusashout.org
Text 'shout' to 85258

St George's House
www.st-georges-house.org.uk/working-with-men-who-
have-been-victims-of-domestic-abuse
Helpline: 01902 421904

Supportline
www.supportline.org.uk

Valley House
www.valleyhouse.org.uk/males-support

Victims First
www.victims-first.org.uk
Helpline: 0300 1234 148

Victim Support
www.victimsupport.org.uk/more-us/why-choose-us/specialist
-services/domestic-violence-services
Helpline: 0808 1689111

Women's Aid
www.womensaid.org.uk/information-support/support-for-male
-survivors
Helpline: 0808 801 0327 (men's advice line)